Worrell, Estelle Ansley, 1929-
    Children's costume in America, 1607-
1910 / written and illustrated by
Estelle Ansley Worrell. -- New York :
Scribner, c1980.
    216 p., [4] leaves of plates : ill.
(some col.) ; 24 cm.

    Includes index.
    ISBN 0-684-16645-3 : $16.95

    1. Children--Costume--History.   2.
Costume--United States--History.   I.
Title.

CHILDREN'S COSTUME

IN AMERICA

1607-1910

WRITTEN AND ILLUSTRATED BY

Estelle Ansley Worrell

CHARLES SCRIBNER'S SONS

NEW YORK

CHILDREN'S

COSTUME

IN

AMERICA

1607–1910

ACKNOWLEDGMENTS

I wish to acknowledge gratefully the special assistance, cooperation, and encouragement given me during my research into the history of children's clothing in America. A special thanks to the Brooklyn Museum; the Museum of Fine Arts, Boston; the National Gallery of Art and the Smithsonian Institution, Washington, D.C.; the High Museum of Art, Atlanta, and the Whitney Museum of American Art, New York. Thank you also to the City Art Museum, St. Louis; the William Rockhill Nelson Gallery of Art, Kansas City; Cheekwood Galleries, Nashville; and the Hunter Gallery of Art, Chattanooga.

I am also indebted to the U.S. Navy, Mr. James C. Tily, the Sears Roebuck Company, the Montgomery Ward Company, Osh Kosh B'Gosh Company, and the Hirschl and Adler Galleries of New York.

A "thank you for your contribution of photographic material through your books" to authors Jean Lipman, Alfred Frankenstein, Inez and Marshall McClintock, Jane Toller, and Milla Davenport, as well as to the editors of Antiques *magazine and* Antique Monthly *and the American Federation of Arts, for their publications.*

To these individuals I also extend my thanks: Mrs. Florence Cavert Smith for sharing her collection of antique baby clothes; Mr. William Colsher of the Nashville Public Library, who is always available when I need help; Marilyn Meehan, my secretary, for working "above and beyond the call of duty" in assisting me with the manuscript; my husband, Norman Worrell, for his help and encouragement, and, finally, my precious father, Sterling Price Ansley, Sr., who made so many sacrifices through the years for so many children.

Estelle Ansley Worrell

Copyright © 1980 Estelle Ansley Worrell

Library of Congress Cataloging in Publication Data

Worrell, Estelle Ansley, 1929-
Children's costume in America, 1607–1910.

1. Children—Costume—History. 2. Costume—
United States—History. I. Title.
GT1730.W67   391'.3'0973   80-19419

ISBN 0-684-16645-3

1 3 5 7 9 11 13 15 17 19   F/C   20 18 16 14 12 10 8 6 4 2

Printed in the United States of America

To my children:

ANNE   MELISSA

ELIZABETH   ANSLEY

CLARE   LOUISE

STERLING   NORTH

and to all those dear little children who

grew up and built a great nation

CONTENTS

CHILDREN'S COSTUME

IN AMERICA

1607-1910

INTRODUCTION

What will children's clothes of today reveal about us and our world two hundred years from now? They will show that we were concerned with our children's comfort and physical freedom of action; and, at the same time, that we were concerned about our own freedom from the drudgery of washing and ironing.

Future historians will most certainly cite statistics on women's careers and single-parent families as being factors in our concern. They will surely comment on the fact that we and our children seemed to value labels to the extent of wearing them even on the outsides of our clothes. They will notice the parodox that, after centuries of laundering diapers, we finally developed mechanical laundry methods—then began throwing the diapers away!

They will notice that sports and the athlete held a very important position in our society. Our interest and pride in our history will be apparent to them. It is reassuring to know that both costume historians and sociologists of the future will think kindly of us because even the most unfortunate of our little citizens dressed with dignity. They will note that even though we had not eliminated poverty, we had at least made free or extremely low-cost clothing available, through charitable agencies, to anyone in need. No child had to suffer the humiliation of dressing in rags as in times past.

Our fascination with shoes will probably amaze future historians. One thing will probably puzzle them, however. They may try to figure out why we were so eager to have a tiny infant declare his sex by his clothes, then dressed boys and girls in unisex clothing. In a world of instant and limitless electronic communications systems, our children, they will exclaim, went around with messages written on their shirts!

What, in the 1980s, exerted the strongest influence on children's clothing in America? One need only look through fashion magazines, newspapers, and catalogs: the impact of our world Olympic games on young fashion becomes instantly apparent. Snowsuits, playsuits, swimwear, coats, jackets, blazers, pajamas, and exercise clothes were miniatures of summer and winter Olympic attire. Along with Olympic sports was the influence of football in boys' fashions, especially sleepwear.

Another strong influence that remained important into the 1980s was that of folk and western historical styles, probably the result of our bicentennial celebrations. The influence of nostalgic styles remains strong not only in both male and female clothes today but in those of all ages, including teens and young adults as well.

Fashion is always the product of the world in which it is conceived and enjoyed. It expresses the spirit of a society and, because fashion is constantly changing, is a mirror of the times.

How a nation's children are treated and educated reveals much about its attitudes toward its citizens. How a people dress their children and how they feel about them go hand in hand. By studying children's costume, it is possible to gain insight into the attitudes of a society toward its young. And by studying a nation's past, one can better comprehend the costume worn by its children.

Fashion can best be understood when viewed in relation to everyday and work clothes, folk styles and traditions, and even the garments of a nation's less fortunate citizens. The fashions of one era are often a reflection of the folk and utilitarian styles of a previous one. And work and folk styles usually complete the cycle by taking something from current fashion. Certainly, how we dress our children for play and work reveals as much about us as does the way we dress them for special occasions. And, how a society dresses (and treats) its poor and unfortunate children reveals something of the value that it places on its individual citizens.

Evidence shows that American children's clothing utilized new European styles and daring or even "shocking" new ideas sooner than did the fashions of adults. Apparently we dress our children in new styles that we ourselves are not always ready to accept. In recent history, young children wore bikini bathing suits before their parents did. The same was true with pantaloons at the beginning of the nineteenth century. Boys' trousers appeared in American paintings with button-fly front openings, whereas men in the same paintings usually still wore the old front flap construction. Girls wore trousers or pantalets before their mothers did and made bloomers part of their regular wardrobe before their mothers did.

Not only does evidence show that American children often wore new fashions before American adults did but also that they wore it at the same time it was in fashion in Europe. There was virtually no time lag between what was first worn in Europe and in America, among the most fashion-conscious well-to-do children. Only a short time passed before homemade or mail-order clothes took up the latest trends.

4/

World events, wars, the arts, our military, royalty of other countries, and scientific discoveries have, through the years, made an impression on the minds of designers of children's fashions.

The fascination with French fashions after the Revolution was to be expected—Americans didn't want much of anything that was English. Then came the War of 1812 to add to those feelings. And, the fashions of France, after her own revolution, were so, well, revolutionary! They just seemed to suit the new exciting America and her changing attitudes toward children.

In a few decades, a new generation of parents had come along who couldn't remember the old feelings toward England. Interest in English society and fashions was rekindled and royalty again influenced American styles.

Things were happening that affected all fashions, but especially little boys' clothes in the second quarter of the nineteenth century. Reforms in Scottish representation in the English court increased the number of Scotsmen wearing tartans. They soon became so visible at court that they caused great interest in plaid fabrics and kilt suits. The kilt was a natural for little boys, since they wore skirts anyway, and this masculine form of the skirt had great appeal for Americans. The kilt suit remained in fashion for many years, into the 1880s.

Interest in plaids was further expressed through girls' clothes after Princess Alexandra appeared in plaid ball gowns about the time of her marriage in the early 1860s to the Prince of Wales, later Edward VII. Royal marriages in England have always created interest in English fashions.

The Crimean War in the 1850s had inspired exotic designs for little boys' clothes, with Turkish braids and tassels. By 1860, American Zouave militia uniforms, patterned after those of native soldiers from French Algeria, were reproduced in little boys' Zouave bolero suits. Girls' bolero suits, cloaks, and dresses took inspiration from both the Turkish and Algerian styles.

An interesting fashion in plaid bolero and kilt suits was the result of adding the Zouave jacket to the tartan kilt. These suits were then usually embellished with exotic black braid and tassels from the Turkish styles. The unusual combination of three different folk and national styles actually resulted in the most charming of ensembles. Designers of talent can take elements of style from even distant parts of their world and by instinct, timing, and artistry create works of art.

Giuseppe Garibaldi, the Italian liberator, visited London in 1864 and was received with such enthusiasm that he influenced fashion for both adults and children. His red shirts, tucked bosom shirts, fondness for gold and black braids, and striped shirts all made an impact on American children's fashions for decades. Red and striped shirts became almost synonymous with the western settlers.

The build-up of America's "new navy" and changes in regulation naval uniforms during the 1880s and 1890s had an impact on children's clothes, not only in the classic sailor suit but in hats, coats, and dresses. America's fascination with nautical styles has been a recurring theme in fashion ever since.

Teddy Roosevelt mediated the Russo-Japanese War in 1905 and won the Nobel Peace Prize. Perhaps that is why some high-necked smocks for little boys were called Russian suits in advertisements and catalogs from about 1905 to 1910.

One scientific product at the turn of the century to have a profound influence on fashion, sports clothing, infants' and toddlers' wear, and all manner of accessories was rubber. Not only did rubber play a part in fashion, but it helped to change our attitudes, too, by allowing very young boys to wear trousers and thus discard the skirts they had worn, out of necessity, for so many centuries.

Probably not even the introduction of our modern synthetics has had as profound an influence on children's clothes as did rubber. The reason is simply that synthetics did not change the design or concepts of clothing as much as they changed the methods of caring for them. Adults, being freed of washing and ironing, were the ones most affected. Children hardly noticed the change except that mothers probably made less fuss about their keeping clean.

The main developments in children's clothing since 1910 have been in fabrics and materials, as a result of the introduction of iron-free and wrinkle-resistant fibers and the use of synthetics. Knits were already developed by 1910; comfortable, freedom-of-action designs for play clothes were here; waterproof diaper covers allowed trousers for infants and toddlers; and soft, warm, protective sleepwear allowed freedom even during sleep. There also were weatherproof clothes for out of doors, especially designed and protective garments for sports, shoes for every sport and occasion, and soft knit undergarments.

It has been observed that in the world of fashion women entered World War I in the nineteenth century and emerged from it in the twentieth. It is evident that their children had already entered into the twentieth century by the end of its first decade.

— 1 —

SCARLET CLOTH &

HANGING SLEEVES

1607-1700

Children of the seventeenth century in America were dressed like miniature adults—and were expected to act like their elders, too. There was great interest in clothing; even the most religious settlers might dress their children in expensive, heavy, ornate garments. Owning a large wardrobe was reason for pride, even though a father was taxed according to the way he outfitted his family and himself.

Although clothing was expensive and a family might be well to do, nothing was thrown away. Children's clothing was made from the reusable parts of grown-ups' worn-out garments, since cloth was precious and items of ornamentation treasured. Buttons, lace, and trimmings of all kinds were carefully removed from old clothes and used over and over again.

Play was considered a waste of time, and even sinful, by the most religious and conservative colonists. But the more fun-loving Dutch settlers brought with them an educational toy enjoyed by children today: alphabet blocks. The Dutch are also credited with having brought sleds, ice skates, doll houses, golf, and the custom of making Easter eggs.

Infants' toys were not only provided for practical reasons such as for teething and learning but for religious or superstitious reasons too. Stick coral (referred to as gum stick), animal teeth, bones, and windpipes were fashioned into toys, necklaces, and teething rings for babies and toddlers. Silver handles or bells were often added to such toys for beauty and because silver or gold in a baby's hand was believed to bring him riches in later life. Whistles, either handmade or imported, were a favorite toy throughout the century.

Connecticut, Massachusetts, and Virginia passed sumptuary laws governing clothes, but New York did not. In Virginia in 1621, a resolution was made to "supress excess in cloaths" and to prevent any but high government officials from wearing "gold in their cloaths." In New England in 1634 it was illegal to have lace, silver, gold, or embroidery on any apparel. Punishment for disobeying the law was forfeiture of the clothes. Slashes in the sleeves, embroidered caps, hatbands, belts, ruffs, and beaver hats were also against the law.

Other sumptuary laws were passed in New England in 1639 and 1651, but they proved so difficult to enforce that they were finally discarded. Ministers continued to preach against these excesses but had little more success than the government officials with their laws. One of the reasons many colonists had migrated to America was to bring up their children in an atmosphere with more individual freedom than they had known in their old country. American colonists weren't prepared to tolerate restrictions on anything as personal as clothing.

A Massachusetts law of 1640 required all boys and girls to be taught "the spinning of yarn." A child could do the spinning with a hand distaff while walking or sitting. In the 1640s, Virginia established flax houses, where children were taught not only to spin but to card and knit as well.

Stockings were hand-knit and vegetable-dyed in "goodly supply" by women and girls, with blue, red, yellow, and tan being the favorite colors. They were knitted not only for a girl's own family members but for local merchants as well, who sold them. If one could afford imported silk stockings, they were available from England, where they had been produced on steel looms since 1600. But even girls who could acquire silk stockings still required a constant supply of hand-knit ones.

Toward the end of the century, three colonies passed laws in defiance of the Navigation Acts, which had required every woman and child to spin a certain amount of flax each day. Children continued to do a great deal of the spinning, however.

Youngsters in early America were always dressed beside the fire in rooms so cold that bread froze on the table or ink froze in the inkwell. Babies and toddlers were considered "unwisely and improperly" attired without a close-fitting little linen or lace cap, so in cold weather these caps were often sewn fastened on the head and the little ones wore them at night and for days at a time, until they needed washing.

Boys as well as girls were known to wear muffs to keep their hands warm in the very cold churches of New England. But even in the most extreme temperatures, a baby might be baptized with frigid water when only two to five days old. He was usually wrapped in a scarlet christening blanket with embroidered Bible verses and gold lace on the edges, because red was believed to keep an infant from harm. Some churches had wooden cages (similar to today's crib or playpen) with a slatted top for holding the babies during services.

A little boy had to wear skirts until he was toilet trained. When he was "dry" and old enough for his first breeches, it was cause for celebration. The child would be dressed in his new masculine clothes, including a small-scale sword, and paraded before the family and friends, who made a fuss over him. He was encouraged to strut and act as manly and adult as he could.

Long hanging sleeves were a part of the garments of both boys and girls as fashion, but they served an important function as well. They were convenient leading strings to be held by an older person to assist a child learning to walk. They also were employed for restraining him after he learned to walk and run, lest he stray or hurt himself.

Shoes were usually made at home by the father or by a traveling cobbler, who repaired old shoes and made new ones. One old inventory revealed that a young boy required twelve to fourteen pairs of shoes a year. By the last half of the century, most New England towns had a weaver, a tailor, and a shoemaker. The local blacksmith was popular with the children, since he probably knew how to make the new metal ice skates in his spare time. Skates had previously been carved of bone.

Starch was very important in early colonial clothing. Aprons, collars, cuffs, and caps were starched stiffly, folded, and pressed in a mangle, which resulted in folds and creases. These creases were a part of the character of children's clothes at this time.

Although clothes were kept clean and crisp, bodies were not equally clean. The soft chemise undergarment was put on primarily to protect one's garments from being soiled. The linens were usually the only parts of one's costume to be laundered. Children cleaned their teeth with a sage leaf, then washed their mouths with lemon juice to freshen the breath. Herbs, flowers, and spices were dried and made into sachets, which were then placed in the corset or held in one's handkerchief. Clove balls and sachets were hung or stored with garments not in use to make them smell sweet when worn.

Figure 1 The costume of American colonists' children was much like that of English, French, and Dutch youngsters—all of whom were dressed in miniature copies of adult garments.

The Early 1600s

In imitation of grown-ups, this little boy wears a small sword hanging from a girdle (belt) around his waist. Before he was out of diapers, he would have worn a skirt with this doublet.

Men's and boys' breeches were in a state of transition at the beginning of the seventeenth century, so several shapes were seen. This little boy wears the full trunk hose and leg cannions made up of strips of cloth, braid, or lace. These hose or upper parts were worn over a linen undergarment much like bloomers, which showed between the strips. They were stuffed to make them hold their

(1)   *(2)*   *(3)*   *(4)*

shape. Cannions were composed of several strips sewn together horizontally around the thigh as shown.

His doublet has shoulder wings and peplum made up of small flaps; at the beginning of the century, these were always six across the back and three on each side of the front. Extra hanging sleeves were worn over the sleeve at the back of the arm. More than fashion, they were used by adults to lead, restrain, or assist a young child. Braid decorates the collar, peplum flaps, and the center front seam of the sleeve.

Ribbon garters hold his white stockings in place, while his square-toed shoes tie over the tongue flaps with ties of matching ribbons. His hair was combed straight back from the face, sometimes slightly bouffant-style to form a kind of pompadour, in the same manner as that worn by men.

Figure 2 Young boys not only dressed like their fathers but were expected to act like them, too. They might be sent to college by the age of twelve or thirteen, and great importance was placed upon erect posture and a serious attitude toward life.

Breeches were still padded or stuffed with "wool, flaxe, or cattelle's tails" to make them retain their shape. A young boy wore full knee breeches pleated into the waist, tapered, and just slightly gathered at the knee.

At the end of the sixteenth century, stand-up collars and ruffs were becoming softer and turning down or "falling." Although still starched and standing, the edges and points of this boy's collar are curved down. His doublet has shoulder wings but no hanging sleeves. (After hanging sleeves were no longer fashionable for adults, they remained stylish for young children and elderly people.)

Braid trims the front of the bodice, the sleeve seams, and the skirt tabs. This boy wears lace cuffs. Boys' coats were sometimes worked with all-over crewel embroidery designs of blue, black, or brown yarns.

Ribbon garters and bows hold his hand-knit stockings that might be blue, red, yellow, or tan. His shoes are tied with ribbons for dress wear. Strings or leather strips were used for everyday wear or work. Boys are known to have required twelve to fourteen pairs of handmade shoes a year.

His hair is combed straight back from the face, as is the little boy's.

Figure 3 It was considered unwise and improper for a baby to be without a cap on his head. Caps of linen or wool were often beautifully embroidered and handed down from child to child, even generation to generation.

Dark red was a favorite color for dresses, with yellow or blue being worn also. Fasteners were usually drawstrings. This dress, with a plain neck and sleeves, is similar to that of the young girl in Figure 4, but without collar or cuffs. The neckline is covered with a kerchief tucked under a belt that has a bell fastened to the end.

Like our present-day baby furniture, the enclosed chair serves as chair, table, and play area. A dowel at the front holds a series of rings for the baby to spin and slide and eventually, perhaps, with which to learn to count. Baby walkers were already being used at the beginning of the century.

Sea coral, like that in the baby's hand, was a favorite toy and teething ring throughout the century. Less expensive ones were plain, but some were elegantly set in fancy silver or gold handles with little silver bells attached. Silver or gold in a baby's hand was believed to bring him wealth in later years.

Figure 4 A 1640 law required that all children, both boys and girls, be taught "the spinning of yarn." Young girls also were taught to card and knit. They not only knitted stockings for their own family members, but often made them for local merchants to sell. This little girl holds a distaff for hand spinning, often carried around by children while they attended to their other chores.

Similar to the boy's doublet, this little girl's bodice points in front and has shoulder wings to cover the ties that hold the sleeves in place. One dress might have several pairs of extra sleeves in different colors or stripes. Dutch settlers' children wore bright colors; the English used brown, tan, or red, while the French often wore blue or yellow. This girl's collar is "falling," as described in Figure 2; her cuffs are little starched ruffs.

A sheer, lace-trimmed white apron is pinned to the bodice of her dress and, as a result, called a pin-a-fore apron. French children usually wore only white embroidered caps and aprons, whereas those of Dutch descent might wear light blue, yellow, or white ones, starched crisply. Amber beads were believed to prevent croup.

The Mid-1600s

Figure 5 A little boy had, out of necessity, to wear skirts until he was completely dry. Some boys continued to wear them until five or six years of age. This little boy wears a bodice with the peplum tabs on the outside of the skirt instead of tucked inside. Except for these tabs being on the outside, his outfit has much the same appearance as the dress of the little girl in Figure 6. Although boys and girls might wear the bodice either way, little boys were more likely to leave the tabs on the outside. When he begins wearing breeches, this boy might continue to wear the same doublet (bodice), since the skirt or breeches tie onto the body as shown in Figure 9. A bodice might open in either the front or back, with front closures usually preferred for boys. Both the skirt hem and bodice tabs are edged with dark braid. His collar and cuffs are sheer and lace-edged.

His doublet has long hanging sleeves, which were used as "leading strings" to assist or restrain him. These hanging sleeves were as commonly used as were the actual strings (shown in Figures 16 and 22) that were attached to the dress or doublet shoulders.

He still wears a lace cap like that worn by the baby in Figure 8. These little

(7)

(5)

(6)

(8)

(9)

caps were sometimes fastened so that the children could not remove them, especially in cold weather. Since children slept in them, caps might therefore remain on the child's head for several days at a time until laundered.

Figure 6 Crisply starched sheer aprons, collars, and cuffs were a mark of pride at this time, especially among French and Dutch colonists. It was the Dutch who invented starch and brought it to the colonies. This little girl's apron has a bib in front with lace at the waistline as well as around the hem. Her blue dress is trimmed with a heavy corded braid down the front sleeve seam and a plain flat braid around the skirt hem. The bodice laces up the back.

She wears a tiny sheer cap on the back of her head over her long, curly hair.

Her collar and cuffs (like those of the little boys of Figures 5 and 9) are part of the soft white chemise undergarment worn next to the body, with the cuffs folded back over the dress sleeves. The chemise usually came well down onto the thighs and sometimes for girls was even longer. It, and aprons, were laundered, whereas the outer clothing was rarely, if ever washed.

Figure 7 The young girl here wears the more conservative style of clothes commonly seen on English colonists. Her dark dress has small puffs at the tops of the sleeves and fastens down the bodice front with hooks. A low, wide neck is covered by a soft kerchief made of the same white linen as the pleated apron. She wears tiny white cuffs on her sleeves.

A hood of either white or black was usually worn under the high, wide-brimmed English-style hat. The more conservative and religious the person, the plainer was the hat band. These cloth hoods were also worn without the hat.

She holds the baby's stick coral described in Figure 3. Although boys went to school, girls were barely educated at all. They were taught needlework skills at an early age, so pincushions and scissors suspended from their waists or necks were a regular part of their costume. The scissors belonging to this young girl are inside a small scissors case. These holders, of metal or needlework and sometimes beautifully decorated, were highly prized possessions. Several pairs of scissors were recently unearthed during excavation of Wolstenholme Towne colony in Virginia.

Figure 8 A wolf's tooth on a ribbon worn around a baby's neck was used for teething, but it also was supposed to bring him good fortune in life. Deer teeth were used in this same manner, as were bones. He also teethed on stick coral, which was often set into a fancy silver handle with a silver bell at the end. A dried turkey windpipe might also be used for a baby's teething toy at this time.

Yellow was a popular color for baby dresses, as was red. This baby wears a yellow dress trimmed with coral red braid on the bodice, sleeve seams, and skirt hem. The full sleeves fasten under shoulder wings. The little starched, stand-up collar is lace trimmed, as is the sheer apron bib and skirt. The shoes are yellow with red ties.

He sits in an elaborately carved and turned chair-on-a-chair, popular in the early part of the century. A bar across the front, inserted into holes or slots in the arm rests, keeps him from falling out. High chairs were usually pushed up to the table, but the idea for a tray across the front was still decades in the future.

Figure 9 This little boy wears a simple solid-color doublet with twelve peplum skirt tabs. The collar is lying flat, since the stiff, stand-up styles of the beginning of the century were no longer fashionable by mid-century. The collar and matching cuffs are of lace, for dress-up. They would be plain for play or for the country. There are no wings at the shoulder; by this time new sleeves are sewn in. Buttons were of silver, wood, or covered with crochet or cloth.

The full breeches stop above the knee, where the stockings are tied with garters. These breeches are pleated at the waist instead of being gathered, and are held up by string ties that fasten through the doublet skirt tabs. Museum doublets reveal small round skirt tab buttonholes.

The large tongues on the square-toed shoes are almost covered by ribbon ties. Expensive dress-up shoes might be white or light blue, but everyday ones were brown with string ties. The alphabet blocks in front of him were a toy brought to America by the Dutch colonists.

Figure 10 Stomachers were wedge-shaped pieces of wood covered with crewel embroidery. Inserted into the dress bodice to hold the body flat and straight, they were sometimes built into the bodice, sometimes worn under laces and at other times were part of the corset. This one is inserted into the embroidered dress front, which fastens down the center over it with hooks and eyes. The dress neck is wide and low like those of Figures 20 and 21.

This little girl wears the fashionable large "falling band" (collar) of the third quarter of the seventeenth century, shown in Plate 3 in its various shapes and sizes. The band or collar is edged with lace.

Many small darts formed the flared, sheer cuffs from a straight piece of cloth. Her full sleeves are open at the front seams and caught at intervals with ties, revealing the chemise underneath. These openings or slashes were frowned upon by the Puritans; wearing a costume with more than one was illegal in New England by 1634. Enforcement of the laws against them was so difficult that they were discarded before the 1660s.

Her apron was stiffly starched and pressed so that the creases showed. Her bodice has extra hanging sleeves reaching down to the hem of her long skirt train. These long sleeves often had pockets in their ends for carrying small articles.

(12)

(10)

(11)

(13)

(14)

Long curly hair had become the modish look for both girls and boys by this time, instead of being hidden completely by caps. The large plumed hat on the floor was often worn over the small white cap.

In her hand she holds a horn book. Paddle-shaped, of wood, it had a printed sheet with alphabets and syllables, covered by a thin, transparent sheet of horn for protection.

Figure 11 Long hanging sleeves at the back of the arm fall to the skirt hem. These sleeves, when held by an older person, were used for assisting young children to walk, run, or climb, as well as for restricting their wandering or keeping them from getting into trouble.

A little boy still in diapers wears a skirt tied to his doublet. When trained, he will wear little breeches, which will be tied up under the tabs, as in Figure 9. The wide, lace-edged collar and cuffs are part of the chemise undergarment. No openings or slashes appear in the full sleeves; the front seam is closed all the way to the wrists.

A popular embellishment of the period was ribbon bands across the center front seam of the skirt and body. They were fringed on the ends, and the same ribbon edged the skirt hem. His close-fitting cap, like his sister's, allows his hair to fall in soft curls around his face. He wears a wolf's tooth on a ribbon around his neck, as described in Figure 8.

Figure 12 Throughout the Middle Ages and into the sixteenth century, babies had been wrapped and bound like the child's doll on the floor (left foreground). Although not actually wrapped and bound in such a manner, this infant is securely fastened inside a long, capelike swaddling garment. These gowns fastened down the front with double button closures, as seen here, or with ties. Such garments prevented the little one from sucking and drooling on his hands, a very real problem in a room cold enough to freeze ink in its inkwell or liquids on the table. It also kept his body warmth inside, since he was also wrapped in several long skirts or "wrappers."

An interesting cap-and-bib combination head covering is shown here in two slightly different versions. The younger infant wears one that is quite long in front and closes in the back where the cap crown is drawn up with a drawstring. The baby in the chair wears a shorter, pleated one with a front opening.

Figure 13 The ring-shaped toy in this toddler's hand is a popular early baby rattle made of a turkey windpipe. It was inflated, stitched end to end, and dried with a pebble inside. This toy was more popular in America and other remote areas than the silver rattle for sale in Europe at the time.

This child wears a dress of black velvet trimmed with scarlet ribbon bows on the sleeves. Little hanging sleeves are lined with scarlet. (One hangs through the chair on his left.) The white chemise sleeves underneath are also tied with scarlet ribbons. A little stomacher (described in Figure 10) is worn in the front of the bodice, covered by the bib of the long sheer apron.

Spiral and ball-and-reed turnings form the stretchers and spindles of this mid-seventeenth-century high chair. The legs are spaced so that the chair widens at its base, to prevent it from tipping over. A rod could be inserted into the arms across the front, as in Figure 8, to keep the baby from falling out.

Figure 14 Doublet skirt tabs had grown larger and fewer in number at mid-century. There were two large ones at each side in front and four in all across the back. By the early eighteenth century, the tabs will have grown still more to become flared coattails. The chemise underneath shows through slashes in the full sleeves. Its large "falling band" collar and cuffs might be plain or lace-edged. The family's religion and wealth dictated the degree, although a child of French settlers would probably wear more lace than an English child.

This boy's breeches are tied onto the doublet through small buttonholes worked into the waistline. Breeches, having lost most of their fullness, were becoming knee breeches, and would change very little throughout the eighteenth century. Garters are tied around his stockings below the knees. His shoes are tied across the tongue with wide ribbons.

Both suits and stockings were made in a variety of colors and fabrics at this time, such as black, brown, purple, red, or blue, in stripes or "spotted cloth." Wool serge, broadcloth, satin, velvet, or brocade might be used, according to the occasion and the wealth and/or religion of the boy's parents. The ribbon decorations described in Figure 11 were used on boys' doublets and breeches also.

His hat might be plain or decorated with ribbons and plumes like the one on the floor in the foreground.

*The Late
1600s*

Figure 15 Worn for a time during the 1660s and 1670s were petticoat breeches consisting of a full skirt, sometimes divided, worn over very full linen breeches, with ribbon loops usually decorating the center front opening. This brown petticoat was pleated rather than gathered, as some were.

This boy's brown doublet has the slashed or open sleeve seams caught at their hem with small ties. There are no skirt tabs on it, making the full doublet similar to a bolero, with the chemise shirt blousing out underneath. The large falling band collar was still fashionable, though starched collars had given way to these soft ones.

When this boy wears a hat over his long wavy hair it will look like that of Figures 7 or 14. His tan stockings are held up by tied garters, while his brown shoes have instep ties across the tongue flaps. (After 1680 the long full coat of Figure 23 would evolve and remain in fashion for many decades for older boys.

(15)

(16)

(17)

(18)

(19)

Little boys would continue to be dressed in "old-fashioned" doublets until the early eighteenth century.

Figure 16 The most outstanding part of this outfit is the baby's "pudding" cap, known in France as a *bourrelet*. The name apparently came from *bourrée*, meaning dance, because the movement of a toddler's first steps somewhat resembled dancing. Sometimes the entire cap was padded, but most often the padding was only in a thick roll or cushion that circled the head. This padding protected the head from injury when the little one fell. Babies still fall frequently at the toddler stage today, but in the days of long skirts and petticoats it must have happened almost every time a child tried to crawl or stand. Antique baby clothes usually show signs of heavy wear at the front hem, caused by its being caught between the floor and the child's knees or feet. Some museum dresses have the front hem completely worn to tatters.

This baby boy wears a brown skirt and bodice with red and yellow striped sleeves over a white chemise. His collar, large and squared at the corners, covers the bib of his linen apron. His little yellow shoes have red soles and ties.

Also noteworthy are the "leading strings," or ribbons sewn to the back of the dress bodice, being held by the young boy. In Europe, these strings were usually satin ribbons as much as four or five feet long and one to two inches wide. In America, they were often made of linen and decorated with crewel embroidery.

Figure 17 Not only was the red blanket or cloth laid across the cradle hood for protection against drafts, but it also was added because of the belief that scarlet laid over the head would keep an infant from harm.

Infants wore a linen shirt with several linen petticoats and wrap skirts underneath a "barrow coat." This was a flannel blanket wrapped snugly around the body to up under the arms. The long part below the feet was turned up and pinned, swaddling him securely. In really severe weather, he would be wrapped up to his neck, as is the baby in Figure 12.

Cradles usually had holes in the sides, sometimes heart shaped, or small knobs called *bokelles* for fastening cords. These cords served to keep an infant from kicking off his covers and to keep him from falling out of bed, at the same time. In times when the temperature of a bedroom often was below freezing, exposure in damp clothing could bring on sickness or death.

One clue concerning the origin of an old cradle is said to be the size of its hood. Colder climates required more protection, thus had deeper hoods. Southern climates allowed small decorative hoods or none at all.

Wicker cradles were commonly used also, because they could be burned after an infant had an infectious disease or died from some unknown malady. They were cheap and could be replaced by a new hand-woven one.

Figure 18 Toward the end of the century, young girls wore curled and wired locks of their own, or pinned false hair over their ears. Corkscrewlike curls and wires caused the locks to bounce when the head was moved. Ministers preached against these "heart breakers," as they were called, and denounced "intolerable pride in clothes and hair" as being sinful, but to little effect. The rest of this girl's hair is pulled toward the crown and wound into a topknot. Her "heart breakers" are tied with ribbon bows.

Red velvet was a favorite material for little girls' dresses such as this one with its wide, short sleeves open at the front seams. They were often decorated with gold lace and edged with red satin ribbon. A large collar of fancy lace is here pleated at each shoulder to make it conform to the child's shape and lie down flat as it goes around to the center back.

Long hanging sleeves are suspended at the backs of this girl's arms. One American child's portrait of 1670 shows the hanging sleeves folded up and pinned to keep them from dragging on the floor. These very long sleeves were used for leading strings as often as actual strings were (see Figure 16). The sleeves are known to have had pockets sewn into them, so a child would have a place to carry toys or other items. A chemise undergarment shows through the sleeve opening and at the lower arm, where it ends in lace-edged ruffles tied with red ribbons.

This little girl wears a sheer lace-trimmed apron with a bib and carries a folding fan.

Figure 19 At bedtime, young children were given mulled cider or simmering beer to warm them, because bedrooms often had temperatures below freezing. In the morning, they cleaned their teeth with a sage leaf and washed their mouths with lemon juice to sweeten the breath.

This little girl, ready for her day's lessons, wears a dress similar to that in Figure 18. The brown dress has red ribbon ties at the open front sleeve seams that reveal the white chemise underneath. The sheer chemise has very full sleeves ending in ruffles at the lower arm.

Her apron has a high-necked bib with the armholes falling out over the shoulders, forming little cap sleeves. The armholes, pointed waistline seam, and hem are edged with narrow lace.

She wears the very popular cloth hood on her head favored by grown women at this time. It is basically a half-circle with the straight edge going over the head and the curved edge gathered in around the neck. The corners tie in front. Sometimes a fitted cap was worn underneath and, at other times, a large black hat was put on over it, as in Figure 7. Her shoes are brown with red ties and squared toes.

—2—

LEADING STRINGS &

SILVER BUTTONS

1700-1770

Not only did girls of all ages wear corsets during the first two-thirds of the eighteenth century, but so did many young boys. Stay makers advertised stays (corsets) for children made of muslin and polished steel, bone, wood, or tin. Grownups were preoccupied with training or even forcing children to sit and stand upright. Children were often strapped in chairs or stocks for hours at a time to force their backs to grow straight. Parents were known to have strapped young children with back boards and steel collars in their unrelenting efforts to enforce erect posture.

Although religion played an important part in their lives, colonists' attitudes were Calvinistic concerning clothing and wealth. Being able to afford lots of expensive and stylish clothes was an indication that one was among God's favored, and clothing was therefore something to take pride in.

A length of fabric cost four times as much in the colonies as it did in England, and taxes had to be paid by anyone using a spinning wheel or loom at home to make cloth for their own and their children's clothes. That is, they had to pay taxes if English officials *knew* they were making cloth at home. It was difficult, if not impossible, to enforce such laws. Things got so bad that in 1729 it was even declared illegal to wear cotton. By 1736, the laws had to be repealed because they were so openly violated.

The first American fabric printer opened a shop in Boston in 1712, producing hand-blocked cloth. All printed fabrics were hand blocked until after 1750, when it was discovered that copper-plate printing could be used on cloth. Some of these hand-printed colors were quite lovely and successful, except for the greens, which could be produced only by overprinting blue onto yellow. It would take until the early nineteenth century to work out formulas for reliable green inks.

Fighting with the French and with Indians had been going on since the 1690 massacre at Schenectady and would end in Quebec in 1760. (The last six years of the conflict are known as the French and Indian War.) The fear of massacre, which certainly affected the lives of youngsters, continued after 53 people were killed and 111 taken prisoner at Deerfield, Massachusetts, in 1704. Young children were no longer allowed to work in the fields, because they were too small to protect themselves from Indians. When they reached age twelve and had been trained to bear arms and other weapons, they were ready to help with the crops.

There have always been numerous reasons for keeping a toddler within sight and under some control, but in times of such dangers it seemed even more justified. With forests coming to the very edge of a village or one's lands, there would be dangers enough without Indians. With a constant fear of the death or abduction of one's children, it's understandable that leading strings were sewn or pinned to almost every little dress. Not only were they held by an older person, but lead strings were likely tied at times to a tree or fence post. Since they often measured as much as five feet in length, this could have given a child a play area of about eight feet. Inside the house, a young child was sometimes given mobility by placing him in a "go cart" or standing stool very much like the baby walkers used today.

Parents didn't worry about keeping a child's feet dry, since it was believed that shoes with thin soles to let the water come in freely would make them tough; children's feet were even dipped in cold water to toughen them. But even though cold liquids were believed healthful to the body's exterior, it was deemed unhealthy to drink cold liquids. An old almanac warned that children's beer should always be heated. It was the custom, on cold nights, to warm the bedsheets with a bed warmer and give the child a drink of warm cider or beer before tucking him into bed for the night.

Well-to-do colonists sent their children to English schools to study from English books and learn English ways for, after all, America *was* English until the Revolution. Those wealthy colonial children who didn't go off to school in England went off to school in New England.

At the beginning of the eighteenth century, a schoolboy's wardrobe might include a dozen shirts, eight cravats (four with lace), and a half-dozen waistcoats. It also usually included red, blue, black, and white stockings, along with at least a half-dozen pairs of breeches. Hats, gloves, handkerchieves, a dozen pairs of shoes, and combs rounded out his wardrobe. One of the most interesting items that a boy took off to school with him was his sewing kit, including several dozen gold, silver, and black buttons with lots of silk thread for mending. Of the dozen and a half handkerchieves a boy took off to school with him, many were short-lived. It seems that a favorite sport of a schoolboy was to tie a large knot in a handkerchief and hit other boys with it.

Girls were also sent off, to boarding school or to board with a relative or friend while attending school. A young lady of eleven or twelve might take with her a dozen gowns of lawn, cambric, or silk, a red petticoat, one good hat with a fine band, a hoop, two aprons, a cloak, and one good white corset. Her accessories might include six pairs of shoes, a dozen pairs of stockings in both cotton and wool, and ten pairs of gloves.

To complete her wardrobe, she would also need a mask, a fan, several handkerchieves, and new earrings and clasps. For mending and replacing lost items, her sewing box would include twelve to eighteen buttons of different kinds and colors, silk thread, and yards and yards of ribbons. She might also take to school with her one of the new toothbrushes being sold in some apothecary shops.

From 1700 to 1730

Figure 20 Lacy aprons were considered fashion rather than work garments in the early 1700s. Often sheer, they might be tucked on the bib, as is this one, or embroidered. The wide lace used around apron skirts was expensive and usually imported. When aprons wore out, the lace would be ripped off and used again on some new article of clothing.

Early in the century, skirts were straight in front but very full and long in back. Overskirts, open in front, trailed in quite long trains, even on young children. The corset stomacher here, described in Figure 10, is long and pointed, giving a long-waisted look to this fashionable little girl.

Sleeves now were close fitting at the shoulder and upper arm, and then flared out at the elbow. Usually large pleated cuffs were added, as shown, but occasionally sleeves were plain. The soft white chemise undergarment ruffles showed at the sleeves and neck.

Earth tones, such as brown, rust, amber, coral, and many shades of red and orange, were popular at this time. Black was used for children's clothes, too, as were striped fabrics of black, white, and earthy tones.

This girl's hair is pulled back from the face in a small pompadour and decorated with a standing ruffle called a *fontange*, which was the vogue for women for a time.

Figure 21 Velvets, brocades, taffetas, satins, and coarse homespuns were used for dresses. This girl wears a dark color with a bodice that is long and pointed and has a wide, low neckline. Sleeves were fitted at the shoulder and flared at the elbow, usually with large, heavy looking cuffs pleated in front to make them conform to the curve of the arm. The ruffles on the chemise undergarment had become quite large and full and were usually made of a wide lace.

The sheer apron bib, which fits over the stomacher, and its full skirt are em-

24 /

(20)

(21)

(22)

(23)

25 /

broidered. Thread and yarn colors at this time were still mostly earth tones and blues, with very little green used.

This girl's hair is pulled back and up into a small pompadour decorated with ribbons. Ribbon, flowers, and combinations of both were very fashionable in the American colonies, usually being preferred to the *fontange* shown in Figure 20.

There was a charming tradition in New England during berry-picking season. Children of the towns were divided into teams and given baskets decorated with colored ribbons representing the different teams. There were contests to see who could bring in the most berries, which grew in abundance.

Figure 22 Satin ribbon leading strings were attached to the the back of the bodice at the shoulders for helping or controlling a little child's walking or wandering. With dangerous forests just outside of town, and with horses, mud puddles, and manure in the streets, leading strings could give a certain freedom, yet at the same time keep a child under control. These strings, sometimes crewel embroidered, might be as much as five feet long. They are being held here by the older boy.

Little boys and girls were attired in much the same clothes, with those of the boys usually being somewhat plainer—but not always. This very little boy, who is still in diapers, has a long train on his skirt like those of girls. His chemise, worn underneath, has ruffles extending beneath his bodice sleeves.

His lace apron has a bib that covers the stiff pointed dress bodice and comes out over the skirt and apron skirt. The soft cloth cap is much like a man's night cap. Little boys also wore turbans and, in Europe, some were even known to have worn the pleated *fontange* in Figure 20.

Figure 23 Holding the little boy's leading strings, an older boy shows the new coat and knee breeches that males would continue to wear for many, many years. The coat would grow quite full before the Revolution, and then become narrower. Here, narrow in the shoulders and upper arms, the coat flares out quite fully at the tails, with extra fullness pleated in at the side backs. The sleeves flare at the lower arm and fold up in large heavy cuffs, so heavy, in fact, that they had to be buttoned in place. Braid embellishes the buttonholes on the coat front, cuffs, and pocket flaps.

Neckties or cravats had become the latest male fashion. (To wear one properly, place the center of the long cravat at the front of the neck. Take both ends to the back, cross them, continue toward the front, and loop one end over the other as shown.) The chemise, which had become the shirt, had a band at the neckline and opened at the chest.

This boy carries the new tricorne (three-cornered) hat that would remain popular until the end of the century. His hair is wavy and long in imitation of the fashionable middle-part wigs worn by men. The instep of his shoes no longer fastens with ties across the tongue flap; instead, the newly fashionable buckles were used.

*From 1730
to 1750*

Figure 24 Just home from his lessons or school, this young boy carries his drawstring book bag. These bags, usually made by a student's mother, would remain virtually unchanged over the next two hundred years. The Sears Roebuck Company pictured one in their mail-order catalog in the early twentieth century that was almost identical with one in a 1744 print in the Metropolitan Museum.

The neck of this coat stands high and the sleeves turn back into full cuffs that are buttoned in place. Coat skirts had grown quite full, with stiffened pleats sewn in at the side-back seams. Although similar to that of Figure 23, this coat has plain, undecorated buttonholes. It is of a plain brown wool, but for dress wear it might be of red, blue, or yellow in velvet, brocade, or satin. It has buttoned pocket flaps such as those in Figure 23.

Of special interest here is the apron—a large triangle with the top point buttoned onto a coat button at the chest. Strip belts are fastened at the waist, wrapped around the body, and tied in front, holding the apron in place. White, black, or unbleached linen, as well as woven striped cloth, was used for this practical apron worn by both men and boys during the eighteenth century.

When this boy wears a hat, it is a tricorne, as in Figures 23 and 40. His hair is pulled back in the cadogan style and tied with a black ribbon, leaving a fringe of curls around his face. His shoes have the newly fashionable small buckles instead of ties over the instep, and his stockings are brown.

Figure 25 Just in from the garden or a trip to town, a young girl wears the flat-crowned, wide-brimmed hat of the period. These soft, floppy hats were made of cloth and decorated with flowers or crewel embroidery. The crown on some hats was no more than a padded circle sewn on top; on others, it might be as much as an inch high. They were held on by ribbons attached at the crown and tied under the chin. A small, white, close-fitting cap was often worn underneath the hat.

The striped dress is much like that in Figure 28 but with the large cuffs of Figure 21. Her apron bib is pinned onto the dress, making it a pin-a-fore. She wears on her hands mitts like those in Figure 28.

Figure 26 Baby walkers, sometimes called go-carts and standing stools, had already been used in Europe for at least a hundred years by the beginning of the eighteenth century. They are, incidentally, still in use today in much the same form as this one. Their design, wider at the base than at the top, prevents them from tipping over, while keeping the baby back an arm's length from things he

(25)

(27)

(24)

(26)

(28)

shouldn't touch. The tray around the top holds his toys, which might be the coral of Figure 3 or the turkey windpipe rattle in Figure 13.

Baby dresses for either boys or girls were like those of girls and women. The neck is wide and low and, although hidden by the walker, the little bodice front is pointed at the waist. This dress is pale yellow; the chemise underneath is white, with its sleeves and neck ruffle showing. This baby wears a small white cap because he is protected by the walker from falling and bumping his head. When out of the walker, he would wear the pudding cap in Figure 16.

Figure 27 This boy's full coat and triangular apron are like those in Figure 24 except that he has the very latest style sleeves, which are split at the sides and have no cuffs. His coat is brown, lined with red; the apron is black.

His hair is combed straight back on top of his head and down the back, and even the sides behind his ears are also combed back. The side hair to the front of the ear is cut short and curled toward the cheeks. The top and back hair is caught with a black ribbon and put into a black "wig bag." (This cadogan hair style was popular with grown men and with soldiers on through the Revolution.) At times, the ribbon or a black cravat encircled the neck, being tied, then tied around the hair.

Playing cards was an immensely popular pastime; this boy is building a house of cards.

Figure 28 Print fabrics were available after 1712, when the first American fabric printer opened a shop in Boston for his hand-blocked prints. This low-necked dress fastens down the front with hooks and eyes over a stomacher underneath, as described in Figure 10. Dresses at this time had become charmingly simple but would grow complex again in a few years. This apron, worn under the bodice point, is embroidered all around the hem. Satin was a popular fabric for crewel-decorated aprons, as were sheer muslin or linen. These elegant little aprons were dress-up; plain ones were put on for work.

The cadogan hair style was copied by girls, so this one's hair is pulled back and tied with a ribbon at the neck. She wears drop earrings and a bead necklace. Sheer, lace, or taffeta fingerless mitts of varying lengths were worn on the hands at this time; black lace was especially stylish.

Figure 29 Still in diapers and skirts, this little boy wears an interesting mixture of male and female dress. His gray bodice with its large buttoned cuffs and metal buttons on the front is patterned after a man's coat, while the neckline and pointed waist are like women's dresses. He wears a chemise that shows at the wrists but not at the neckline.

The skirts are gray also and flared instead of gathered, making the outfit look

From 1750 to 1770

(29)

(30)

(31)

(32)

like a man's coat. A black sash, its ends decorated with embroidery, is tied up under the bodice point.

His shoes have the new buckles instead of ties, but they still have large tongue flaps. His hair style is one popular with the military. The side hair is rolled into sausage curls over the ears, while the rest is tied in back with a black ribbon that then ties around his neck.

Figure 30 New style coats, before and during the 1750s and 1760s, had lost some of their previous fullness, while fronts were already beginning to curve or cut away toward the back. Cuffs had become smaller, too. Braid, embroidery, or lace decorated the fronts, hem, back split, and cuffs, sometimes in elaborate designs. Waistcoats were long and cut away at the corners, too, and were always trimmed, even with plain coats.

This chemise or shirt has frills at the neck opening and a soft white cravat tied around the neck, as described in Figure 23, then tied in a knot that blends in with the ruffle of the shirt.

The new slender knee breeches had narrow bands below the knee with little buckle fasteners. White stockings were always worn for dress occasions, tan or gray for play.

This boy's hair is worn in the fashionable cadogan style described in Figures 24 and 27. By this time, well-to-do colonial children were dressed as fashionably as children in Europe. Ships were crossing the seas more often, bringing goods and fashion news to the colonists.

Figure 31 Children and babies wore dressing gowns like their mothers' robe à la française or sacque. It was worn over a chemise, a corset, and petticoats, or at times a dress, depending upon the time of day and the weather. The sacque was straight in front and fitted in the shoulders, but flared out at the sides. Extra fullness was pleated into the back, and the skirts flowed behind in a train.

This toddler wears the padded pudding cap described in Figure 16 for protection to his head should he fall. The name was probably the origin of the term "puddin' head." It is easy to imagine one affectionately calling a toddler "little puddin' head."

Commode, or "necessary," chairs for children had been used in the previous century, but early in the eighteenth century someone thought of adding rockers. Some of these chairs had a hinged seat, which would convert it to an ordinary rocker, whereas others had a padded cushion for the same purpose. Some of these little chairs were elaborately carved, but others had decorative cut-out designs such as this one.

Figure 32 Simplicity was the mode for girls' dresses at mid-century and during the third quarter of it. This girl's bodice is decorated only with little pleats at the shoulders, which add a small drape under the neckline. This is in rust color, but yellow, blue, brown, and plum were popular colors also. The sleeves have flounces or ruffles of the same cloth. The white chemise undergarment shows in a ruffle at the neckline and adds two lace ruffles underneath the sleeve flounce. Sometimes there were two sleeve ruffles as well.

Skirts were plain at this time, with sheer aprons worn only occasionally. Velvets, taffetas, and the new printed linens were popular fabrics.

This young girl wears her hair in the stylish cadogan, tied in a satin ribbon at her neck. Small white caps and wide-brimmed hats, or colorful satin hair ribbons, were worn with this dress.

— 3 —

"SUNDAY FINERY" &

STRAW HATS

1770-1800

Portraits during the last third of the eighteenth century mirrored changes taking place in attitudes toward children. There was less insistence that a child be a miniature adult in appearance and behavior. The idea that a child's body was proportioned differently from full-grown physiques and thus required at least some freedom of movement was new. Children would still be corseted and their backs braced, with clothing still copying that of adults, but their own special needs were slowly being recognized. However, some parents were still obsessed with erect posture, and little girls often had knitting needles inserted into their corset fronts to poke them if they slumped over too much.

Writers philosophized about child rearing; youngsters were becoming more respected as individuals in the family and in society. Paintings of children with a dress off one shoulder, a sash untied, or little bare feet showing were the fashion. Informal family groups in which young children were shown playing with a toy, climbing over someone's lap or furniture, or embracing a family member were tremendously popular. For the first time children were painted with twinkling eyes and laughing faces.

It was still the custom to remove lace and other trimmings from a garment before giving it away. Many were given away, never thrown out. Even when a garment was worn out, the usable sections were cut up for new jackets, waistcoats, and children's clothing. (In the English royal court, ladies were ordered to remove lace from their dresses before giving them to the servants, to reuse it on new dresses.) Even in the best society it was acceptable to alter children's clothes as a child grew, and to plan for future growth by building in tucks, deep hems, and drawstrings.

Toys and play were no longer considered very sinful, and more social activities were encouraged. Young girls had "coming out" parties when they turned twelve. These were always garden parties or dances, and boys were rarely included, the girls dancing with each other. Dress for these occasions was always a girl's best clothing. (This practice still occurred in some areas of the South up to World War II.)

Playing cards was still a favorite pastime, even though it was frowned upon or illegal in some towns. Though cards were called "the devil's picture books," friends often congregated at one another's homes for an evening or Sunday afternoon of card games. Musical get-togethers were favorite amusements, too, and children routinely received music lessons as part of their education and social training at this time.

As the Revolution neared, British goods, including cloth, were boycotted in some ports. There was much patriotic talk and even songs written about dressing in "clothes of your own make and spinning," even though, in making their own cloth, women defied the strict laws against home weaving. A mother could raise the flax and wool, make it into thread and dye it—but not weave it! The law said it was to be sent to England to be woven; then, back in America, the colonist had to buy the cloth. Being forbidden to make their own cloth for their children's clothes was the last straw of tyranny for many colonial mothers.

During the war, young girls suffered from shortages of the gauze cloth so popular for hats, hair styles, and dresses. Two other favorites, green slippers and silk, had to be sacrificed too. The lack of pins was a serious hardship, and children's aprons and scarves had to be fastened with thorns or spines of plants. This shortage did not affect the fastening of baby diapers, however, because they were tied, not pinned. Before the war was over, clothing and accessories were so scarce that children were wearing their Sunday finery for the most ordinary wear.

After the Revolution, Americans again received fashion plates from England and France showing the latest styles being worn abroad. These fashion plates would eventually lead to the publication of fashion magazines.

At the end of the century, straw hat manufacturing was begun in America. The leghorn hat so identified with Americans was worn by everyone of fashion.

Little boys wore the shocking "vulgar" pantaloons before adults were ready to accept them. Many older men would never accept them, remaining in knee breeches or "small clothes" throughout their lives. There were political overtones associated with pantaloons, with long pants symbolizing rebellion and even lawlessness in the minds of more conservative citizens. But little boys were relatively free of such associations, and, besides, the pantaloons' comfort and freedom made them naturals for their active bodies. Boys would grow to manhood at the close of the eighteenth century thinking of pants as just another perfectly natural article of male clothing, which they were eventually.

34 /

The baby carriage was first manufactured in England in the 1780s by makers of horse-drawn carriages. Since the British horse-drawn carriage was considered the finest in the world, it was natural that the British baby carriage, or "pram," would follow in the tradition, becoming admired and sought after the world over. The earliest prams were like wagons or horse-drawn carriages, but they developed into their unique form before long. Walking dresses were the fashion for girls and ladies, so the pram brought about an interest in infant dresses, to be displayed while strolling with baby on the common. Bonnets and large gauze hats or plume-decorated ones were coordinated with bright silk sashes and colorful shoes for the little ones' afternoon outings.

Figure 33 Both boy and girl toddlers were dressed in soft muslin or gauze frocks with necklines so wide and low that they often fell off one or both shoulders, as seen here. A number of portraits from the period show cherubic youngsters with bare feet and carelessly worn dresses.

From 1770 to 1780

This little one wears a dress of thin, off-white muslin with tucks sewn across the bodice and around the skirt hem. Sometimes, instead of tucks, ribbon was sewn around the skirt, as in Figure 34. The neck is self-bound, the sleeves cuffed. A lilac-colored satin sash is long enough to serve as leading strings.

Little bangs and side fringes of hair are brushed toward the face with the remaining hair brushed toward the back and softly curled.

Paul Revere was one of the silversmiths who created rattles, toys, and teething rings of silver and sea coral like that in the toddler's hand.

Figure 34 Gauze was often woven with a thick–thin design, giving it a striped look. In this little girl's dress, the gauze appears pink-and-white striped as a result of the pink slip underneath showing through the thinner stripes. Several rows of white ribbon or self-bound fabric are sewn around the skirt hem, and one row edges the neck. The sleeves are fitted at the shoulder and slightly gathered at the elbow.

Instead of ribbon, this sash is made of several yards of fine, salmon-pink gauze tied into a bustle and train. Her turbanlike bonnet has white gauze over the crown, and a little flower pin decorates the center front.

Lace-up shoes of red, blue, or black were commonly seen with these little dresses. Her hair is cut short and brushed toward the face.

Figure 35 This baby boy wears a low, wide-necked muslin dress. The sleeves, similar to those of Figure 34, are folded back into wide cuffs. The skirt has several tucks around the hem, which will be let down as he grows. There is no sash around his waist.

What appears to be a collar on the dress is actually the flap on the little

(33)

(35)

(34)

(36)

linen undershirt, worn by babies for over a hundred years. Made of linen, it had flaps at the front and back of the neck that folded out over the neckline of the dress, protecting it from stains.

Little red or blue high-top shoes were commonly worn. Babies at this time often wore large black hats of felt or beaver, with a close-fitting linen cap sometimes worn underneath.

Figure 36 A "mouse," or soft mauve color, was popular, as were gray and brown. A little girl wears an embroidered mauve dress with a bodice that has a shirred front panel. Embroidery as well as shirring was often used on these front panels. The neckline is edged with a dainty ruffle, the close-fitting sleeves with a shirred band at the elbow.

Sashes might be satin, tulle, or embroidered cloth bands, such as this one, in soft blue or yellow. This has a floral center design with satin edges, and it ties at the back to form a little bustle.

This girl's hair is cropped quite close at the top and sides, with the long hair in back held by a ribbon. A wide-brimmed hat with ribbon ties lies on the floor by her feet. Her shoes have large tongue flaps and small buckles over the instep.

Figure 37 Dainty ruffles and ruchings (shirred bands) of soft sheer silk make this dress exquisitely feminine. Three rows of shirring decorate the front bodice and sleeves, while a single row edges the front of the split overskirt. The ankle-length underskirt is quilted satin. This dress was often made of cotton, with a quilted muslin petticoat. Satin sashes were worn with both silk and muslin dresses.

Like their mothers, girls wore their hair powdered, frizzed, and arranged in "high head" fashion. This girl's bonnet has a pleated ruffle band that curves up into a point in front. A satin ribbon band and rosette on the cap match the sash. Blue, yellow, lilac, pink, brown, and gray were high-fashion ribbon colors. Green colors were not used much, since green dyes were not reliable until after 1813. This girl's shoes are buckled over the instep as those of the boy in Figure 40.

Figure 38 Sheer cottons or silks with stripes of heavy opaque weave were fashionable. Worn over petticoats of pink, blue, or yellow, their effect was very pretty. Usually, a wide satin sash matched the petticoat. This little girl's dress has a plain bodice and sleeves with wide ruffles at the elbows and around the neckline. A wide tuck at the hem will be taken out to lengthen the dress as she grows. An interesting ribbon headband is tied around her bangs and long soft hair, coordinating with the dress ribbons.

The pointed bodice was being replaced at this time by the straight waistline seam. The waist was beginning to be raised just slightly too, forecasting the high-waisted dresses to come.

(37)

(38)

(39)

(40)

Figure 39 Muslin was used for soft, simple, yet elegant little dresses such as this one. It has several groups of tucks around the full skirt and a cornflower blue ribbon sash. Blue shoes match the sash.

The bonnet, covered with lace and gauze ruffles, was originally designed to fit over the high head of hair fashionable with young girls and women. After little girls' hair styles became more natural and soft, the bonnet was simply worn over the soft new style with the bangs and back hair showing.

Capes with hoods were the popular wrap throughout the century. Black, lined with white satin, was a stylish combination, as was blue lined with yellow. Capes might be edged with lace, as is this one, or with braid or embroidery. The hood was quite full, in order to fit over the large bonnets.

Figure 40 Young boys' coats followed men's styles, so when adult coattails curved toward the back, so did those of boys. The full-skirted coats that had lasted for so many decades gave way to the cutaway, split in back and collarless. Although this boy's coat has cuffs, cuffless sleeves such as those of Figure 27 were worn too. Pocket flaps remained popular.

Waistcoats or vests were made of satin or silk, richly embroidered for formal and dress-up occasions. Plain broadcloth or homespun in black, brown, dull green, gray, or tan was preferred for everyday wear and work. Stripes, running either horizontally or vertically, were popular for waistcoats too.

This boy's shirt has full sleeves, a neck frill, and ruffles at the wrists. A cravat is tied around the neck as described in Figure 23 and then into a knot, which blends into the frill. His breeches button up the side of the leg and have small bands at the knee fastened with buckles.

This cadogan hair style, pulled back and tied, has sausage curls over each ear. The hat is the tricorne, worn till the end of the century by boys of all ages.

Figure 41 Girls often had "coming out" dances or garden parties when they became twelve, to display their very best clothes.

From 1780 to 1790

Dresses had by this time reached a state of utter simplicity and daintiness. This young girl wears one of creamy muslin or linen, with only the tiniest hem edging the neckline. Her elbow-length sleeves are simply hemmed, as is the skirt. The wide satin sash is tied in a large bustle bow. Dresses of gray, blue, pink, and lavender as well as cream were fashionable.

Straw hats had to be imported until the 1790s, when they were first manufactured in the United States. This girl's hat dips down on each side, presaging the bonnets to come.

At the end of the century there was a fashion for little jackets over these dresses. The jackets were masculine, even military in design, much like little boys' jackets. When put on over a dress, the result was much like the outfit in Figure 100.

(43)

(41)

(42)

(44)

(45)

Figure 42 By the time a girl was twelve, she was considered a woman. Sometimes she might mature by eleven. This young lady wears the fashionable clothing of adults. The dress, with its new long fitted sleeves, is dull green, but blue or red and white stripes were also in vogue. The neck, quite wide and low, is filled in with a sheer ruffle. The chemise was still worn underneath at this time, so the ruffle might be attached to the dress neckline or be a part of the undergarment. A coral or salmon pink satin sash is tied at the side.

This wide-brimmed hat is trimmed with plumes which were usually dyed in either dark or bright colors, in brown, red, gold, blue, or pink. Hat crowns grew deeper during the last part of the century. This girl's hair falls in soft, vertical curls around her shoulders, while the front hair is cut in straight bangs.

A gauze scarf was sometimes worn over the bodice, tucked into the neckline or crossed over and tied in back like those in Figures 45 and 46.

Figure 43 Babies' dresses, whether for boys or girls, always followed women's fashions. This infant has on a charmingly simple muslin one with the sleeves folded back into cuffs. This neckline is plain, though dresses often had a small ruffle around the neck opening. Often a little shirt worn underneath had flaps that folded out over the dress, as in Figure 35.

The ribbon across the baby's skirt is one of two leading strings attached to the back of the dress. (They are described in Figure 22.) These strings often matched the satin ribbon sashes, and might be embroidered was well. A close-fitting linen cap is worn under the wide-brimmed hat, decorated with much gauze and ribbons. Red- or pastel-colored shoes were very fashionable.

Figure 44 Little boys' coats, cut away like those of their fathers, usually came down to the thighs and were squared at the corners, as shown in Figure 50. Red or blue were favorite colors, often paired with short calf-length pantaloon breeches, usually of yellow nankeen.

Light-colored piqué vests were worn over large-collared blouses. Sometimes a ruffle-edged scarf, like those worn by girls, was tucked into the neckline over the collar, as shown. This little boy wears his hair cut short and brushed forward. His buckled shoes are worn over white stockings. Boys' hats were either tricornes or wide-brimmed beavers with plumes.

English farmers who had migrated to the American colonies had brought with them the practical smock. There are paintings to verify that the smock was still worn by men here for many years, up to the Civil War. Little boys, especially rural ones, are believed to have worn smocks also. (One can be seen in Figure 136, on page 96, as worn when it became a part of children's fashion.) Black smocks were favored by those of German descent, cream muslin or green by English, and blue by those of French. The term *blue collar workers* grew out of the blue smocks worn by French factory workers who brought the idea to America. At any rate, little boys did wear smocks at this time for play or when in the country.

Figure 45 Although the straight waistline was the mode, the pointed bodice was still being worn. This young girl wears the bodice commonly seen during mid-century. Her sleeves are short and flounced in the mid-century manner also. Pink or yellow taffeta and cream-colored muslin were the preferred colors and fabrics.

Children's skirts were often pulled up in front and pinned as shown, or tucked under the bodice point to keep them clean and out of the way during play. Sometimes they were pulled up and toward the back, or up in the center front.

A soft scarf is worn around the shoulders, crossed and then tied in back. This little girl wears hers loosely, falling off one shoulder. Around her neck is the popular black cord tied in a bow. One end has a small locket fastened to it that at times was placed down inside the neckline.

The very shallow hat crowns grew deeper toward the end of the century but were often almost completely concealed with gauze, ribbons, or plumes, as is this one.

Figure 46 Muslin dresses were worn for many occasions, with a satin ribbon sash for dress and no sash at all for play. Skirts were pulled up in drapes to get them out of the way and keep them clean. This little girl has her dotted muslin skirt pulled up to the back and pinned or tied into a bustle, with the white petticoat showing below.

The bodice is plain, with a wide neck and simply hemmed sleeves, like the baby's dress in Figure 49. A scarf goes snugly around her neck, crosses in front, then ties in back. Scarves were plain, as in Figure 45, or edged with lace or self ruffles like this one.

The ruffle on this white cap curves into the band at the center front, where it is accented with a pink bow.

Figure 47 Sleeves became shorter, as did dress hemlines, after the Revolution. This girl models a dainty dress of sheer muslin or gauze. Gray, light brown, yellow, pink, or blue were popular colors, as was natural or white muslin. Her sleeves have cuffs with banded edges; the neck is very low and wide.

In this period skirts were either tucked, banded with ribbon, or made of cloth woven in a thick–thin design. This was particularly attractive when the transparent skirt was over a slip of pink, blue, or yellow taffeta or silk. The wide sash ties in back in a large bow, forming a bustle, with the ends falling almost to the skirt hem.

Bonnets and hair styles grew huge, as shown in Figure 48. Even when young girls wore their hair in soft natural styles as this girl does, big bonnets gave them

(48)

(47)

(46)

(49)

(50)

43 /

the large-headed look of their mothers. Bonnets had increased in size, of course, so they could fit over the high hair styles. This one is draped with gauze, lace ruffles, and little feathers.

These shoes have the new larger buckles over the instep.

The younger girl at the harpsichord is dressed in a similar outfit.

Figure 48 The waistline would gradually move up as the end of the century approached. Here it is only slightly raised above the natural waistline. This bodice also predicts the full bosom of the coming styles. It is gathered at the neck and waistline and held in at the midriff with a wide satin sash tied in back as that in Figure 47. The sleeves have fullness too, which is gathered in with drawstrings at the elbow and upper arm and tied with deep pink ribbons.

This young lady wears a black cord tied in a bow at her neck. It was fashionable to suspend a locket or cameo at the end of one of the ties; the locket or cameo was sometimes worn inside the neckline or tucked behind the sash.

This girl's hair is teased and crimped into a tall pompadour with the corkscrew curls around the neck left soft. The number of curls each season was dictated by fashion; it might be from one to five or six.

Figure 49 Such simple little muslin dresses as these are pictured over and over again in portraits of the 1780s and 1790s. This one is so simple that its sleeves are hemmed without cuffs. The neckline is plain and hemmed, too, with the ruffle of the chemise undergarment pulled out over it. A little linen undershirt with its flaps folded over the neckline was worn also, as in Figure 35. There is only a simple hem in the skirt, without tucks, and the bright colored sash is quite wide. Red and bright blue sashes were popular for boys, pink, yellow, or lilac for girls.

For infants, bonnets were also large and high, as those of women, even though there was no hair piled up inside. A large ribbon rosette accents the center point of this bonnet, which is like that of Figure 46 shown from the side a bit.

Baby shoes were most often red or black but were sometimes made in blue or yellow.

Figure 50 Bright red, blue, or a dull green were the favorite colors for little boys' suits. This boy's cutaway is faced with black, which shows when the lapels are turned back. The vest matches the coat and ankle-length pantaloons. The interesting feature of this suit is the use of brass buttons for decoration as well as for fastenings. They are used on both sides of the coat and on the pocket flaps and cuffs. The vest is double breasted. These bright colored coats with metal buttons were inspired by the military uniforms of the Revolution.

Large blouse collars were sheer, with sheer or lace ruffles resembling a woman's scarf. Shoe buckles grew quite large in the 1780s, whereas the tongue flaps grew smaller.

44 /

Figure 51 In the last decade of the eighteenth century, children's dresses reached the state of utter simplicity shown in this charming little drawstring muslin. It was worn by children in the French court and by English aristocracy, as well as by little children in American villages. It was often seen without a sash or trimming, as shown here, but sashes were worn.

Charles Willson Peale's painting of the *Stoddert children* in 1796 shows the girl's sash drooping on one side, revealing the drawstring construction of the dress under it. The only variation was in the space between the rows of gathering, and whether or not there were turned-up cuffs on the sleeves. Usually, there were several tucks around the hem, so that the dress could be lengthened as the child grew. Scarves were sometimes crossed over the chest and tied in back, giving much the same look as that in Figure 46.

This bonnet is particularly noteworthy, an interesting transition between the eighteenth-century mob cap and the nineteenth-century sunbonnet. The band has flared and widened a bit, making the bonnet almost like the one in Figure 46, worn in reverse.

Little kid slippers dyed in bright or pastel colors, as well as black, were worn with these frocks.

Figure 52 Infant dresses were much like the girl's dress in Figure 51, except that they often had only one row of drawstring gathers at a high waistline and one at the neckline. They usually had tucks around the hem for lengthening, and plain or cuffed sleeves. For special occasions a satin sash might be tied in the back or side, in a large bow.

This baby's cap is much like that in Figure 51, but with a narrower band. It ties under the chin with a wide ribbon bow. A well-dressed infant probably had little kid shoes dyed to match the bonnet ribbons. American mothers were partial to red, as well as pink, blue, yellow, and lilac.

The baby carriage was invented in England at this time. Since it was first built by carriage makers, the early ones were like wagons and horse carriages, either pulled or pushed.

Figure 53 This little girl wears an all-white dress without a sash. It has a slightly raised waistline and a lace-edged sheer ruffle standing up crisply at the wide neckline. Her sleeves, coming to just above the elbow, also have crisply pleated sheer cuffs with lace edges. This is in contrast to the softness of the dress on the child to her right.

The ankle-length skirt had one or more tucks for decoration as well as for practicality, since it would be let down as the child grew.

This child's hair is worn long in a soft natural style with bangs parted in the center. For a time, little girls' hair was styled to look soft and fall freely over their shoulders, but during the early 1800s, feminine hair styles became tightly arranged again and eventually were even oiled.

(51)   (52)   (53)   (54)   (55)   (56)

Figure 54 When little boys grew old enough to discard their dresses, they wore little suits with button-on pantaloons, such as this one. They might be of black, brown, red, dull green, or, for very dressy wear, pastel-colored nankeen.

The little jacket was usually double breasted, with brass buttons. Some had collars, but others had only lapels and were collarless. The wide blouse collar covered the jacket collar, if there was one. Sometimes a woman's-style scarf was tucked inside the neckline, and at other times both a blouse and a scarf were worn.

Pantaloons buttoned onto the jackets with the same brass buttons as those on the jacket. Some pantaloons had a drop seat; others were made with only a front drop panel. Both a front and seat panel might be provided in some. These little pants were quite short, ending above the ankle. (For details of their construction, see Figure 59.) Wide satin sashes were often worn around the waist and tied in a large bow at the side or back, in the same manner as those of little girls.

Large black hats of felt or beaver were seen on even very small boys. They were usually decorated with plumes. This little boy holds his hat in his hand.

Figure 55 Dresses of "spotted" muslin, embroidered gauze, thick–thin woven cottons, and silks were worn over colored slips. Salmon pink, coral, and blue were favorite colors for these slips and matching sashes. Black cummerbund belts, as commonly seen as sashes for a time, might be beaded or embroidered.

This young lady wears a white, sheer, embroidered dress over a blue slip with a black cummerbund. It is similar to that of Figure 48 but shows the waistline moving up to become the Empire waist.

Under the full, drawn-up sleeves are the new taffeta mitts or sleeves. These glovelike garments varied in length from short to elbow length to the full sleeve going all the way to the dress armhole. They usually had a drawstring at the upper arm to hold them in place. White, black, and pastel colors were used, and sometimes they were the same color as the dress sash and slip. Mitts might have the entire hand exposed or just the fingers, as in Figure 28. They were sometimes like gloves with fingers, too.

Hair styles became more natural, with bangs and long soft tresses for a few years.

Figure 56 Boys' coats, like those of men, were sharply cut away into tails and usually double breasted, as were the vests worn underneath. Collars stood up high, and lapels were wide. Vests had lapels also. These coats were either broadcloth or leather for everyday wear and most occasions. For very formal wear and for court wear in Europe, they were made of velvet, with a contrasting color for the collar and lapels.

Although very little boys were wearing the new pantaloons, older boys and men would continue to wear knee breeches for a time. The new pantaloons were still considered vulgar and shocking by conservative people. Breeches were often of soft deerskin, with a band and buttons at the knee.

This young gentleman wears boots with canvas fold-down tops. His long soft cravat was placed with its center at the neck. It then was wrapped toward the back, crossed, and continued around to the front, where it was tied in a bow. His hair is almost the same style as that of the young girls, with its long back and front bangs.

— 4 —

PANTALOONS &

PEARL BUTTONS

1800-1840

Trousers for both girls and boys were the most outstanding fashion development during the early nineteenth century. Very small sons of fashion-conscious mothers had already adopted pantaloons by the end of the eighteenth century. Soon all boys would be seen in them. After 1810, pantaloons would lose some of their fullness and grow longer too. During the 1830s a strap sometimes went under the foot. Nankeen was a favorite fabric for pantaloons; it was estimated that a million dollars' worth of yellow nankeen was imported by the United States in one year alone.

With pantaloons came an interest in striped stockings to fill the space between pants and shoes. There was a fancy, too, for buttons on boys' suits, not just for fasteners but as decoration. It no doubt grew out of the fascination for things military during and after the Revolution. (Some of the earliest recorded toy soldiers in America were imported after the war.) Buttons eventually adorned necklines, waists, jacket fronts, sleeves, and trousers, and their use continued beyond mid-century. There was an interesting similarity between this fashion and the outfits of the English "pearlies," who extended the idea of button decoration into a well-developed folk art.

Girls began wearing their feminine version of the pantaloon around 1800. Pantalets were needed under the soft sheer dresses of then-current fashion. By 1810, when skirts had grown shorter, pantalets remained ankle length, showing below the dress. They became part of the fashion look and were considered both an under- and an outer garment. On older girls they were not always actually trousers but often just tubes with drawstrings around the leg, below the knee. This fashion was short-lived, because they kept slipping down around the ankles at the most embarrassing times. Pantalets would eventually be known as drawers, because they were drawn on over the feet.

Calico, first printed in Philadelphia in 1804, was commonly employed in little girls' frocks and pantalets. Green dyes and green fabric-printing inks were improved by 1815, resulting in, for one thing, the custom of sewing bright green linings inside girls' bonnets.

By 1825, there were machines for printing borders on fabric. After 1827, the new manganese oxide dyes improved yellows, oranges, and browns, and, by 1837, better blue dyes were also to be had. New developments in dyes usually showed up soon afterward in a fashion demand for certain fabrics and colors.

A locomotive built in New York made its first passenger run in America in 1830, carrying fifty passengers at twenty miles an hour. It was a historic trip that affected American clothing, because train travel would be an important factor in making the United States a leader in producing modern sportswear. By mid-century, children's clothing would show the railroads' influence on fashion.

The mackintosh, a waterproof cloak, invented about 1825, was worn by young boys in the 1830s. It was always lined with plaid and often had a shoulder cape or two. The use of plaid linings in boys' raincoats remains a tradition.

Education for girls was becoming a reality for many who could not have dreamed of it a few decades before. Girls' seminaries were opening in towns around America. They were directed toward homemaking, needlework, crafts, and manners for "finishing" young ladies. But girls were acquiring a taste for education, and it would be only a matter of time until they demanded more serious studies. Even very young girls and boys would, by mid-century, have an opportunity to learn. The kindergarten concept had been developed in Germany in 1837 and was already creating interest in America.

In a growing country, everyone had to work, including very young children. One chore of the younger ones was to thread the needles for their mothers, grandmothers, and aunts during quilting bees. Each woman had as many as twenty needles stuck in her own pincushion. The child threaded them all, then went out to play until it was time to return and rethread them. How much time this must have saved the quilters! Eight women could finish one quilt and sometimes two in a day if the designs were simple ones. Quilting bees continue in some areas of America today.

So many babies and young children died that they were considered "little visitors" until age six. If a child was strong enough to live to six, he was then thought of as a permanent member of the family. Many portraits of children now in American museums were memorial paintings done after a child's death. Artist William S. Mount, upon deciding not to paint from death anymore, objected that "death is a patron to some painters."

In the 1890s, Alice Morse Earle wrote that even young children were dressed in mourning clothes, including "veils on their bonnets and crepe on the hems of their pantaloons." They could even purchase toy coffins for playing with their dolls. (One museum recently displayed a carved toy funeral procession, with funeral sleigh and mourners.) Throughout the nineteenth century there were sentimental paintings, lithographs, and engravings with titles like "The Burial of the Pet," showing children playing funeral games. It was a natural rehearsal for life for them.

Amelia Bloomer would shock the world in 1840 by appearing in public in a shortened dress and pantalets gathered in at the ankles, but little girls and boys had been wearing these gathered pantalets for years, and the uproar must have seemed foolish to the little ones. Children's clothing in America has often reflected new attitudes and new ideas before adult fashions.

Figure 57 In the early 1800s, not only did little boys wear the "coarse, shocking" new pantaloons before grown men did, but portraits painted at the turn of the century show young boys were already wearing long trousers, too. (It would be another decade before trousers were "taken up" by fashionable gentlemen. Some older men, in fact, were never able to accept them and continued to wear knee breeches to the ends of their lives.) As a result of their wearing long pants during childhood, boys naturally would be at ease with them in their own adulthood.

This little double-breasted suit jacket has quite large lapels but little or no collar. Even when there was a small collar, it was always covered by a large frilly blouse collar.

The very large buckles on this little boy's shoes are typical of the 1780s through 1790s styles for gentlemen. This boy's hair is cut short and brushed toward the face.

Figure 58 A very dressy little suit of satin or velvet was saved for special occasions. Sometimes the suit was all of the same fabric and color; sometimes the jacket was darker than the trousers. The short jacket was snug fitting, with a double-breasted closing and long fitted sleeves. A fancy blouse of soft white cloth was trimmed around the large collar and at the wrists with a wide ruffle. The cuff ruffles fell down onto the hands. These ruffles might be lace, self fabric, sheer organdy, or any fabric with embroidered or scalloped edges.

This young boy wears shoes with large silver buckles and small tongues. He carries a top hat with a slightly flared shape, which he will wear over his soft wavy hair and straight bangs.

Figure 59 Little boys' button-on suits were styled much the same at the beginning of the century as they had been a decade before, as shown in Figure 54. The

FIGURES 57-62

(57)

(58)

(59)

(60)

(61)

(62)

52 /

short jackets were double breasted, with large lapels and sleeve cuffs. Several buttons fastened the pantaloons to the jacket. These pants had a band around the middle that buttoned in front, with a drop panel fastening over that. Sometimes they had drop seats also.

The wide sash was no longer worn over this suit after 1800. Blouses also changed with the new century, with collars growing wider, and squared in shape. They fell all the way out over the shoulders, with lacy or sheer ruffles adding still more width.

The latest style shoe was the flat little slipper replacing the buckled shoe.

The soft "page boy" hair style would give way to the new, shorter styles of early and mid-century, but it returned to fashion in a few decades.

Figure 60 White "spotted" or dotted sheer over a pink lining was a charming and popular fashion for very little girls at this time. This dress falls straight from the gathered neckline to the hem. The neck is quite wide, going clear across the chest from armhole to armhole. Little sleeves go across the shoulder, where they are pulled up into a swag by a string of red beads. They are edged with a sheer embroidered ruffle.

Several rows of narrow tucks, a flat embroidered sheer band, and white satin ribbon bands encircle the skirt above the hemline. A sheer embroidered ruffle edges the bottom. All these dots, bands and tucks stand out against the pink slip underneath, for a delicate and feminine result.

Around the neck of this very little girl hangs a silver whistle with little bells on each side. It is held by a long string of red beads like those on the sleeves.

Her little sheer close-fitting cap has a double ruffle around the face and a pink flower decoration. The ties are narrow pink ribbon. Her shoes are red high-tops laced with red ribbons.

Figure 61 Dresses for little girls were sewn in two basic designs during the first decade of the nineteenth century. One style had a high waist, like that in Figure 62, while the other fell straight from the neckline to the hem, as shown in this dress and that of Figure 60.

Utterly simple is this soft, all-white muslin frock. It has no decorations on the skirt, and no color underneath. Its only embellishment is the sheer embroidered edging on the sleeves and that gathered around the wide neckline. This neckline is so wide that the neck is bare all the way to the shoulder, where the sleeve begins. The upper back of the dress was necessarily narrow, with the sleeves extending toward the center back, in order to keep them from dropping down off the shoulder.

This little girl wears red beads, with a large amber stone in the center. Her flat slippers are also red.

Her hair is cut short around the face and brushed forward, the back hanging in soft curls.

Figure 62 The gathered full-bosomed look of adult dresses was imitated for young children, as illustrated here. The high-waisted bodice is gathered at both the neckline and waist. A crisp, sheer embroidered ruffle stands up at the round neckline. The straight sleeves come to the elbow. The satin sash was going out of style and was soon to be discontinued, although a few portraits show it still being worn during this decade.

Woven thick–thin sheer fabrics were still fashionable, as shown here, with the opaque bands going almost all the way up the skirt. Tucks gave the same effect when the sheer skirt was worn over a contrasting-color underskirt.

Soft wavy hair and straight bangs had been popular ever since the 1770s, and would continue to be worn for a time.

Figure 63 As boys' jackets grew shorter, so did girls' coats, until they became the little spencer jacket. The spencer remained the favorite wrap for women and girls until 1830. It started in England and came to America almost immediately. The jacket ended just below the bosom, where it was gathered in with a band or drawstring. There was usually a standing collar or frill at the neck and sometimes shoulder wings at the armhole. The sleeves were quite long, coming down onto the hands, with a cuff or ruffle. Velvet was the favorite fabric, with green, purple, black, orange, and dark red the popular colors. Lightweight or summer spencers were usually made in chintz.

Dresses had become high waisted, with short, medium, or long sleeves, like those of Figures 65, 75, 83, and 90. Most of these dresses had borders, or fancy swags, ruffles, or poufs around the hem. The borders are a characteristic of the period.

This young lady's shoes are flat-heeled slippers with ribbon ties. These kid slippers often were dyed to match the spencer or the bonnet ribbons. Her bonnet has the new high crown and pulled-down brim, to make this a very fashionable outfit for a young lady.

Shawls and stoles were also commonly worn at this time. One painting of the era shows a young lady in matching cornflower blue spencer, slippers, and bonnet ties with a white dress. Over this she wears a yellow stole.

Figure 64 Conservative people in New England, the South, and rural areas were not so quick to accept the new Empire fashions. Portraits painted in those areas at this time often depict clothes of the 1780s and 1790s. This dress, from a New England portrait signed and dated 1802, still has the chemise. It shows at the low neckline with a standing ruffle and at the sleeves where its cuffs fold back over those of the dress. A medium color taffeta was used for the dress, a soft satin

(64)

(63)

(65)

(66)

(67)

for the wide sash. Gathers at the neckline and waistline give fullness to the bodice.

Soft curls fall around this girl's shoulders, with one of them pulled to the front, apparently by accident but actually artfully planned. Her soft bangs are parted and combed to the sides. Her black slippers are low cut and flat heeled.

Figure 65 By the middle of the decade, waistlines had gone as high as they could, while necklines were quite low. Gathers at the neckline and waist make the little bodice puff out at the bosom. Sleeves were beginning to grow larger at the shoulder and taper toward the elbow, with a foretaste of the large sleeves coming in the 1830s.

Skirt fullness was moving to the sides and back, with dresses becoming flat in front. Even though the sash was not used much anymore, large bustlelike bows were still often attached at the back.

Calico dated from 1804, and this dress from an 1808 portrait is proof of its immediate popularity. This is dark blue and gray calico, in an all-over circular pattern.

Square-cut flat slippers and fancy stockings were worn with calico. This little lady wears large loop earrings to accent her soft hair style. Her bangs and sideburns are thin and wispy, and the back hair is curled outward.

Some dresses at this time had stand-up collars, like that of Figure 73.

Figure 66 The spencer jacket had originally been an item of clothing for men when it was first designed in England. (The ladies quickly took to a feminine version, as shown in Figure 63.) Frenchmen were wearing the short jacket too, so American men and especially boys were seen everywhere in it. Eventually, tails would be added, as in Figure 84, and finally skirts, as in Figure 106.

Young gentlemen of the period wore jackets of blue, red, or black, with double-breasted fronts, although the covered buttons were rarely fastened. Sleeves were now gathered at the shoulder and tapered to fit the lower arm. They were so long they came down onto the hands and wrinkled a bit at the wrists.

White vests with rounded collars were, however, always worn buttoned. Shirt collars, stiffly starched, stood up off the coat lapels, while cravats were tied in a bow. These ties might be white for formal wear and either red or black for informal occasions.

This young man wears the new long trousers over black riding boots, but flat low-cut slippers were worn also. His hair is parted near the middle with a little wave over the forehead.

Figure 67 A rather short-lived feminine costume was the chemise dress worn at the end of the first decade of the nineteenth century. It was seen on both fashionable mothers and their daughters, even though many people considered it shocking.

Made of a soft, clinging thin linen or sheer cotton, it was often pulled on the body while damp, so it would conform to the body's shape. This girl's chemise has a high neck with a standing ruffle, more modest than the low neckline of her mother's outfit. Two rows of pleated ruffles edge the skirt hem. Her slide necklace is long, with tassled ends.

These early pantaloons were the aspect of this costume that would survive after the chemise was set aside. In a few years they would become the lace-trimmed pantalets of Figure 83.

This very fashionable young girl wears her hair in the Grecian style, with ringlets around her face. Her shoes are lace-up high-tops, as high-style as her chemise and pantaloons.

Figure 68 Little boys all across America wore the short jacket, vest, and pantaloons. It was, you might say, a national costume. Much about the outfit was reminiscent of sailors' uniforms. After the War of 1812, this look became universal.

Jackets might be brown, green, or black, but red seems to have been the preferred color. Although usually double breasted, these jackets were rarely fastened. When closed, they would have been a snug fit, like that in Figure 58. They had either a small collar or were collarless.

Vests were always white, gray, or buff colored. The shirt or blouse underneath always had an open collar, starched to stand up from the jacket. The cravat or tie might be black, brown, or red and tied either in front or in the back, as shown here. When no tie was worn, the top three buttons of the vest were left open and turned back into lapels.

Pantaloons still had the front drop panel and fastened onto the blouse. Either red and white or blue and white striped stockings were worn. They might be striped either vertically or horizontally. When a hat was worn it was usually a top hat. Fashion-approved shoes were a lace-up style similar to an oxford.

Figure 69 Museum exhibits of little boys' suits reveal that the vest was sometimes attached to the coat front for a false vest. Since children's clothes had become more sensible and comfortable by the beginning of the nineteenth century, it seems appropriate to discuss the construction of the pantaloons and waists. Little waists were either buttoned to the pants or, as shown here, sewn to them. A little drawstring or button-on blouse, as in Figure 70, was put on over this basic waist. It might have long sleeves, short ones, or no sleeves at all. In hot weather, some were just a dickey.

Although this sewn-on waist was more an undergarment than a shirt, it was

(68)

(69)

(70)

(71)

(72)

(73)

worn by little boys in the west and south. Little black boys often were pictured barefoot, in muslin or calico pants and waists like this.

Figure 70 Linen shirts were sleeveless, short- or long-sleeved, depending on the weather and climate. This small boy shows one without sleeves. Collars might be plain, edged with self ruffles, as shown, or with lace.

This boy's ankle-length pantaloons have a drop-front construction. When the blouse buttoned onto the pants, the underwaist was not needed to hold them up, but it would be required for this drawstring style. (Various other types of front and back pantaloon construction can be seen in Figures 59, 80, 86, 99, and 134.)

One American painting of 1819 depicts a barefoot young black boy wearing an outfit with a vest buttoned up over a short-sleeved blouse. Another well-known painting, of 1810, shows a boy, his back turned, wearing a long-sleeved blouse and vest with the pantaloons from Figure 99. In both paintings, the boys have removed their jackets.

Figure 71 As much a part of the American scene as the boys' pantaloons and short jackets was this simple dress and apron that was worn either straight or pulled up in one of several ways. This draping was primarily for aesthetic reasons, but it did also serve a practical purpose: children had one less skirt to worry about during play. Since these aprons usually fastened with two or more ties in back, like that of Figure 98, they could also be put to use to hold up the apron's skirts. Here, the lower ties, tied together, are caught up and joined with the top ones in a panniered design. Blue, brown, gray, black, and red were the colors most often used for these protective garments.

For dress wear, bonnets had bright colored satin ribbon ties, but play hats or everyday ones were always tied on with a red scarf. It might be a fine red silk scarf or just a cheap cotton bandanna, but it was always red.

Figure 72 Instead of low necklines, many girls' dresses had high necks with a ruffle called a betsy, after Queen Elizabeth's ruff.

Necklines on aprons varied from high to wide and low. Some were gathered in with a drawstring, as shown here. Instead of the ties at the middle of the back being pulled up, as in Figure 71, the bottom corners at the apron hem were sometimes caught in the ties, pulling the apron up into an even more distinct swag.

Another variation in dressing up the straight little apron was to wrap the waistline ties around the body and then fasten them in front, to simulate an Empire waistline, as illustrated.

Soft lace-up slippers high up on the instep were worn by women and girls. They had pointed toes, and somewhat resembled the oxford shoe of today. Usually in black or red, they were worn for many occasions.

Figure 73 Girls wore open collars for a time, as did boys, giving the clothes a modern, casual look. This girl's dress has an Empire bodice with the fashionable a band around the arm and a small ruffle at the edge. Around the bottom hem is a wide tuck to provide decoration, and to allow for the girl's growth.

Aprons with drawstring necks were also pulled up in the center front to form side panniers, as shown here. This must certainly have been done for purely aesthetic reasons, since it exposed the dress underneath at the front, where it most needed to be covered. These aprons were practical, though, since many were made in dark colors such as black, brown, and gray, as well as in more quickly-soiled cream muslin.

The American cloth sunbonnet as we know it today had evolved by this time. White at first, they were soon produced in colors and the new American-made calicos. Various methods of stiffening the brim were tried, from quilting to starching to inserting paper or cardboard inside.

This young girl's shoes are the new lace-up oxford style that appealed to girls and their mothers. They were usually in black or red.

Figure 74 Long straight dresses continued to be worn by toddlers and very young girls throughout the 1820s, but the details of decoration always followed current adult styles.

By 1820, fancy hemline embellishments were seen everywhere, ranging from dainty tucks and lace to elaborate swags and ruffles. This very little girl's sheer dress from about 1818 shows the current fashion in the three stiff, uniformly rippled ruffles around its hem. They are stiffened and padded at the edges, creating an opaque band in their sheerness. Another crisp ruffle follows the neckline; this is higher than some popular necklines of the previous decade. Little puff sleeves and large satin ribbon bows on the shoulder predict the large sleeves to come. A pink slip is worn under the sheer white dress.

A sheer matching cap has a crisp ruffle around the face, with a large pink satin bow on top. The shoes are high-top lace-ups dyed red.

Figure 75 Waistlines had moved all the way up to the bosom by this time, while sleeves were so brief that they barely covered the shoulder. It was said that these delicate garments could be folded small enough to fit into the popular little drawstring pocketbooks like that shown here on this young lady's arm. During the first few years of their vogue these slim skirts were plain, but later all kinds of fancy trims were used at the hemline, as illustrated in Figures 74 and 76.

Stoles and shawls were worn winter and summer, in all weathers and climates, as were short spencer jackets, as shown in Figure 63. One 1815 portrait shows a button on each dress shoulder for attaching the scarf, stole, or shawl to keep it from slipping off.

(75)

(74)

(76)

(77)

(78)

(79)

In every era of fashion there is a stylish manner of wearing the current mode, so how one wears her clothing can be as important as what she wears. The stole was always draped casually over one arm and under the other, as demonstrated by this young lady.

Of special interest is this girl's hair style. The hair on the top and sides is pulled back tightly into a braided knot. That to the front of the ears, around the face, is pulled to her right, where it is curled into little ringlets held by a comb. A large decorative comb adorns her hair at the crown.

Her drop earrings have the same red stone as the slide of her gold chain necklace. She wears rings on her index fingers.

Figure 76 One of the most feminine outfits of all times for young girls is this little muslin frock. The tiny sleeves are covered with rows of narrow, gathered lace. Around the skirt hem are row upon row of gathered lace wider than that on the sleeves. Above this lace is a row of pink rosebuds and green leaves entwined together. The sash at the high Empire waist is bright pink satin.

With her dress, the young girl wears the very fashionable stole of a moss green color in the "proper" manner, over one arm and under the other. Her slippers are pink kid.

These little dresses were usually of cream muslin, but they were dyed, too, in colors such as salmon pink, yellow, or blue. Less dressy ones were made of the new calicos.

The bonnets in Figures 63 and 71 were worn with this dress and that of Figure 75. The spencer jacket of Figure 63 was still seen too.

Figure 77 One very fashionable form of long trousers for little boys in France was the bloomer type, shown here, which was drawn in at the ankle. They were not well received in America, but they are known to have been worn here.

Usually, a rather feminine tunic topped these drawstring pantaloons. It was high waisted and puff sleeved, like girls' dresses. This little boy wears a tunic with a high standing collar and a skirt that opens part way, for a coat effect. Just as with girls' dresses, there are tucks around the hemline.

This boy's soft slippers are flat heeled, with very pointed toes. He wears a cameo at the neck. The whole outfit has a rather exotic feeling about it.

Figure 78 Since little boys' clothes were influenced by those of their mothers as much as by those of their fathers, the male waistline soon moved up. Trousers became so high waisted that they came up onto the chest. These little high-rise trousers buttoned onto a short vest.

The cutaway coat is so short that the tails in back barely fall below the natural waistline. The front covers only the chest. Buttons and buttonholes outlining the coat front are mainly for decoration; they were rarely, if ever, fastened. Yellow nankeen was a favorite fabric for these suits, as also was yellow and white checked cotton.

Blouses at this time were frilly, with ruffles either around a collar or standing up at the neck and running down the front as shown.

Hair was cut short all over and brushed toward the face, forming little curls or points on the cheeks and forehead. Shoes were lace-up oxfords with pointed toes. Only two widely spaced eyelets were used for the laces.

Figure 79 Older boys, up to eight or nine years of age, wore high-waisted suits cut along more masculine lines. This cutaway tailcoat is double breasted though never buttoned. The tails come down almost to the knees. Dark colors were contrasted in these suits with light colors in double-breasted vests or waistcoats. The long trousers are quite slender.

Open collars were still the fashion, but with a ruffle added in this period. Soft cotton lawn was a favorite fabric, with white the preferred color.

Shoes were lace-ups coming up high on the instep, and with flat heels.

A new hair style called the Brutus was worn by both men and boys. It was cropped short and brushed toward the face, onto the cheeks. Some portraits show the hair on top arranged to stand up and out over the forehead in a kind of forward-brushed pompadour. Sometimes the hair was oiled.

Figure 80 Since little boys' clothing was affected by women's styles, this pantaloon suit has the high waistline of current feminine fashion. The pants end above the ankle, with splits at the sides. They fasten to the little short waist with buttons all the way around. Side openings allow the back to become a drop seat.

The waist has the wide, open lace-edged collar of women's dresses. Sleeves were long and reached down onto the hands. These suits usually had white muslin waists, with pants of a light or medium-dark color.

This lad's shoes are lace-up hightops. His hair style is a soft pageboy with bangs parted in the middle.

Figure 81 The suit for little boys had many variations of detail, but this short jacket and ankle-length trousers were seen all across America for decades.

Here a little boy wears a dark suit with small buttons very close together on both jacket and side openings of the pants. His blouse has a wide lace ruffle around the open collar. He holds the buff top hat with black grosgrain ribbon band worn by fashionable men at this time. His Brutus hair style of the period, as popular for children as for adults, is cut short and brushed toward the face. Ribbons are used as ties for his low-cut shoes.

Red was still a favorite color for these suits, as were dull green, brown, and

(80)

(81)

(82)

(83)

(84)

black. The waistcoat or vest was still usually white or a light color. One old draw-ing in the Metropolitan Museum of Art depicts two boys in outfits like this. One has a black jacket, red vest, and plaid trousers, while the other displays a red jacket with red and yellow calico trousers. Both children wear lace-up shoes and lace-edged blouses like the one illustrated here.

Figure 82 Pantaloons that narrowed or were drawn in at the ankle were in vogue for a short time. (A very young boy is shown in them in Figure 77.) They are known to have been worn by boys up to fourteen years of age.

This young gentleman's tunic and pantaloons are dark velvet. The tunic flares like a frock coat. The blouse underneath features an open collar like those of Figures 80 and 81. Waistcoats or vests were usually of a light striped fabric. When this boy wears a hat, it is a top hat like that in Figure 81.

At the beginning of the nineteenth century, both men and boys favored the high–low or half boot. It fitted the foot snugly, laced up at the ankle, and was flat heeled, with sharp, pointed toes. It could be bought in colors dyed to match the blue, green, brown, or black suits.

This long hair style is the one usually seen on younger boys. In fact, the entire outfit was somewhat feminine in line and was usually associated with young children. It seems to have been foreshadowing the frock coat of mid-century.

Figure 83 Tartan scarves, crossed over the breast, were seen on girls and women of all ages. Lightweight silk or cotton scarves were worn in summer, with wool ones in winter. Percale dresses had puff sleeves and wide necklines on the very short-waisted bodices. Skirts, quite full in back, became slender and gently flared in front. Bands of tucks, ruffles, and lace were used on the lower skirt, sometimes going almost halfway up. This young lady wears lace-trimmed and tucked pan-talets fastened around the leg with drawstrings just under or just above the knee. They were not yet actually one-piece trousers at this time.

Soft little lace-up boots with flat heels were dyed in colors to match the bon-net ribbons. Gloves or mitts were often yellow, orange, lime green, or other bright colors. Bonnets had tall crowns and ribbon or plume decorations in front.

Figure 84 By about 1820, tailcoats had replaced the cutaway for older boys. The coats were usually double breasted, although single-breasted ones were seen. High collars usually had boning in them to keep them upright. Open collars were so popular for a time that shirt collars were often opened out over the coat collar. Vest collars were also boned to stand up. Sleeves were so long that they came down onto the hands. Brown, blue, and green were favorite colors for coats; vests were light or striped.

Pantaloons were usually of corduroy, leather, or nankeen, and were favored in yellow. Red watch fobs were considered a handsome accessory, hung from the vest, even when the wearer had no watch.

High–low boots, with pointed toes, laced up snugly around the ankles. They were often dyed green or blue to match the coats.

Hair was oiled and brushed down onto the forehead and cheeks.

Figure 85 On little boys' suits, buttons were still more for decoration than for utility, in the 1820s. These are of metal on a dark green suit. Noteworthy are the pointed collars and lapels of this period. Some jackets had complicated points on both collar and lapels, and even at a point between.

Underneath the jacket, this young man discloses a blue and white horizontally striped vest, with self lapels and little covered buttons. Below the jacket hangs a watch fob on a bright red ribbon, like that of the boy in Figure 84. Sometimes these ribbon fobs were worn even when there was no watch, because it was part of the fashion.

Shirts still had stiffly standing open collars, worn without ties. Shoes were either low-cut slippers, as illustrated here, or the high–low boots in Figure 82.

Although boys' hair was still brushed forward and lifted in a forward pompadour, it was not kept as flat and oily as it had been during the previous decade.

Figure 86 Little high-waisted pantaloon suits remained popular, but the newer design tastes had waistlines a bit lower.

Instead of either the front drop panel or the drop seat, this suit has side openings. As before, the pantaloons fasten to the jacket, with the same dark buttons as those on the sides. Still more buttons can be seen going around the back of the neck. (Similar decorative use of buttons can be seen in Figures 94, 122, and 131.) Dark green, red, and yellow were favorite colors for these high-waisted suits.

The blouse collar is fluted and starched here to stand up around the neck, but some portraits dating from this time show soft ruffled collars. This boy's shoes are soft lace-up boots coming up over the ankle. They were often black, but sometimes dyed red or green.

Figure 87 Baby dresses in general still had no waistline, but fell straight from the neckline to the hem.

This little muslin dress has a narrow lace ruffle around the wide and low neck. Its small sleeves are drawn up in a swag effect, with narrow blue ribbons tied at the shoulders.

The close-fitting cap has a double ruffle gathered full enough to stand up around the face. A blue ribbon bow on top matches the cap ties and sleeve bows.

Amber beads, once believed to help protect an infant from illness, were still

(85)

(86)

(87)

(88)

(89)

(90)

worn by babies during the first half of the nineteenth century. This infant wears a double strand. (Portraits of this time show infants' shoes dyed red, blue, yellow, or black.)

Figure 88 A child's dress, charming in its simplicity, is made of muslin, lace, and eyelet embroidery. The waist is hardly more than a band across the chest, as are the tiny sleeves. A row of pointed lace edges the neckline and folds over onto the bodice and sleeves. The sleeve edges show another row of the same lace.

Straight in front, the skirt has fullness gathered in at the back. Two rows of hand-embroidered eyelet encircle the hemline, ending in a row of pointed lace at the edge.

Coral ribbons tied at each shoulder match the coral-dyed lace-up boots. A green plaid turban with plumes is worn over a white cap and decorated with coral ribbons to match those on the dress. A dark blue ribbon around the toddler's neck holds a locket. Whistles and teething rings were hung around the neck in the same manner.

Figure 89 This plain little dress was made up in all kinds of fabrics, such as calico, flannel, percale, or muslin, and was useful for all occasions. Both bodice and skirt were flat in front, but the skirt gained fullness in back. There were a number of variations shown in portraits of the time: a contrasting bodice, bands on the skirt, edging on the neck, a scarf over the bodice, and ruffles and aprons. It is shown in yellow with red trim, blue with lavender, cream with pink, and olive green with pink. This skirt hem is scalloped, with hand-worked buttonhole stitching in a thread darker than the dress. Sometimes the neckline of these simple frocks had the same scalloped design. A ribbon sash usually coordinated with the thread of the scalloped edges.

Little lace-up boots were black or dyed a color to match the dress.

This little girl's hair is pulled back into a braid wrapped into a bun at the back of her head. Ribbon bows are made to stand up at the crown, in simpler imitation of the large Spanish combs most likely worn by her mother.

Figure 90 Another dress commonly seen in portraits painted during the 1820s had a higher neckline than those of recent years and long, close-fitting sleeves. One to three sheer, stand-up ruffles always outlined the neckline, as shown. They were sometimes embroidered or scalloped on the edges. Matching sheer flounces always edged the sleeves and covered part of the hands.

This dress is high waisted and snug fitting in the bodice. The slender skirt has extra fullness sewn in at the back. Sometimes the bodice and skirt were of different fabrics. Sometimes a print fabric was used, as shown, with a border added at the hem. Short-sleeved versions of this dress appear in some portraits and museums. Favorite colors were dull green, dark blue, bright red, and pastel colors.

Corkscrew ringlets, often oiled, were always arranged across the forehead and on the cheeks in this Grecian hair style. Some written accounts of this period called these oiled bangs the Indian style, in reference to girls of some southern tribes who greased their bangs with bear grease.

This little lady's slippers are flat, square cut, and dyed to match her dress.

Figure 91 Sleeves began to grow larger, as a foretaste of the enormous sleeves of the 1830s. Skirts were beginning to grow fuller too, but most of that fullness remained in the back.

Bright red was a favorite color, with black trim. This dress has a full, gathered bodice and very full sleeves that droop a bit rather than standing up at the shoulder line. Black binding is used at the neck and sleeves, then repeated in several bands around the skirt. There is an interesting tradition concerning the skirt bands, which were once called rural bands. For centuries in Europe and the British Isles, rural women had shown a liking for this decoration. Their skirts had usually been red or green and the bands always black. This tradition was not only handed down from our early colonial settlers, but was brought here by nineteenth-century immigrants.

This little girl wears black low-cut slippers on her feet and beads around her neck. Her hair is pulled to the sides and arranged in rows of horizontal curls around her face, in imitation of adult hair styles.

Figure 92 Very young boys and girls wore this simple little frock. It was usually made of cream muslin or bright red cloth and hung straight from neckline to hem. Slender in front, it was somewhat full in back. Sleeves were puffed, though small. A sheer embroidered ruffle around the neckline was its chief embellishment. Sometimes the ruffle stood up crisply at the back and sides, but at other times it was sewn to lie soft and flat against the dress.

This little girl wears black slippers with red ribbon ties. Even the soles of these slippers were colored red in one old portrait.

Boys usually wore their hair cut short during the 1820s. Girls' hair styles were influenced by their mothers'. Shown here is a universally popular style for very young girls, even today. It has bunches of curls tied at each side of the head and little wispy bangs.

Figure 93 "Skeleton" suits—slim, with long trousers—were seen on little boys all over America. Here we see a beige high-waisted suit with black braid trim. The bodice is like that of girls' dresses, with a short full "skirt" or ruffle at the

(91)

(92)

(93)

(94)

(95)

waistline. Above the ruffle can be seen the black buttons that hold up the trousers. The neckline is wide and the sleeves puffed.

The trousers fasten at the sides with black buttons, as in Figure 86. One new feature to appear at this time is pockets on the trousers front.

Black braid is sewn around the trousers hems, the sleeve bands, and ruffle edge. The V-shaped design on the bodice is of braid, copying women's dress bodices at this time. It fastens with buttons down the back.

This boy's hair is cut short and brushed forward. His flat black slippers tie at the instep with black cords.

Figure 94 The Eton suit was to become a classic with little boys in America. This one has the characteristic short, straight jacket with fitted long sleeves. The use of buttons as decoration on boys' clothing was continued until 1850. On this boy's suit, the buttons, intended for use as fasteners, are sewn onto the edge of the jacket. On the jacket's left edge are buttonholes. Farther back on the jacket bodice, the same pearl, or self-covered, buttons were sewn on in a curved design following the jacket bottom around to the back.

The use of buttons on little boys' suits probably began in imitation of the buttons on soldiers' uniforms during the Revolution. It was this decorative use of buttons that inspired the folk clothing of the English "pearlies," who became famous for their extravagant use of pearl buttons.

Yellow cotton nankeen was used for the jacket and trousers, white piqué for the little pointed vest, and soft white lawn for the ruffle-edged blouse. The trousers not only have the front drop panel but also side openings to form a drop seat. These slippers are like those in Figure 93.

This boy's forward-brushed hair is lifted at the center front, like then-current hair styles for adults.

Figure 95 Both boys and girls wore this charming toddler fashion. It is quite low at the neckline, without even so much as a band going over the shoulder. A small sleeve, attached at the lower armhole, goes across the upper arm. Around the neckline is a dainty embellishment of little points buttonhole-stitched at their edges. This appears again on the sleeve edges, but nowhere else. The hemline is plain. Made of cream muslin, such dresses were soft and comfortable and easy to care for.

Little slippers of black, red, or a pastel color were usually seen with this dress.

This little girl's hair style is pulled into a bunch of curls at the back, like a modern ponytail. The front bangs are sectioned off and curled. They have been lifted up and forward into a kind of pompadour, like that of the boy in Figure 94. This hair style is noteworthy because the treatment of the bangs is more typical of a style from her father than of her mother.

Figure 96 Throughout the nineteenth century, boys' trousers either buttoned onto waists, in the case of young children, or were held up by suspenders. Although belts were occasionally used, the belt loop was not a part of trousers until the twentieth century, except on a few innovative sports uniforms. At first, suspenders were just two separate straps that buttoned to the trousers, as shown here. By 1850 they would have double elastic fasteners on the ends, as in Figure 164. Sometimes only one suspender or brace was used, because the other was lost or broken. Or perhaps only one was put on in the first place, because one could hold up the trousers.

Shirts were wide across the shoulders, falling over to form a drop-shoulder line. Sleeves were gathered full. Throughout the eighteenth and nineteenth centuries, shirts opened only over the chest, not all the way to the shirt bottom, as twentieth-century shirts later did. Cravats of red or black, or red cotton bandannas, were tied under the soft collars. Shirts were white, red, green, blue, or black.

Trousers were either ankle-length pantaloons or the new long trousers rolled up. Heavy brown leather shoes were worn, as were black boots like those in Figure 135. This hat is the mid-century flat-crowned straw hat. Although mid-century paintings and drawings often show barefoot boys in these clothes, they rarely show them without some kind of hat.

Figure 97 Aprons were a necessity for protecting long dresses in times when dyes ran and faded, and laundering methods were drudgery. As during the seventeenth and eighteenth centuries, aprons were still an important item of children's clothing. The apron illustrated here was worn during several decades. It could be adapted to whatever waistline was fashionable, because the ties were simple. They went over the shoulders, crossed in back, then wrapped around the waist, tying in front, resulting in a high waist.

Sunbonnets had developed by the early nineteenth century into the form we know today. Brims were either starched or quilted to stiffen them. Some museum examples reveal slots in the lining of the brim for inserting cardboard or folded paper for stiffening. Sunbonnets varied in depth of brim, fullness of the crown, and in the size (or absence of) a neck ruffle. This ruffle was quite large, as those of farm girls or western travelers, who had to be in the hot sun for long periods. Necklines of early nineteenth-century dresses were generally wide and low, and it was necessary to protect the neck from sunburn.

It is possible that this was originally an adult apron, to be worn around a woman's waist. Put on a child for kitchen or garden chores, the ties went over the shoulders, raising the hem up off the floor. Every mother at some time or other has put one of her own aprons on her child in the kitchen or garden in order to protect the child's clothes.

(96)

(97)

(98)

(99)

(100)

Figure 98 The all-over apron was used during the entire nineteenth century, for maximum protection of dresses. It had large loose armholes and was usually straight, although fine ones might be slightly flared at the hem. The neck sometimes had a drawstring like that of the little apron of Figure 72 or a collar, as shown.

Long ties at the back could be wrapped around the body and fastened, giving this apron a waistline such as that in Figure 97. As styles changed, these ties could simply be resewn at any level so that the apron remained in current fashion.

Seen on children on farms, in families traveling west, in the cities, and on children of textile mill workers, this apron was worn by all age groups in all parts of the nation.

The bonnet was commonly seen with ribbons and flowers for dress wear, or a red bandanna was worn across it for work. It might be sewn of cloth or made of straw and had many variations.

This girl's shoes are the flat-heeled lace-up shoes so widely worn through midcentury.

Figure 99 Although many little suits had a drop-front panel, as in Figure 59, and many had drop seats or side openings, there was a less complicated way of fastening the trousers. It was done simply by overlapping the center back seam and adding buttons, as illustrated here. (Girls' and women's pantalets and drawers were still fastened in this manner in the early twentieth century.)

This little boy wears trousers fastened by buttons onto a muslin bodice. A blouse was usually worn over this, as illustrated in Figure 70. Many small-town and rural boys, slave children, western settlers, and city youngsters wore this underbody and simple trousers, without blouse or jacket, in hot weather. This ancient method of fastening trousers is still used in many parts of the world today.

Figure 100 The jacket over a dress or skirt, with an apron, might have been worn during any decade of the nineteenth century; it was universally popular.

The fashionable little jackets of mid-century, shown in Figures 157 and 158, had their rural counterpart in this simple outfit. The jacket, unadorned and practical, has no braid trim, lace collar, or ruffles. The skirt and apron are also untrimmed. Although these little jackets and skirts were simple, they were rarely dull. Often a different color was used for the jacket, the skirt, and the apron, for a gay result. Rust, gold, green, red, blue, brown, and black were favorite colors. Printed calicos were used too.

Red bandannas were often added around the neck or across the straw hat to secure it, adding still more color. Stockings were red, brown, or black, while the lace-up boots were usually brown or black. Black as well as red ties on the hat were often seen.

Figure 101 In the 1830s, plaids and checks were very much a part of the fashion scene in America.

This pink and white cotton plaid frock has a high waistline, though it is considerably lower than those that swept the country through the two previous decades. The bodice is gathered both at neckline and waist. The bodice, skirt, and waistband were cut on the straight of the fabric, while the short sleeves, cut on the bias, make a diagonal plaid. A self-binding edges the neckline while a dark braid or ribbon bands the sleeves, skirt hem, and waistband.

Pantalets of white organdy are edged with a self-ruffle, lace, and pink floral ribbon. The young lady's slippers are deep pink kid with little wooden heels and ribbon ties.

Bonnets were of sheer organdy, with lace-edged ruffles and yards of ribbon. Striped ribbons were a favorite trim. It was fashionable to leave the bonnet ties loose and hanging free, with the ends curled as shown. Sometimes the decorative bows were on the inside of the ruffle to show off the face, instead of outside, as shown here.

Figure 102 As waistlines moved down, so did necklines again, with many of them bared all the way off the shoulders. Adult dresses at this time had diagonal lines on the bodice, which some children's dresses copied. The diagonal line on this frock is created by a ruffle that begins at the waistline and moves at an angle over the shoulder, widening as it goes. Sleeves, no longer dainty, grew during the decade, to become huge, like those in Figure 113.

White organdy or lawn pantalets reached down to the ankle. Some were edged with lace or tucks without ruffles. Plain black or fancy dyed slippers contrasted with white stockings.

Lockets were worn around the neck on a long black cord and tucked either into the bosom of the dress or under the belt. Amber or red beads were usually worn along with the lockets. Little scissors, thimbles, or monocles were sometimes suspended on a cord in this manner, too.

A popular hair style consisted of a middle part and rows of horizontal sausage curls down each side of the face. The back hair was pulled back tightly and fastened in a bunch of curls.

Figure 103 During this period, calico, as popular as gingham checks and plaids, was first made into pantalets matching the dress. Shown here is a dress with the new sleeves, full at the shoulder and tapered toward the wrists. The bosom is full and the neckline square, with an organdy ruffle at its edges. The skirt, full in back and narrow in front, has a flounce at the hem.

The Titus hair style, similar to the Brutus style worn by men and boys, was cropped short and brushed toward the face. Sometimes only the side and top hair

(101)

(102)

(103)

(104)

(105)

was short, with the back wound into a knot. The short cut does appear in a number of contemporary portraits of little girls.

Figure 104 A little organdy or sheer muslin dress has a great deal of lace insertion and rows and rows of tucks. Inset in a V design on the bodice, the lace follows then-current adult styles. Lace goes around the neckline and the sleeves, where it is inset in a similar V design. The skirt is gathered all the way around, whereas the bodice is flat, without gathers. Satin ribbon bows decorate each sleeve.

The pantalets are noteworthy, being gathered in at the ankles like the early pantaloons of Figures 67, 77, and 82. They have drawstrings about one inch from the bottom, so that ruffles form around the ankles. The ruffles are edged with the same lace as the dress.

This toddler has his short hair brushed toward the face. He wears soft little slippers that come high over the instep.

Figure 105 Sleeves grew to huge proportions during the 1830s. They were full at the upper arm, but then tapered to a fitted wrist and fell down onto the hands. It was the custom to fasten a ribbon around the sleeves at the wrists to hold them in place. Sometimes these ribbons had buttons for more secure fastening. Here we see red striped ribbons with brooches pinned on. A similar red brooch is pinned at the neckline. The full gathered skirt has three bands made up of tiny tucks alternating with wide tucks. The skirt hem and sleeves of this muslin dress are edged with narrow lace, while the square neckline is edged with a wide lace-edged ruffle. This neckline was often worn plain.

Around her neck this young lady wears the fashionable chain or cord that holds a locket, which is shown tucked under the belt in some portraits, into the neckline on others. Monocles, small scissors in cases, and thimbles were also suspended from these cords, as was the pince-nez.

This girl's hair is arranged in long corkscrew curls pinned back behind her ears. She accents it with a large bone comb tucked in at the crown. Her slippers are bright red, with little wood heels, and tie with fringed ribbons.

Figure 106 The frock coat, sometimes called the redingote, was the very latest fashion for young gentlemen at this time. It would become so much a part of the American scene that it continued to be worn till the end of the century. It could be had in either single or double-breasted models. The flared skirts or coattails came to just below mid-thigh, with pockets set in at an angle at the sides and a split in center back. Sleeves were slightly full at the shoulders. Tan, green, and white were favorite colors. These coats were sometimes made of deerskin.

The shawl-collared vest was somewhat short waisted. It was buttoned over

(108)

(110)

(106)

(107)

(109)

(111)

a tucked shirt with a stiff standing collar. The cravat of striped silk was tied in a casual knot in the manner of a bandanna.

Trousers were slender and came down over the shoe and even out onto the floor at the back, as a result of their curved hems.

Although still brushed forward, the newest hair style was curved toward the sides a bit and down onto the cheeks, as illustrated here.

The proper hat to top off the frock coat was the flat straw, similar to that of Figure 111, or the top hat. Black riding boots were seen on older boys; slippers or lace-up shoes were for younger ones.

Figure 107 Little boys wore full-skirted frock coats, too. This one of black wool broadcloth has a black velvet collar. The self-covered buttons are spaced close together on the double-breasted front, running all the way to the shoulder seam.

One interesting difference between the coat of Figure 106 and this one for younger children is the false waistcoat (vest) front attached inside the coat. It is of tan piqué and fastens with small pearl buttons.

A waist like that in Figure 69 is sewn to the trousers. The waist buttons down the center back and across the back, where the drop seat fastens. A blouse similar to that in Figure 70 is worn over the waist and under the vest. With the trousers fastened to the waist and the vest attached to the coat, a little boy was practically sewn into his clothes.

Flat-heeled black slippers for boys often had ribbon rosettes. Curls were the newest thing in boy's hair styles; they gained in popularity during the 1850s and 1860s.

Figure 108 Capes and mantles were made in a variety of fabrics. This boy wears a box coat with two matching capes attached. It is a bright red and dull green plaid, with the red predominating. Although the capes, like the coat, are cut with the plaid design running straight up and down, the longer cape is cut at an angle at the bottom. This causes the cape to fall in points in front, as illustrated.

The collar stands up at the neck, and the larger cape has self-covered buttons matching the coat's. The upper shoulder cape has no buttons. The coat falls to just below the knees. Mackintosh or waterproof coats were first worn about 1830.

This young gentleman shows the new hair style, which, though still brushed forward, now has a side part. His sideburns are brushed out onto the cheeks in forward-curled sideburns.

Figure 109 Boys up to the age of three were still outfitted like little girls. This little boy's muslin dress has a high waist and full bosom. The sleeves are the new full style tapering toward the wrists. One difference between this dress and a little girl's is the lack of lace and ruffles here. The neck is bound plainly with muslin, and the hem, too, is plain. The matching muslin pantalets are also untrimmed. The only color is in his bright red lace-up shoes and red beads.

This toddler's hair is cut short and brushed forward onto the cheeks and forehead.

Rocking horses were a favorite toy for little boys at this time. They would move up in popularity, as well as in workmanship, quality, and realistic appearance during mid-century.

Figure 110 Though other styles would come and go, the short jacket would remain a wardrobe fixture for young boys for several decades. There was a countrywide fascination with fancy pointed lapels, beginning around 1810 and continuing into the 1840s, though it crested during the 1830s. The points were put in at the seams where the collar joins the lapel. Most of these short jackets were double breasted, but single-breasted ones were also in fashion.

Vests were usually of white or light colors such as yellow, gray, or tan, with shawl collars. Trousers were long and slender, with straps to go under the foot. White, buff, gray, and yellow were favorite colors. Shirt collars were worn out over the coat collar, with cravats tied in soft bows.

This young boy wears the newest hair style, still brushed forward, but with a side part and sideburns curled onto the cheeks.

Figure 111 This version of the short jacket has rounded lapels and a collar without fancy notches. It is double breasted but was rarely seen buttoned. There is a little fullness gathered in at the top of the sleeves, but they are close fitting.

This light-colored vest closes with tiny self-covered buttons placed close together. It has a collar but no lapels. The shirt has a tucked front and a standing soft collar. A black cravat is tied in the back in a manner worn by adults.

Trousers opened at each side instead of in front and were cut full in the seat. Low splits in the side seams helped the long trousers curve over the foot and down behind the heel, to the floor. Some trousers at this time were designed with straps under the feet.

During the 1830s, a hat, which was very shiny and usually of a light color, such as gray or tan, came on the scene. The material had a brushed nap, so it was called a silk "beaver" hat. The hatband was a cord with tassels at the ends.

Figure 112 Worn by both boys and girls, this charming little dress is more complex than many during this decade. The bodice is made of rows of vertically tucked sheer muslin, alternating with bands of satin ribbon. The neck is very wide and edged with tiny lace. Alternating bands of lace and muslin form the sleeves, which are edged with lace, too, while two rows of lace are inserted in the full skirt.

(112)

(113)

(114)

(115)

(116)

Blue ribbon was generally used on boys' dresses and pink on girls'; but yellow, red, and lilac were also chosen for either at times.

Pantalets were worn under the dress, and often high-top lace-up shoes were dyed to match the ribbons. The close-fitting cap has a double ruffle of organdy and lace around the face. Ribbon rosettes and bows repeat the ribbons on the dress.

Figure 113 Outstanding features of ladies' seamstressing at this time were diagonal tucks on the bodice and huge drooping sleeves. This young girl wears a youthful version of the popular dresses. Necklines might be plain, or collared. This sheer organdy collar stands up at the sides and back. Another characteristic of dresses of this period was the use of decorations around the skirt, which might be tucks, lace, or ruffles.

Ruffled pantalets were a part of the fashion look, also; this girl wears white organdy ones. Her flat slippers tie with ribbons around the ankles, and she carries a folding fan and a straw bonnet like that in Figure 118.

Especially interesting is her hair, because of its startling modern look. It is cut quite short, parted in the middle, and pushed behind the ears where the straight ends flip outward.

Figure 114 In just a few short years, Amelia Bloomer would shock the world by wearing a short dress and gathered pantalets like these, but both girls and boys had worn them for some time.

Light blue was a favorite color for dresses, with dark blue, brown, and even black also being worn by children. Wide collars and berthas were often added over the huge sleeves, for a horizontal effect. Early in the century, dresses had been designed to make girls look tall, but now the full skirts and broad sleeves added to the width. Though these sleeves were large at the upper arm, they were fitted below the elbow. The neck of this dress is filled in with sheer white organdy, with a little standing collar.

The skirt, flat in front and quite full at the sides and back, is trimmed with narrow bands of brown braid. Underneath the dress, this girl wears pantalets gathered in at the ankle, in the style of the beginning of the century, as seen in Figure 67.

This girl's hair is parted in the middle and pulled behind the ears. She wears a locket on a cord around her neck.

Figure 115 The dress waistline continued to move down toward the natural waist till the end of the decade. This little girl is turned out in an interesting transitional style, with its full bosom and wide waistband giving it both an Empire and a natural waist at the same time. Its only trim is the white binding at the neckline and waistband and the sheer white sleeve ruffle. The neckline is completely off the shoulders, and the short sleeves are quite full. Red was a popular color at this time, judging from several portraits from the period.

This little girl's pantalets were given added charm with several rows of sheer organdy ruffles on the lower legs. Her slippers are black, and her necklace is several strands of red beads. Her hair is parted in the middle and pulled behind the ears.

Figure 116 A most delicate look is achieved by the use of sheer white muslin or organdy and dainty lace for this infant's christening dress. The lace forms a panel at the front center of the skirt but angles out on the bodice to the neckline, in keeping with the vogue for diagonal lines on girls' and ladies' dresses. Narrow lace edges the neckline, while several rows of wider lace form bands across the panel at the hemline. Narrow cream satin ribbon is used for a sash.

The matching cap is sheer and lacy, with a tiny ruffle around the face and ribbon ties to match that of the dress sash. Little white stockings and pastel-colored shoes finish off the costume.

— 5 —

TAILORED SUITS &

SHORT SOCKS

1840-1870

The Victorian age began with Victoria's coronation in 1837. The camera came into use in the 1840s, recording, for future generations to treasure and study, what some American children were wearing. One new fashion to come along at mid-century must certainly have made a major impact on youngsters: the new fashion of cleanliness. It was suggested by fashion magazine articles and soap advertisements that everyone should bathe daily!

Elias Howe's lock-stitch sewing machine was used in American homes by 1843, with mothers sewing clothes for their children as well as themselves. Fashion publications began to give directions for making the newest children's styles. After the Civil War, the new paper-pattern business would sell millions of patterns for children's apparel.

The growth of railroads in America was tremendous at midcentury. Although the main east–west lines would not be joined until 1869, in Utah, there were hundreds of smaller railroads connecting small towns and cities in a network over the nation. The railroad was to have a great influence on American clothing because of the need for casual but attractive sports clothes. Coats and suits were often designed specifically with travel in mind. Canal-boat travel was common in the East, and stagecoaches were running regular routes in most other areas.

A favorite amusement of children was to run to the station or railroad tracks when it was time for a train to pull into town. If it wasn't due to stop, the children went out just to wave and watch. When trains did stop, the station was a social gathering place. It was also the place to catch up on the latest news, fashions, and gossip. Railroad stations were a favorite subject for artists' paintings at this time, and railroad engineers became heroes to small boys everywhere. A new play item, first produced at mid-century, was to become an all-time favorite for generations of children—the toy train.

Sports suits for boys featured the new sack coat without a waistline seam. At first called a box coat, this new straight coat came about because of the increased travel. Its popularity was given impetus by its being worn by the Prince of Wales, who visited the United States in 1860. Sack coats are still worn today.

The tailored suit for girls, first worn in the 1850s, was destined to become a classic too. First promoted by Charles Frederick Worth, an English designer living in France, it soon was taken up by American girls. Eventually it became the jacket, skirt, and shirtwaist (blouse) that American girls have made famous on every continent, and was a part of the worldwide trend to sports clothes and a more relaxed life-style.

Walking, exercising, and traveling affected design of children's and babies' equipment and toys too. Many complex wheeled toys were invented so that young children and infants could travel, since it seemed as though the entire nation was on wheels of some kind. The baby carriage, patented in America in 1829 and first produced here in the 1830s, became a common sight by the 1850s. Velocipedes (tricycles) were popular for the little ones, but only older boys could ride the new bicycle or "boneshaker" invented in 1866. It had an enormous front wheel and no brakes at first, and would not be adjudged safe for girls or little boys until the end of the 1880s. The bicycle would eventually exercise a tremendous influence upon children's fashions.

The modern safety pin was designed and manufactured at mid-century. However, baby diapers would continue to be tied, rather than pinned, until the twentieth century.

Short socks began to appear in artists' portraits and canvases during the 1840s, although long stockings would remain the most common legwear until the twentieth century. For many years, abbreviated stockings appeared only on young children, with the older ones gradually being seen in them.

Elastic had been put on the market after being invented in 1836 by Charles Goodyear. It was used at first only for shoes and garters; it would be a few years before its possibilities were recognized. Boys' shoes sometimes had elastic insets at the sides so they could be slipped into easily.

America's Christmas celebration, as we know it today, began at mid-century. Exchanging gifts at Christmastime had been growing in popularity since the Revolution, and it would become an established tradition during the 1840s. "A Visit From St. Nicholas" ("Twas The Night Before Christmas") was first published in a newspaper in the 1820s, and then published in book form by 1837. Charles Dickens's "A Christmas Carol" was published in 1843. Almost every town had a toy store by this time, or else the general store stocked toys at Christmastime. Christmas trees were put up in parlors everywhere and decorated with bright colored ornaments and candles. One clothing item to be forever associated with

Christmas is the stocking, the first of which were the colorful striped and patterned stockings of mid-century.

It is worthy of note that at mid-century little girls' fashions and their toys were very closely associated. Paper dolls became an instant success when published at mid-century. The first magazine to print fashion paper dolls was *Godey's Lady's Book*, in 1859. Soon other magazines followed, and young girls everywhere played with paper dolls having fashionable wardrobes. There were other toys as well, aimed to "develop a young girl's design taste and ability." One such utilized pieces of cloth and cardboard cutouts, enabling a girl to design her own paper doll fashions.

Another toy directly associated with sewing and little girls was the jump rope. The game was enjoyed back in colonial days, but, from the 1840s to the 1860s, the world of childhood went through a fad for elaborately made jump ropes. Braid, knotting, or crochet was used to cover the handles, with tassels or tinkling little bells suspended from them. Ropes were crocheted or knotted with bright colored yarns. Patterns and directions for making them were published in ladies' fashion magazines, and many a mother or grandmother created the most elegant of jump ropes known to history. Fashion prints commonly showed little girls holding jump ropes.

Dolls, too, became more than just toys at mid-century. Elaborately dressed, they were always pictured in fashion magazines, implying that no well-dressed little girl could possibly be without one. One development at this time, which paralleled the evolving new assessment of children and child development, was the new baby doll. Children's "toy babies" had actually always represented ladies and gentlemen, not young children. The realization (or at least appreciation) that a child's body is proportioned differently from an adult's was part of the new attitude toward children, their education, clothing, and even play.

During the Civil War, cotton production in the South was virtually stopped, while wool production was increased and increasingly modernized in the North. Clothes were exorbitantly expensive, especially in the South. Toward the end of the war, bonnets for little Southern girls were practically nonexistent. If a girl was fortunate enough to have one, it was probably homemade, from natural materials. Clothes were made from scraps or used fabrics, and everything was handed down from child to child. Shoes were one of the most difficult items to acquire, as everything of leather was used up. Old saddles and luggage might be used for new soles for whatever shoe tops people could salvage.

On the positive side, the practice of sizing clothes developed as a by-product of the manufacture of Union army uniforms, since records had to be written down about men's clothing measurements. These findings and the study of them would, of course, eventually lead to sizing and labeling children's garments as well as those of adults.

Figure 117 The chemise of former years was still sometimes worn underneath dresses as the 1840s began. Here can be seen the sheer embroidered ruffle belonging to a chemise as it falls out over the neck. The dress has the large drooping sleeves and slightly raised waistline of the previous decade, a style that would continue in favor for a few more years. It is in rust, with two rows of black braid at the waistband and two more rows around the hem. Between the two braid rows on the skirt is a large decorative cord sewn into the cloth from the back side. This serves to stiffen the full skirt as well. Another cord is stitched into the bodice across the chest, where it curves slightly, following the neckline.

The pantalets have numerous rows of tucks. White stockings and slippers of a matching rust color are worn.

Middle-part hair styles were commonly seen at mid-century. The long curls of this little girl's hair are pushed behind her ears.

An elegant toy of the time was the jump rope. Several fashion magazines, which began in the 1840s and 1850s, published directions for fancy crocheted jump-rope handles. Some had bells or tassels added.

Figure 118 The use of tucks and drapes on the bodice would continue into the 1860s, although it is considered characteristic of this decade. Horizontal and vertical tucks became as much used as diagonal ones. This girl's bodice has several horizontal pleats, or large tucks, caught at the center with a band of the same fabric.

These drapes over the bosom always have the appearance of being applied, rather than having been built into the original bodice construction. The dress has the off-the-shoulder neckline and huge sleeves of the period. One uncommon feature of this beige dress is the use of large pleats in the skirt, instead of the usual gathers. No trim or collar is used.

The simple white pantalets have a wide hem and one row of lace insertion set into the legs. White stockings and square-cut black slippers are worn.

This little girl's bonnet is natural straw with brown satin ribbon band and ties. The straw is woven in a lacy design, with a scalloped edge.

Figure 119 Similar to the one in Figure 118, this dress has the same large pleats in the skirt. Large drooping sleeves are tapered to the wrist. The bodice has two groups of vertical tucks, with a plain band in the center. It is of a dark color such as plum, forest green, brown, or blue, with a plain white collar at the high neck.

The pantalets, also like those of Figure 118, have one row of lace inset at their hems. Square-cut black slippers are worn with white stockings.

This young girl wears the characteristic middle-part hair style pulled back into a knot at the nape of the neck.

(119)

(118)

(117)

(120)

(121)

(122)

PLATE 1

(6)

(11)

(14)

(15)

(16)

During the seventeenth century, scarlet was a favorite color for young children's clothes, with yellow, blue, and brown popular also. Soft linen garments were worn next to the body by both girls and boys, with starched aprons put on over dresses to keep them clean.

The little girl in Figure 6 is shown in a blue dress with her best lace collar, cuffs, and apron. The tabs of the doublet in Figure 11 are shown here being worn outside the skirt. An older boy in Figure 14 grasps the little boy's hanging sleeves for leading strings. He models his "Sunday best" lace collar and cuffs, along with his plumed beaver hat.

Boys' high-waisted doublets gave way to loose coats and flared sleeves during the second half of the century. The boy in Figure 15 shows the coat and petticoat breeches worn between 1660 and 1680 in America. They evolved into the long full coat after 1680. He sports his best collar, edged with lace, while the toddler in Figure 16 beside him is in his padded puddin' cap and striped sleeves.

PLATE 2

(23)

(24)   (32)

(22)

Little boys and girls were attired in much the same clothes during the early eighteenth century. Dresses and aprons usually had leading strings attached at the waist or shoulders, for use in keeping a child safe from harm. The little boy in Figure 22 wears a yellow dress and lace apron, with blue satin leading strings.

At the beginning of the century, boys' coats took the form they would continue to have for more than half a century. The boy in Figure 23 shows a red velvet coat with braid-trimmed buttonholes and pointed pocket flaps. A lad in Figure 24 models the full coat in a plainer version. It was often protected by a triangular apron buttoned to a coat button. This coat sometimes had the new fitted sleeve with splits seen at mid-century.

Early and mid-century dresses were simple but charming, as is Figure 32. Blues, yellows, and earth tones were popular colors.

(55)

(40)

(34)

(39)

(44)

(56)

Although children were still laced into corsets and braces, their clothes were becoming softer and allowing more freedom of movement.

The thin muslins, gauzes, and linen used for girls' dresses were often woven in thick–thin patterns that were quite beautiful when a colored slip or lining was used underneath. The little girl of Figure 34 wears a striped gauze dress over pink. A thick–thin effect was also achieved by sewn-in tucks in the sheer fabrics of Figure 39. Capes were often lined with bright colors, making them reversible.

Toward the end of the eighteenth century, boys' coats lost much of their fullness and began to slope or were cut away toward the back, as shown by Figure 40. Waistcoats were often beautifully embroidered, as is this cream silk one. Little boys' coats were cut away like those of their older brothers, as shown by the child in Figure 44. He wears the revolutionary new pantaloons that older boys were not yet wearing.

After the revolution, girls' waistlines began to move up toward the bosom, as in Figure 55, and boys' coats continued to slope more steeply toward the back, as demonstrated by Figure 56. Collars were added to both coats and waistcoats, whereas waistcoats were shortened.

(63)

(106)

(58)

(76)

(114)

Boys' pantaloons were the most outstanding fashion of the early nineteenth century, with the short jacket also a new idea. The little boy in Figure 58 shows the ankle-length pantaloons, short velvet jacket, and striped socks of the period.

Girls' waistlines rose to extreme heights at the beginning of the century, as demonstrated by Figures 63 and 76. These young girls also show the short spencer jacket and stole that were favorite wraps during the first half of the century.

The frock coat was introduced before mid-century. It was essentially the short jacket with a flared skirt added. Shown here and in Figure 106, it would continue to be worn until the end of the century. Waistcoats grew quite short, and starched collars stood up at the neck. Trousers, for older boys, became so long that they touched the floor in back.

Little girls were dressed in gathered pantalets long before Amelia Bloomer gave them a new name and new meaning. The little girl in Figure 114 models blue ones to match her blue dress.

(130)

(156)

(174)

(184)

Although the short jacket was a favorite of little boys throughout the last half of the nineteenth century, it always conformed to changing collar and lapel styles of adult fashions, as did the shirt and waistcoat. The young boy in Figure 130 shows a jacket and shirt with the new standing collars. Waistcoats usually had shawl collars.

An increase in Scottish representation in the English court created interest in plaids and checks during the second quarter of the nineteenth century. Princess Alexandra stimulated still more interest by her plaid ball gowns. Girls in America were commonly seen in plaid dresses worn over hoop petticoats, as the little girl of Figure 156.

The Crimean War inspired exotic braid-trimmed fashions for little boys, as did the new American Zouave militia uniforms. Zouave suits such as those of Figure 174 were featured in the most elegant fashion magazines.

Girls wore exotic bolero suits too. The young lady of Figure 184 wears her jacket, straw hat, and striped stockings with the very popular red blouse.

PLATE 6

(188)

(211)

(217)

(225)

(243)

Train travel brought about an interest in casual sports clothing, as did a visit by the Prince of Wales to the United States. The new sack coat shown in Figure 188 would remain in fashion, with only minor changes, till the present.

The extreme fullness of girls' skirts in mid-century was swept toward the back and up, to form the bustle of the 1870s. It was not uncommon for a dress to be made of two or three different fabrics, with several different trims. The basque bodice of Figure 211 is shown over a dress with the fashionable draped overskirt.

Little boys' jackets were styled after the new sports jackets, too, with the blouse collar worn outside, and a large bow-tied cravat, as in Figure 217.

Dresses had either very low waistlines or no waistlines at all and were made in a variety of fabrics, from dark woolens to delicate laces and satins. The young girls of Figures 225 and 243 show the dressy feminine fashions of the 1880s. The girl in Figure 243 wears a fashionable little white piqué coat with eyelet and ribbon trim over her dress.

PLATE 7

(262) (265) (267) (276) (277)

The bicycle brought about several new fashions, including the new and shocking divided skirt eventually called culottes. The young cyclist in Figure 262 models pleated culottes here instead of the full Turkish trousers. Over her culottes (divided skirt) she has added the reefer coat of Figure 271 to form a bicycle suit. Along with the billed cap, a wide-brimmed sailor hat with sheer veil was very fashionable and would soon be worn for automobile riding too.

The girl in Figure 265 shows the new bolero jacket of the 1890s, which might be worn over dresses or with skirts or culottes. Its new body-fitting shape gave it virtually the same appearance as a dress.

Middies were worn outside trousers as a result of new navy uniform regulations. The already tremendously fashionable sailor suit continued its popularity with many variations seen on little boys, such as this scalloped version from Figure 267. Sailor overblouses inspired little boys' overblouses in all styles, such as this Little Lord Fauntleroy velvet suit in Figure 276, shown here with the jacket.

Reefer suits such as that of the little boy in Figure 277 were made in feminine versions, too. This one of eyelet piqué or flannel is beautifully scalloped. The little girl's mob cap has the characteristic front dip and tall ruffle of the period.

(286)

(288)

(309)

(316)

Knickers were the latest fashion for boys, with those of little boys being worn above the knee. "Russian suits" were often seen with high leggings over the button shoes, as in Figure 286. These little suits were probably inspired by Teddy Roosevelt's mediation of the Russo-Japanese War in 1905.

Double-breasted overblouses were seen with the popular "military" or standing collar, as well as with the sailor collar from Figure 288. Billed caps and dark stockings were favored for boys everywhere.

Shoulder and neck interest remained in fashion throughout the decade, with both round and square necks being seen. The frock in Figure 309 is shown here in a slightly different variation with a square neck and extra ruffles around the armholes. It could be either a sleeveless dress or a jumper worn over a guimpe.

V-necked yokes were as popular as the squared and round ones. The dress in Figure 316 is shown here in a delicate printed lawn fabric with a deep V-neck and tucked yoke, for a very romantic effect.

Figure 120 Black and brown were popular colors for children's clothing at this time. Here a very young boy wears a black broadcloth smock with the skirt open in front. It has the same full drooping sleeves of girls' dresses and a sheer white ruffle at the neck. Its main feature is the black velvet wing or panel that begins at the waistline and grows wider as it angles out over the shoulder. The rich black of the velvet contrasts nicely with the dull black of the smock.

Plain white trousers with little splits at the side seams are worn underneath. White stockings and black, square-cut slippers carry out the black-and-white color scheme.

Outstanding also is the shiny little black-billed cap of European origin. It has a gold band across the front and black cord and tassel ties. European-inspired caps and folk smocks would grow more and more popular during the next two decades. In his hand the little boy holds the string for one of the new pull toys widely advertised and sold at this time.

Figure 121 The use of European-style smocks for little boys continued into the 1860s, when many had shoulder yokes outlined with ruffles or fringe. Several portraits from the 1840s show similar versions of this pleated smock. The version illustrated here is of muslin with a yoke and ruffles; the bodice is pleated and held in place with a wide black belt. Black trousers and black slippers with ribbon rosettes are worn with it.

One period portrait shows a blue smock with black fringe around the yoke, worn over white trousers. Another painting of the time shows a black smock with black fringe topping white trousers. This had two rows of fringe around the sleeve, at the elbow.

A black or natural straw cap shaped like that in Figure 120 was worn with this outfit. The side-parted hair styles for boys were here to stay. This boy has his hair curled over the ears.

Figure 122 This smock is cut like a coat, resembling both a man's frock coat and a woman's dress of the period. It is black velvet, with large sleeves that taper toward the wrists, as in Figure 119. The pearl buttons are purely decorative, since the bodice is cut with a V opening and could not fasten. A sheer white ruffle stands up around the front and neckline. A false vest front is sewn into the smock and fastens with identical pearl buttons.

Under the smock, this boy wears tan trousers and little lace-up boots. He, too, wears the new side-part hair style, in this case brushed toward the cheeks to form pointed sideburns.

Figure 123 The new sleeve of the 1840s was large at the lower arm and close fitting at the upper part. Shirring was immensely popular for a time, and was com-

(126)

(123)

(125)

(124)

(127)

(128)

mon on sleeves, bodices, and even around skirts. The tucked bodices just naturally evolved into shirred ones, as tucks grew smaller and closer together. This little bodice is made up of many small tucks. The sleeves are tucked at the upper arm, with several rows of stitching across the tucks to hold them flat. The tucks are released just above the elbow into full lower sleeves. Two wide tucks go around the full skirt of this bright red dress.

Over the dress is a gray apron with the straps crossed in back and then tied in front to form a waistline. White, tucked and lace-edged pantalets are worn underneath, with white stockings and black slippers. The little girl's hair is combed with the stylish middle part, with bunches of curls over each ear anchored in place by ribbons.

Figure 124 The waistline had dropped back to the natural waist on infants' dresses by now. This simple printed ankle-length cotton dress has a full gathered bosom, with self-binding at the neckline and a sewn-in waistband. There are no tucks or lace; its only embellishment consists of blue ribbons tied around the sleeves to draw them up into small swags. It is much like the dress in Figure 125, except for the sleeves. The dainty print fabric has a miniature pink, blue, and green leaf design on a white background.

Black slippers with ties and white stockings are worn with the ankle-length dress.

Parted on the side, this hair style has a rather modern look.

Figure 125 Here is another baby dress, following the same lines as that of Figure 124, with its sewn-in waistband at the natural waist and its full bodice. The sleeves have a ruffle at the edge ending just above the elbow, and then another self-ruffle about midway up the upper arm. The dress is pale blue muslin without ribbons or lace of any kind.

Bright red boots contrast colorfully with the dress. The baby's hair is brushed straight back.

Figure 126 This dress illustrates the characteristics usually associated with women's fashions of the 1840s. The young girl here models the new bodice that is shirred from the waistline point up to just under the bosom, where the fullness is released. The neckline and shoulder seams are gathered, to take in the fullness again and fit the neck. The sleeves are shirred down to the elbow, where the fullness, released, is then gathered in once more at the lower arm. These sleeves are pushed up to the middle of the lower arm. They can be pulled down to the wrist, to look like those of the little boy's suit in Figure 128. Narrow lace edges the neckline. Stripes, checks, and calico prints were favorite fabrics, with browns and blues the favorite colors.

Pantalets with lace and tucks were worn underneath. Black slippers and white stockings complete the costume. The young lady's hair is arranged with a middle part, with the back hair pushed behind the ears where it falls softly over her shoulders.

Figure 127 Still commonly worn, but more representative of the styles of the 1830s than of the forties, this frock has a tucked bodice and off-the-shoulder collar. The tucks resemble small double pleats and cover the entire bodice front. Full ruffles edge the sleeves. A bertha collar grows wider at the curve of the shoulder and falls out over the sleeves. Outlined in black lace, it also has a black ribbon rosette at the center front.

Over the lavender dress, the little girl wears a sheer black apron with a pointed waistband. It is edged with black lace and has a small pocket, holding a green handkerchief. Her bead necklace is amber colored. She has on the familiar white pantalets, white stockings, and black slippers. Her hair is pulled back tightly behind her ears and fastened, with sideburns brushed out onto the cheeks.

Figure 128 Both male and female fashions are reflected in this little boy's suit. The black blouse has the latest-style sleeves, with the shirred upper arm and very full lower arm. They are like those of Figures 123 and 126, but are longer, coming all the way to the wrist. His collar is the open type favored by very young boys at this time.

Black buttons attach the blouse to the full pantaloons, which open at the side to form a drop seat.

The hat is very up to date, with its flat crown and wide brim. It is tied on with a black silk cord matching its cord and tassel decorations. The shiny black square-cut slippers have bow ties. The child holds the string of a typical pull toy from the mid-nineteenth century.

Figure 129 Simple little muslin frocks with off-the-shoulder necklines appear in so many children's portraits during this and the following decade that they must have been worn in all parts of the nation. Very young boys as well as girls wore them.

This bodice has only slight fullness, and the sleeves are straight. A flat lace edges both sleeves and neckline. It was a hallmark of fashion, judging by the many portraits, to paint the dress with one shoulder falling down onto the arm, as shown here. The look was always of studied casualness. Two large tucks encircle the hemline of the gathered skirt.

White pantalets, white stockings, and high-cut black slippers complete the outfit. Red shoes were commonly worn too. Vertical corkscrew curls start high

(133)

(130)

(131)

(129)

(132)

(134)

93 /

at the side of the head and fall onto the shoulders in a favorite hair style of mid-century. The little girl holds a reticule purse.

Figure 130 The ever-popular short jacket was constantly updated to conform to adult fashions. The updating might change the collar, lapels, or sleeves. This jacket has a standing collar and rounded lapels to make it the latest style. It is double-breasted, though never fastened.

Vests were pale colors such as white, buff, yellow, or gray, in cotton or brocade fabrics, usually with shawl collars. Shirts had standing collars, with just the corners turned down over the popular black cravat.

Trousers were neutral or green colors, sometimes of corduroy, tweeds, or stripes. Although the buttoned-front fly was being worn in Europe at this time, it was still only occasionally seen in America.

This young boy has on low-cut slippers over white stockings. He might add either a top hat or the flat wide-brimmed hat of Figures 111 and 128.

The frock coat of Figure 106 was still worn during this decade and would remain in favor for many years.

Figure 131 Again we see buttons used for trim as well as function, on this child's suit. The short, dark jacket has white pearl buttons outlining the neck, front, and bottom edges, going all the way around the back, similar to those on the suit in Figure 86. The neck is wide, with the ruffle of the blouse pulled out over the jacket neck.

More pearl buttons dress up the trousers, where they are used to fasten them to the blouse. They also fasten the front drop panel.

Low cloth boots were usually worn with these suits. Of broadcloth or wool, they were sometimes combined with leather and dyed colors like soft green, yellow, tan, or black.

This child's hair is cut short and parted at the side.

Figure 132 Cut on the same lines as women's dresses, this little boy's dress has side-front seams on the bodice. They are outlined with the same bias binding as the sleeve cuffs and neckline, with a little belt set into the center front panel. The dress is made of a small blue and white plaid.

Boys' dresses at this time were often quite short, revealing white trousers or pantaloons underneath. Occasionally, boys' pantaloons had ruffles, but usually they were more tailored, like these with two small tucks around the bottoms to allow for the child's growth.

White stockings and low black boots are those commonly seen at this time. His hat is the wide-brimmed, flat-crowned straw seen on men as well as boys. It has a black band and bow.

Although he wears a dress, this lad sports a fashionable masculine side-part hair style.

Figure 133 Pleated skirts were as important a characteristic of dresses during the 1840s as pleated and tucked bodices. The pleats of this untrimmed skirt are about 1½ inches apart all around the waist. The bodice pleats are framed in a curved panel and gathered just a bit at the center. White lace is gathered at the neckline and sleeve edges. There is also a row of black lace sewn flat onto the sleeve, just above the white lace. Pink ribbons run from the neckline to the sleeve edge and tie at each shoulder of this peacock blue dress.

The fad for tying satin ribbons around the wrists is shown here. These wrist bows did not always match the ribbons on the dress. Low boots were dyed in colors such as blue, pink, or red.

This young girl wears the popular middle part with corkscrew curls starting high on the head. Instead of being pulled back tight, the hair is waved at the forehead.

Figure 134 The huge sleeves of women's and girls' clothes inspired the full sleeves of this little boy's black suit. They are tapered to fit the lower arm. The blouse curves down at the lower back, where it buttons to the trousers with three medium-sized metal buttons. The large lace-edged blouse collar is like that in Figure 107 shown from the front.

This back view shows the full, even baggy seat of these suits, caused by taking five pleats at the waist. Side openings allow the back to drop down when needed. The same metal buttons are used for fastenings.

Instead of covering the ear, newer hair styles in this period cut the hair around the ear, leaving it exposed. Front hair was still often brushed forward. The black boots are lace-ups.

Figure 135 Young boys' clothes show that they were wearing trousers with the new button-front opening before it was widely accepted by adults. At first, buttons were exposed, as shown here. Trousers often fastened up the lower leg, too, with buttons facilitating pulling them on over boots. Straps or braces had developed stretch ends after 1836, when Charles Goodyear invented elastic.

On canal boats, on river craft, in eastern cities, among bands of western settlers, and just about anywhere else in the United States, one might see boys of all ages in these folk garments. The drop-shouldered shirt opening only part way down the front was standard wear for dress and everyday wear, from the Revolution on throughout the nineteenth century. Cravats and ties changed, as did the treatment of the collar, but the shirt changed little. Here a boy has the collar open and tied with a red cravat or bandanna. The red cravat was brought to America

(135)

(136)

(137)

(138)

(139)

(140)

by French immigrants at the beginning of the century; the red cotton bandanna that evolved from it was to become an American folk symbol.

This boy's cap is like that issued by the U. S. Army in 1841. It had originated in Prussia during the Napoleonic wars and come to America with European immigrants earlier in the century. It was widely worn in all parts of the country, adopted by males of all ages, until the end of the century.

Boots had straps inside on each side for pulling them on. Sometimes they were made of beautiful striped or floral grosgrain ribbon over a heavy lining, and were proudly allowed to show.

Figure 136 The smock had been worn by farmers in England and on the continent for centuries. It came to colonial America long before the Revolution, and continued in use until the Civil War. It became a feature of children's apparel because of the decade's fascination with European folk costumes. During the early nineteenth century in England, the smock had developed a distinctive decorative stitching—smocking—that took its name from the garment. It is used here not only on the front yoke but on the cuffs as well.

Little boys used the smock as a play cover-up, usually to protect clothes. The jacket and blouse were removed and replaced with this practical little garment. An attached waist held up the pantaloons, as shown in Figure 69. This little boy still wears pantaloons, rather than the newer long trousers.

His slippers are flat and square cut. His hat is the traditional straw, but a variety of hats were seen with the smock.

Figure 137 Shawls found favor throughout the nineteenth century in all parts of the nation, by girls of all economic and social classes. For parties or special occasions they might be lace or embroidered silk, for daytime or play they were of paisley and other exotic designs, usually with printed borders. Or they might also be simple homemade or home-woven ones.

Produced in plaids, stripes, solid colors, embroidered, and printed, they varied in size as well as design. Edges might be trimmed in varying lengths of fringes, ruffles, or scallops. Young girls and children usually held them in place by crossing them over in front, as shown, and tying them in back. Sometimes they were tied around the shoulders, with the corners hanging down in front.

Typical of those of the 1830s and forties, this dress has wide sleeves tapering toward the wrists. It has a conservative high neck and small round collar, like that of Figure 119. This bonnet was widely seen also. It usually was of straw, but might be lined with cloth or even made entirely of cloth.

The aprons in Figures 97, 98, and 100 were commonly worn under these shawls.

Figure 138 For everyday wear in small towns and rural areas and for some cities, these practical clothes were sturdy and warm. This small boy has put on several woolen shirts, one over the other. The outer one is a winter version of the waists in Figures 69 and 99, with a high neck and long sleeves. It fastens to the pantaloons with buttons. Another pair of trousers shows under the pantaloons.

The cap, of European origin (described in Figure 135) is worn over a scarf across the head. Along with keeping the ears and head warm, the scarf crosses under the chin and then wraps around the neck, keeping it warm too. It came in red, tan, and white stripes, with tasseled ends.

The child's mittens and heavy knit stockings are gray, his shoes, heavy brown leather.

Figure 139 The play apron at this time had taken on the look of a smock. It was still gathered at the neck, sometimes with a drawstring, and hung straight from neck to hem. At mid-century, aprons were red, pink, blue, gray, brown, and black. Such basic aprons can be made to conform to any era by updating the sleeves to reflect the current fashion.

This little girl's cap is of interest: it is a feminine version of the ancient stocking cap. Originally made by using a knit stocking and tying a string around it, the resulting ruffle or bunch of cloth could be worn on the inside or outside, as illustrated. The yarn fringe ball on today's caps evolved from this bunch of cloth. Here, a cuff is turned back around the face and a ruffle or flap protects the neck as a result of chin string ties.

Red or black stockings were tucked into heavy brown shoes. The mittens are gray, as those of the little boy.

Figure 140 Immigrants in this period were coming to America from Ireland, Scotland, Germany, and other parts of Europe. Americans were pouring through the Cumberland Gap into the southern and central regions. By the end of the decade, Mormons would migrate to Iowa and then to Utah. It was not unusual to see European folk costumes among these groups, as engravings, paintings, and sketches done at this time attest.

This young girl wears the chemise, or folk blouse, under a dark corset bodice edged with braid. Some of these bodices closed with buttons, some with hooks, and others with laces. The skirt is of a bright color; some were calico, or striped or embroidered fabrics with old-fashioned country-style bands of braid decorating the hemline. Aprons were white or colored. They might be decorated with lace, embroidery, or braid.

There might be many reasons why these clothes were commonly seen. Perhaps there wasn't enough money yet in the immigrant family to buy new clothing, or maybe the clothes served to remind one of home. One must feel integrated into a new culture before letting go of the old one. Most importantly, it might have been respect for ancient tradition and the individual's sense of identity that led to upholding tradition. Whatever the reasons, British and European regional and folk clothes became very much a part of the American scene.

Figure 141 Very young boys, up to four years of age and sometimes even older, still wore dresses in the 1850s. These had become quite elaborate, as here, a small lad shows a fashionable "frock and cloak." It was of a bright color, because aniline dyes had recently been synthesized, so that colors like orange, fuchsia, violet, and magenta had become familiar.

A bodice of ribbon-striped fabric in this garment has a feminine wide neck and dainty sleeves, much like those of Figure 144. It fastens in front with pearl buttons like a vest. The full skirt has small pleats all the way around. The cream ribbon around the hemline matches the narrower ribbon on the bodice and on the scalloped cape.

Noteworthy are this boy's plaid stockings. Judging from portraits of very young boys painted at this time, they were a familiar sight, often in browns, tans, grays, and blues. He also wears pantalets and low-cut slippers with ribbon rosettes. His Scottish bonnet would be more widely worn in the next two decades.

Figure 142 Collarless muslin, calico, and wool shirts with drop shoulders appeared everywhere after the detachable collar came into fashion. Only a narrow neckband finished off the shirt neck. Sleeves were often rolled up during work or play. Stripes, prints, and bright solids were worn, with red being a favorite by the 1860s.

This boy wears pantaloons of early denim cloth, which came undyed and unbleached, making it a coarse, canvaslike fabric. It came to be called denim because it originated in de Nimes, France.

Shoes much like backless scuffs or low-heeled mules were often worn by blacks in the South, particularly in the Mississippi River region. Sometimes they may have been just old shoes with the heels pushed down, but they do appear in many drawings and engravings at mid-century.

Both white and black youngsters were seen wearing such garments, either with bare feet or with black boots replacing the scuffs. This collarless shirt was often seen with suspenders, heavy shoes, and the straw hat of Figure 96.

Figure 143 The wide use of braid and tassels on little boys' clothing grew out of a fascination with Turkish styles during the Crimean War of 1853 through 1856.

A short, flared coat of exotic design with flared sleeves, called a pardessus, appeared at this time for boys. It was often of cotton cloth in colors such as ma-

(142)

(143)

(145)

(146)

(141)

(147)

(144)

100 /

roon, brown, dark green, gray, or tan, heavily trimmed with braids of varying sizes and designs. This coat has one-inch-wide braid on the hem, front, collar, and sleeves. A narrower folded braid binds the edges of the collar, sleeves, and around the front and bottom hem. It even edges the pocket flaps. All the braid and buttons match. Trousers might be blue with a gray coat, or gray with a maroon coat. Sometimes braid was used down the side of the trousers to match that on the coat.

The accompanying cap is of European origin. Originally soft on top, as in Figure 135, it had grown hard, like caps issued with some American militia uniforms at the time.

Figure 144 An interesting transitional dress for a little boy seems to foreshadow feminine styles to come, while, at the same time, it is representative of the 1850s. The bodice is quite off the shoulders, with a drop-shoulder line at the armhole. A curved peak in the sleeve edge is meant to give the effect of swags, which would be drawn up by ribbons. A similar look is created at the hips, as the long bodice curves up at the side seams and out over a full skirt and petticoats. In a portrait in the National Gallery of Art, this garment has a narrow white binding around the neckline, sleeves, hem, and all seams. The light brown bodice has tiny black dots, whereas the skirt is very dark brown, with small white dots. Little boys were often dressed in the frocks of Figure 150.

The little boy's stockings are also worthy of special note: They are the argyle or plaid stockings inspired by the originals of the Scottish Highlands. His hair style is transitional, too, with its new side part and forward-curled sideburns.

Especially designed for young children, the "shoo-fly" rocking horse shown here allowed them to sit safely between two flat horses.

Figure 145 There was such a variety of coats at mid-century that almost any length and shape might be seen around the nation. Slave boys wore striped or checked cotton jackets in summer and wool tweeds, checks, or bright solids in winter. Rural boys, both black and white, waterfront workers, western pioneers, and American boys everywhere wore these ageless garments. Drop-shouldered full shirts opening to the chest remained standard folk wear during the entire nineteenth century.

Red bandannas were a familiar sight on boys throughout the country, cutting across many classes. The bandanna was useful for wiping perspiration, which led to its being called a wipe, but it had other uses. It could be pulled up over the nose in the fields or on the trail to keep out dust from the throat and lungs, or tied around the head or neck to soak up sweat, or tied over the ears in winter for warmth. In an emergency, it could be a tourniquet or a bandage; and it could be a washrag or towel if needed. There are stories of young boys being punished for fighting with bandannas: it made an effective weapon when folded and knotted!

A variety of hats, boots, and shoes might be worn with these simple clothes.

Figure 146 Fashion for boys was inspired by Turkish styles, as a result of the Crimean War. Exotic tassels, braids, and heavy looking garments such as this one were put on even very small lads. The wide neckline of this blue smock is decorated with black braid, as are the flared sleeves set into the drop-shouldered armhole. A heavy, twisted silk cord with large tassels forms a belt. Underneath is a full white blouse with ruffles at the neck and wrists.

Trousers for very young boys for wear with these smocks might be white pantaloons, some even with ruffles or lace trim. Older children usually preferred plain gray trousers.

The billed cap is similar to that in Figure 143, with a flared top where a button holds a cord with a tassel. This boy and the one in Figure 143 sport the new curly hair style.

Figure 147 This somewhat more masculine suit for very young boys has frills but no skirt. A little black velvet jacket fastens only at the waist, where it is gathered onto a waistband. It has short flared sleeves revealing the white blouse sleeves underneath. The very full blouse has ruffles at the neck and wrists.

White pantaloons fasten onto the blouse with the same pearl buttons as used at the side openings. The full back becomes a drop seat, as in Figure 134.

Curls at the cheeks and a side part form the same fashionable hair style as that in Figure 144.

Figure 148 One family portrait painted during the 1850s reveals a mother and three daughters wearing virtually identical dresses like this one. The youngest child in the group is about four years old, and judging from the painting this dress was not limited to any age group.

Definitely off the shoulder, the bodice has a lowered armhole, in keeping with the continuing trend to drop-shouldered dresses. The short sleeves are gathered at the center, causing them to flare out, adding to the sloping shoulder look. Small tucks radiate from the bodice point, demonstrating the popular use of diagonal lines. The waistline point has returned, along with the natural waistline.

Pantalets or bloomers gathered at the ankle were worn under full ankle-length skirts and petticoats.

Figure 149 Adults usually reserved off-the-shoulder dresses for formal wear and for summer attire in southern areas, but it would seem, from their portraits, that little girls wore them all year 'round, for all occasions, during the 1840s and early 1850s. This dress illustrates just how low-cut many dresses of this period were.

(150)

(152)

(148)

(149)

(151)

(153)

It comes quite far down onto the arms, with a band that drops the armhole still lower. It must have been difficult for a child to raise her arms in such a restrictive garment, even though it is charmingly attractive. Skirts grew quite short for a few years in the early 1850s.

The bodice has pleats that radiate from the point at the waistline toward the shoulders. There is also a point in the center of the band around the shoulders. Two puffs are formed by gathers in the elbow-length sleeves, with the upper puff smaller than the lower one, emphasizing the sloping shoulders look. Pleats are used in the full skirt, rather than gathers. Favorite colors for these dresses were pink, yellow, blue, and red.

This young girl wears pantalets with eyelet-embroidered, or "cutwork," scallops, shorter than the pantelets of the 1840s.

Of special interest are the short white stockings that appeared at this time. They were apparently inspired by the new "half hose," or socks worn by gentlemen. Some paintings portray little girls' socks with ribbing at the top, while others appear to be folded over, giving them a twentieth-century look.

Figure 150 Soft little muslin dresses like this seemed to be owned by almost every boy and girl. They appear over and over in museum collections as well as in private portraits done at mid-century. Probably the reason for their having been preserved in all those chests and attic trunks for generations was their exquisite needlework. Often they had as many as sixteen to twenty little tucks around the skirts, plus rows of hand-stitched cutwork or eyelet embroidery, as we call it today.

The sleeves and waistbands were often embroidered, too. They all appear to be much the same, yet, upon close inspection, no two are alike. Upon close examination, what often appears to be machine stitching turns out to be the tiniest-imaginable hand stitches. A magnifying glass usually reveals the cutwork to be worked in the most perfect little buttonhole stitches! Often a trunk produces not one but two or three of these dear little frocks, in stair-stepped sizes, and one can just see the children in the family growing up from one to the next.

The little linen slip worn underneath was usually of the same painstaking and loving craftsmanship. There was rarely, if ever, any color—only white needlework on white.

Figure 151 The diminutive drawn-up sleeves first seen around 1800 would remain in favor even into the 1860s. Although many of these sleeves were drawn up by simply tying ribbons around them, there is a portrait in the National Gallery of Art that shows clearly the drawstring and its resulting shirring on a little girl's sleeves.

This dress is bright red with little raised black dots. A narrow white lace edges the neckline, and dark green ribbons draw up the sleeves. Although the sleeves are like those of earlier decades, the bodice is quite fashionable, with its fitted body and natural waistline. The skirt is rather long, coming to below the calf.

Ankle-strap black slippers fasten with ties that thread through holes in the ends of the straps. Of unusual note are the red stockings, which match not only the dress but the red bead necklace.

The middle-part hair style with corkscrew curls was preferred by most little girls at mid-century.

Figure 152 An interesting variation of the wide neck and shirred sleeve styles was this little boy's dress. The bodice and sleeves are one long piece; this has been gathered to a narrow binding strip that reaches from one elbow to its shoulder, across the chest, and then down the other shoulder and elbow.

The back of the bodice is made the same way and is joined to the front on the arms. A small triangular gusset at each shoulder gives the bodice its proper fit.

The interesting use of buttons as decoration on boys' clothing continues, with small buttons highlighting the binding at the neck and sleeves. A narrow lace edges the neckline, while a wider ruffle appears at the sleeves. Rust, green, and deep blue were favorite colors for boys' dresses.

Blue cloth shoes with blue leather heels and toe tips were often seen beneath the ruffled pantaloons of little boys. The cloth might be wool or canvas, with the ties matching in color.

This child wears his hair cut short and brushed toward the face, in a style that was disappearing from fashion but still occasionally seen.

Figure 153 Seen on girls in every area of the United States, on all classes of people, and in all kinds of fabrics, this simple dress can truly be considered an American folk classic. It appeared on wealthy children and on the poor, and in cities as well as rural areas. It clothed slave children, while at the same time silk versions of it were worn by plantation owners' daughters. It differed only in the fabric used and in minor details of trim. Plain unbleached muslin was often used for slave children's clothing, while calico and gingham were used by just about everybody. Fine white cotton muslin (much like today's batiste) and beautiful lace might be saved for special occasions.

This child's shoes are low-cut slippers with ties or ribbons that wrap around the ankles. One portrait from the 1850s shows such slippers worn with short socks. This hair style is pulled back on top, like that in Figure 149, but it falls in small ringlets instead of long curls at the sides and back. Fancy floral or striped ribbons were used to fasten the hair. The little bead bracelet has a large blue center stone.

Figure 154 The use of diagonal bodice pleats continued well into the 1850s. Waistlines were set not only at the natural waist but appeared to have sunk even lower as a result of the waistline point. This young lady's dress shows the new snugly fitting sleeves with their pointed cuffs. Narrow sheer lace edges the sleeves and wide neckline. The full skirt is pleated instead of gathered.

Underneath are seen the pantalets soon to be out of fashion in favor of the new shorter bloomers. This girl wears the slippers that will also soon be discarded for the boots, which will remain popular until the end of the century.

The outstanding feature of this figure is the girl's hair style. Much like that in Figure 113, it appears very modern, parted in the center, then pushed behind the ears. Most startling are its short length and lack of curl. A similar short hair style in one contemporary portrait shows ribbon bows behind each ear.

Figure 155 Infant and toddler dresses often reflect styles of earlier decades, as does this one, with its wide neckline off the shoulders and the diagonal panels on the bodice. The little sleeves are cut to imitate the drawn-up sleeves worn by babies since 1800. The neckline, bodice panels, and sleeves are all edged with lace. Several rows of tucks are stitched around the skirt. The transparent soft cloth becomes opaque when doubled, forming stripes that are especially attractive when this white dress is worn over a pink, blue, or yellow slip.

The little slippers have ankle straps fastened with ties. Small rosettes decorate the toes.

English carriage makers made the first, and still the finest, baby carriages. Designed somewhat on the lines of horse-drawn vehicles in the beginning, some had to be pulled and others pushed, like the one shown here. Although they had only two wheels, there was a leg or brace under the footrest for support when the carriage was not in motion.

Figure 156   Plaids and tartans were favorite fabrics seen everywhere on children of both sexes. Also commonly seen were scalloped edges on sleeves, collars, and skirts, as modeled by this young girl. Her bodice buttons at the front, where it forms a point. Dropped shoulder lines also form points at the upper arms, continuing down toward the waistline in the familiar side-front seam. This seam appears on virtually every bodice at mid-century, sometimes accentuated with cord or braid. The flared sleeves are edged with scalloped borders like the skirt hem. Skirts had one, two, or several tiers at this time, with braid or scallops at the hems.

A white blouse worn underneath has a matching scalloped collar.

The hair style features the middle part and corkscrew curls so familiar at this time.

Figure 157 Sleeves with several puffs continued in popularity throughout the 1850s, as did tiered skirts. Shown here, a typical dress of the decade has three

(156)

(154)

(155)

(157)

(158)

tiers in the skirt, although there was great variety in the number of tiers used. Each tier or ruffle has braid-trimmed edges. Scalloped edges were very much in fashion, too, as was lace on formal frocks. The bodice has a dropped shoulder line leading down to the pointed waistline, like that in Figure 156. Collars were almost always white and might be large, as shown here, or dainty, as in Figure 158.

This young girl's bonnet is similar to those of the last two decades but much more shallow, not extending out to shade the face. These small purely decorative bonnets were trimmed with much ribbon, lace, and flowers. The boots, of cloth and leather, are the new front-button style.

Figure 158 The idea for the tailored suit began in Paris, when the English fashion designer Frederick Worth began making dresses with matching jackets for women. Eventually, the idea evolved into the matching skirt and jacket combination, or suit. The shirtwaist blouse also developed about this time.

This girl's jacket has the same drop-shouldered bodice as in Figures 156 and 157. The sleeves flare only slightly to the elbow, where a flared flounce is attached. The jacket skirt and the sleeve flounces are cut into small scallops at the edges. Two rows of black braid go down either side of the front buttons, around the waist, and around the sleeves. The matching skirt is plain.

Jackets like that of the little boy's ensemble from Figure 176 were worn by girls also. The back coattails were longer than those in front. The white blouse or shirtwaist here worn underneath has a small scalloped collar and sleeves that repeat the shape and scalloped edges of the jacket sleeves.

This young lady wears the boots that will remain in style until the end of the century. They are side-buttoned cloth with leather toes and heels. Her hat is the wide-brimmed straw usually worn out of doors to protect the wearer's skin. It has a ribbon band and long streamers.

Figure 159 By the 1850s, many of the states had had militia regiments for some years, so there was always a certain amount of interest in military uniforms. The war with Mexico during the late 1840s had created interest in toy soldiers and military uniforms for boys. Most of the boys pictured at mid-century in uniforms are of school age, so apparently the idea of dressing very little boys in military garb was not yet accepted.

It is interesting to note that the style of uniforms seen most often on young boys was reminiscent of those being worn by California vigilante troops and by the unique U. S. Camel Corps, which traveled from San Antonio to California in 1857. Probably news of these groups as played up in newspapers stimulated interest in their attire.

This boy's cap is an early form of the kepi. It is stiff rather than pushed

(162)

(163)

(159)

(160)

(161)

(164)

down in front, like the later Civil War kepis, and has a leather visor. His coat is the single-breasted frock-coat style with a standing collar worn by 1850s militia regiments and continued during the Civil War.

Uniforms with short jackets were also worn, cut on the same lines as the little boy's suit of Figure 160. Two white straps were sometimes crossed over the chest.

The frock coat in Figure 106 was still the fashion for nonmilitary young gentlemen. These were military school uniforms of similar design but the uniform appeared as fashion in many fashion prints.

Figure 160 Although not military in color or decoration, this short jacket is cut on the lines of uniforms worn by U.S. soldiers in the war with Mexico and also by some state militia in the 1850s. It is of velvet, with small buttons close together down the front, and a standing collar. These jackets were usually of maroon or brown, but might also be tan, green, or blue, with either metal or pearl buttons.

Trousers were usually cotton twill, in small stripes or windowpane checks. High-low boots of bright colors were of wool or broadcloth, with side button fastenings. Young boys favored the tam-o'-shanter with fancy ribbon bands. Either tassels or pom-poms decorated the crown.

Figure 161 Capes and mantles and combination capes and coats were considered elegant and proper for young gentlemen. They might be silk or wool, in solids or plaids. This young man wears one of interesting design, not quite a coat, yet not exactly a cape. A short, pointed cape across the back comes around each arm to the front, where it forms a kind of sleeve. The sides of the skirts are split and the hem slopes down in the center, both back and front. All the edges are bound with braid, and the lining is quilted silk.

This boy's trousers, like those in Figure 159, are curved down in back and arch up over the shoe in front. They touch the ground at the heel. His hat, both high crowned and wide brimmed, was sometimes referred to as a flower-pot hat. The silk cord band with tasseled ends hangs over the brim edge.

Figure 162 Seen in early western settlements, wagon trains, rural areas, and cities were these full shirts with drop shoulders, worn under vests. Shirts still opened only to the chest. Some were collarless, like that in Figure 142, although many had collars that were worn open, as shown here. Vests often had shawl collars.

Trousers would not have belt loops till the turn of the century, but trouser belts were occasionally worn if no braces or straps were used. Denim was first used in the early gold mining areas by prospectors, because it was soft but tough. Denim was available unbleached at first, but soon it was woven with indigo blue dyed threads across white. The gold miners are believed to have originated the idea of metal rivets at the points of stress on denim trousers.

Tall boots were worn in rural and rugged areas. They were lined with either tan or red canvas, and the tops were folded over as shown.

Figure 163 The double-breasted shirt was seen on the glamorous, dashing volunteer firemen in eastern cities as well as on a few military men. It was worn by many immigrants from Europe, where it had originated. It had a soft collar and a double panel over the chest, with buttons on each side. Boys usually wore a red or black cravat tied in a large bow at the neck. There was much interest in dressing fashionable young boys in European folk costume at this time. The double-breasted shirt or smock might be worn tucked inside the trousers, as illustrated, or belted on the outside, as shown in Figure 171. Blue and gray were favorite colors, but red, green, and black were seen also. Sometimes a braid edged the front panel and collar.

Trousers either had the old front button panel or the very new front fly, as illustrated in Figure 164. Braces were worn over these shirts sometimes when they were tucked inside.

The boy wears the billed shako cap described in Figure 135. His boots are especially interesting, with their decorative imitation cuffs. Apparently inspired by the fold-down boots shown in Figure 162, they have a tan leather band at the top that is stitched in place. They are lined with bright red, and have colorful striped pull-on straps inside hanging out over the sides. The lower part is black, with squared toes.

Figure 164 Braces, or suspenders, had developed two elastic extensions on the front ends and one on each brace in back by mid-century.

This boy sports not only the latest thing in suspenders but also in trousers—his have the new fly-front opening. The button-front trousers of Figure 135 were the earliest form of the fly opening, but here we see the very fashionable addition of a panel covering the buttons. Period paintings indicate that young boys' clothes adopted the fly before it was commonly used on men's garments.

His shirt, opened only to the chest, has the soft collar and dropped shoulders in general use. Both folded cravats tied in a bow and the new pretied bow ties were popular. This boy wears his cravat tied only once with the ends hanging free in a casual style.

Figure 165 A most feminine frock is this complicated muslin one. The bodice has a yoke of small tucks that extends out onto the upper arm, forming a low shoulder line. Large rose-colored ribbon bows form epaulettes. Eyelet embroidery, medallions, and lace are all applied to the bodice in a zigzag design. Both the cuffs of the long sleeves and the high neckline are edged with lace. A large rose-colored bow is attached at the side of the waistline.

An overskirt is cut into points similarly decorated with eyelet, lace, and me-

From 1860 to 1870

(166)

(168)

(170)

(165)

(167)

(169)

dallions to repeat the bodice design. The skirt underneath is the same rose color as the large ribbon bows at the shoulders and waist. A straight band of embroidery and braid goes around the hemline.

In the 1860s, colored boots often matched dresses or coats, for a coordinated look. This girl wears deep pink ones matching her skirt and ribbons. They fasten down the side with buttons in scalloped edges and have a point at the top front.

Hats were becoming smaller and moving down toward the forehead as hair styles were pulled up in back. The hat brim curled up on the sides, and streamers and other trim usually decorated the back. Parasols were carried by young ladies to protect their skin from the sun.

Figure 166 Aprons were sometimes as fancy as the dresses under them and might be worn for any occasion. This little girl models a pastel-colored frock that still has the wide neck and sloping shoulder line of the two previous decades. Its sleeves are ruffles, accentuating the sloping shoulders. Rows and rows of tucks, lace, and insertion are used on the full skirt. The petticoats underneath are equally elaborate, as are the pantalets.

The sheer white apron's bodice follows the same lines as the dress bodice. The off-the-shoulder bib is edged with lace at the neck, and its curved flounces at the arms fall out over the dress sleeves. The apron skirt has several rows of lace around its curved corners and a ruffle of lace at its edge. The large satin ribbon sash and bow at the waist coordinate with the pastel dress.

The boots are cloth and patent leather; the hat is a flat-crowned straw with ribbon streamers.

Figure 167 Another example of the complex and charming frocks that dressmakers and mothers labored over is this white muslin model. In contrast to the pointed design in Figure 165, this has a feeling of roundness, with its curved corners, puffed sleeves, and round neck. The front V-shaped panels on the "corsage" bodice and skirt are filled in with rows of insertion. Sometimes as many as three or four different sizes and designs of lace were used. The ruffles around the skirt and bodice panels were often flat, being pleated or fluted instead of gathered. At times they were ruchings.

A green satin sash was fashionable, as was pink, blue, or lilac. The narrow-brimmed hat was almost always trimmed with velvet in a color that matched the sash. Wide ribbon streamers hung down to the shoulders in back. Hats were placed straight on top of the head or tilted to the front and usually had rows of lace ruffles on the underside of the brim.

Cloth and patent leather boots were either black or bright colors.

Figure 168 Sack coats were usually shorter than dresses, to allow the dress to show below. Plaid flannel was used for winter frocks, as shown here. The coat is flared from the shoulders to the hem. An attached scarflike decoration goes around the neck and hangs to the hemline, both back and front. It has three cord-edged points at the ends with small tassels ornamenting each point. The three points are repeated in the sleeve cuffs. Blue and gray were the preferred colors for girls' coats.

The small hat with curled brim tilts slightly forward. In gray felt with a velvet band, it has streamers to match the coat. The young girl wears matching kid gloves and canvas and leather boots.

In 1865 fashion magazines still showed girls wearing pantalets, although the new shorter drawers were replacing them.

Figure 169 Aprons and pinafores for very young girls were usually of "brown holland," which was actually more tan than brown. Red braid was a favorite for the sometimes elaborate embellishments. Even "simple" play aprons might require hours and hours of buttonhole stitching on the edges, with sewn-on braid and embroidery. The square yoke, pointed epaulette sleeves, pockets, and skirt hem of this little apron have both a straight row of braid and a row sewn on with decorative loop designs alongside it.

The red dress, like the apron, falls from a yoke at the chest and has no waistline. Directions given in ladies' magazines for making such garments rarely gave patterns, because such needlework was "so easy that any needlewoman will find it unnecessary."

This child wears the little boots with buttons at the sides and points in front, over dark stockings.

Figure 170 Referred to as a robe in *Godey's Lady's Book*, this christening dress was of "French mull trimmed with Valenciennes insertion and puffs." A front panel, or tablier, was set into the bodice front and skirt, down to the hem. It was made of alternating rows of lace and bands of shirring. Rows of lace also edge the entire length of the panel. The wide neckline is out onto the shoulders, and the little sleeves curve up in the center, copying the drawn-up sleeves of earlier times, as shown in Figure 87, page 67. Large white satin bows are used down the skirt panel and neckline. They were also often used at each shoulder on these elegant dresses.

The ladies' magazine that carried directions for making this dress suggested a matching pillow, using the same mull and Valenciennes lace. It also suggested, "For a boy the lining of the pillow should be blue, for a girl it should be pink." This infant's cap is made of alternating rows of lace and shirring.

Figure 171 Interest in European folk styles continued throughout this decade. Smocks were worn by all ages of young boys. This one is rather simple, being

(174)

(176)

(171)

(172)

(173)

(175)

(177)

hardly more than a regular shirt worn outside the trousers and belted. Shirts had always been made quite long, down onto the thighs, as shown here. As with shirts, this smock opens only over the chest, where it fastens with black buttons. The smock was often blue or gray, with white collar and cuffs. The belt and large tie were usually black, although red ties were popular too. Trousers were often light gray or blue.

Boots worn during the last half of the nineteenth century, by boys and girls alike, were often combinations of cloth and leather. These are black leather with black canvas tops.

Figure 172 Figaro jackets, Spanish jackets, corsage bodices, and various other names were used to refer to the little boleros worn during the 1860s. Often they were part of a suit of matching skirt and jacket, but just as often they were worn over dresses. They might appear over white blouses and colored skirts. They usually had either a dropped shoulder line, epaulettes, or some other decoration at the shoulder to give them a sloping look. Sleeves might be short, elbow length, or long, depending on the season. The many methods used for fastening them at the neck included braid loops, ties, buttons, clips, and buckles.

This young girl wears a matching bolero and skirt with a dark belt. Blue with blue satin trim was a popular color combination, as was tan with brown velvet edging. Blue, with gray velvet trim, and white velvet with red velvet trim were suggested in fashion magazines as appropriate for young ladies. White piqué and light gray poplin were used for summer boleros.

This girl wears boots with pointed toes and a large flat straw hat with ribbon streamers. Her hair is in long corkscrew curls.

Figure 173 Russian, Turkish, and other exotic styles influenced boys' clothes as interest in "things foreign" continued in the wake of the Crimean War. Perhaps this was natural at a time when trouble was in the air at home. There was much interest in Garibaldi, the Italian liberator, during the early 1860s, too, and he influenced styles in England and the United States. His caps and red shirts, as well as the exotic braid trim on clothes, were widely copied. This young boy wears a gray velvet coat edged with plum silk cord on front, hem, cuffs, collar, and pockets. Maroon and brown were favorite colors, too. Heavy corded frogs are used for fasteners in front.

This boy's knee breeches are like those in Figure 174. They sometimes matched the coat and might have braid at the outseam.

His shoes are worthy of note. Of leather, they have buttons to the side of the center seam, but no openings. Instead, they have the new elastic insets at the side of the instep so they do not need to fasten. Another unique feature is the fancy pull-on strap of striped twill at the center front. The cap is the European-inspired shako.

Figure 174 Zouave suits were the masculine equivalent of little girls' boleros. The native soldiers of French Algeria (the Turcos) inspired the idea of using the Zouave uniform for French designs. The French in turn gave it to a U. S. militia unit in Chicago in 1860. Soon these exotic uniforms were used by militia regiments from Connecticut to Louisiana. Early in the Civil War they were worn by some state militia. They became so popular with little boys that they remained in fashion until 1885.

Often of velveteen, they were trimmed with silk braid and metal buttons. Brown, green, and tan were the customary colors, with black or brown braid. One fashion magazine suggested a buff suit with coral braid trim on the jacket and knee breeches. The white cotton blouses worn under the jackets often had eyelet embroidery at the neck or collar, with pearl buttons.

Pillbox caps and Scottish tams were seen with these suits, as were side-button boots, sometimes of a matching color.

Figure 175 Cloaks were as much a favorite with girls as with boys. They came in a variety of exotic styles, with trimmings ranging from simple to elaborate. This double-tiered cloak has a hood, but many did not. Black and white stripes, checks, and plaids were the preferred fabrics. Fringe was usually used to enhance the attractiveness of these cloaks, with ball fringe a favorite. One fashion magazine recommended black and white striped cloth, edged with black and white ball fringe. Braid was frequently added above the ball fringes, as illustrated here.

At this time, capes and cloaks were flared, in circular, half-circular, or quarter-circular shapes. This one has a center back seam, so that the stripes meet at an angle. The hood has a center seam also, with a velvet bow on top.

Figure 176 Pearl-colored cloth was a favorite fabric for children's clothing throughout the last half of the nineteenth century. It was a beautiful lustrous cream/gray wool. Lovely in its own right, it was also the perfect background for silk embroidery, braids, satin and velvet trim, and lace.

Made on the lines of young girls' suits, as that of Figure 158, this little boy's ensemble has long coattails in back, with similar shorter ones in front. A black and white twisted braid ornaments the neck, front, coattails, and sleeve cuffs. It also edges the scalloped skirt hemline. Box pleated, the full skirt is calf length. Blue wool and black velvet were familiar fabrics for these suits, as well as the beautiful pearl-colored cloth.

Boots of cloth and leather were customarily worn with the suits as were caps like those in Figures 160, 173, and 174.

There was a garment for young boys that appeared to be the same as the suit while actually being a one-piece coat. The jacket and skirt were sewn together, with the skirt separated in front. It was worn over boys' dresses such as those in Figures 141, 152, and 181.

Figure 177 Capes and shawls were preferred to coats for girls, because they were less likely to compress and flatten the bouffant skirts. Also, the drop-shoulder lines at the dress armholes made coats less desirable than the free-hanging cloaks.

Seen in every length imaginable, from down to the elbow to just above the boot tops, capes appeared in many colors and styles. There was a variety of braid and tassel trim employed for decoration, as well as an assortment of fabrics. Some had hoods, usually with tassels, while others were plain. Canvases of those years show the cape in bright red, yellow, gray, black and white, blue, tan and brown. Wide-brimmed straw hats with ribbon streamers were worn with the hooded as well as unhooded capes.

Of special interest are this young girl's horizontally striped stockings, worn with her high-button boots.

Figure 178 Collarless shirts were among the exotic clothes that young boys were often decked out in, as described in Figure 173. The points at the neckline corners were often rounded, giving them a soft look. Braid occasionally edged the neckline and cuffs, as shown in Figure 187. The front might be tucked or trimmed, sometimes with rows of braid on a panel over the chest, but these shirts always opened only part way down the front. The dropped shoulder line was still apparent on all shirts, as were full sleeves.

Boys up to seven or eight years of age had buttons on the waistline of their shirts for the trousers to fasten onto. The buttons were simply moved down as the child grew in height. Older boys now wore braces or suspenders.

Red was a favorite color for these collarless shirts, but muslin, print calico, checks, plaids, stripes, and other dark solid colors were common also. Slave boys are usually pictured in unbleached muslin or striped shirts in the 1860s.

Figure 179 Aprons were an important item of the wardrobe of little girls for play or fancy-dress outfits. They were so much an integral part of girls' apparel that they were considered fashion and might be designed especially for a particular dress.

The apron shown has braid-edged shoulder straps or suspenders that tie at the curve of the dress's wide neckline. The waistband is edged with braid or lace to match the straps. Rows of tucks or braid encircle the full skirt. Decorative pockets were a familiar adornment, as illustrated by these, with braid-edged button-down flaps. Sometimes they had ruffles around the pockets, and at times lace medallions or embroidery might be added to the flaps instead of buttons. The suspenders tied so far out on the shoulders that they had to be fastened to the dress by ties, pins, or buttons. Often of plain white muslin, aprons might also be in colors like gray, brown, blue, or red. The dress underneath is much like that in Figure 186.

(182)

(178)

(179)

(180)

(181)

(183)

Note especially the plaid stockings, seen on girls as well as boys. They were of either straight or diagonal plaid and were inspired by plaids native to Scotland. This small girl wears rather high-topped boots of cloth and leather. Boots were sometimes made of checked or plaid wool also, with leather toes and heels.

Middle parts and corkscrew curls were the prevailing hair style for young girls at this time.

Figure 180 Aprons or pinafores were not only practical but part of fashion as well. One might be made especially for a particular dress, or designed to match several frocks. This pinafore, for very young girls, offers more protection to the dress than the one in Figure 179. Its design was called old-fashioned, having been seen on girls for decades. (It would continue to turn up in different periods, right on up to today.)

The neckline of the straight, full garment sometimes had a binding holding the gathers, ending in ties at the back. A more practical style had a drawstring, adjustable to fit a growing child or to go easily over either winter or summer clothing. The neckline is wide, in keeping with the then-current trend to wide necklines on fashionable dresses. Lace might be added at the neck or hem, and pockets might be sewn on the front, but this was an apron for hard use and more likely to be kept simple.

Noteworthy is this child's large cloth sunbonnet. Constructed somewhat similarly to that in Figure 98, page 73, it has a deep starched brim to protect the face. A ruffle at the back protects the neck from exposure to sunburn, a practical necessity with wide- and low-necked dresses. Sunburn and suntan were considered extremely unattractive and undesirable during the nineteenth century.

This little girl wears "old-fashioned" pantalets and high-top red shoes.

Figure 181 Boys up to five years old were dressed in bolero suits of white piqué in summer and pearl-colored flannel in winter. (For pearl-colored cloth, see Figure 176.) The skirt buttoned onto a soft white blouse with a small round collar. The bolero and skirt were edged with braid which might be applied in several flat rows or looped and curved into elaborate designs. Black braid was favored, but other dark colors like maroon, brown, or dark blue were common too.

Little cloth or leather boots were worn all year round, with long stockings in cool weather and short socks, as illustrated here, on warm days. Plaid and striped stockings were seen on both boys and girls.

This little boy's hair is short, with soft curls all over the head.

Figure 182 At mid-century, dresses for infant boys as well as girls became quite simple. This very small boy shows one with a natural waistline, high neck, and small white collar. Its sleeves are gathered full at the shoulder and slightly at the wrist under the fold-back cuffs. The ever-popular black braid trim edges the collar and cuffs and follows the hemline of the full skirt. A black ribbon is knotted at the neckline to resemble a man's tie.

Natural leghorn straw was molded into the small "porkpie" hat. It is bound on the edges with velvet. The hatband, rosette, and chin ties are velvet also, with brown, black, maroon, and dark green being the popular colors.

This child also sports the short socks that were to remain proper for children up to the present time. His shoes are lace-up high-tops.

The Victorian mahogany armchair-on-a-table was very modern in concept. It had a center rod to hold the chair in place on the table, so that it became a high chair, which could be pushed up to a dining table. When the chair was taken down, it could be placed on the floor, turning the two pieces into a child-size table and chair set for eating or play.

Figure 183 Coarse muslin, unbleached denim or canvas, and inexpensive calico were ordinarily sewn into clothing for children in rural and mountain areas. Settlers in remote western regions and slave children were dressed in practical clothing made from these fabrics, too.

This girl's plain muslin apron is constructed much like the dresses of earlier years. The bib or bodice is enclosed at the sides under the arms like a dress bodice. This design was certainly more practical than the open-sided bib, because in summer it could be worn by itself as a dress. One painting at mid-century shows a slave child in an unbleached pinafore like this over a brown dress, with its sleeves rolled up.

A solid red bandanna or scarf was often tied around the hair. It should be noted that evidence shows that black women and girls did not wear turbans with large bows on top of the head, as often depicted in the theater and early films. That image probably resulted from misinterpretation of the real life role of the traditional minstrel show comic, and gradually came to be accepted as historical fact. According to facts presented in both paintings and photographs, the turban was tied either front or back, with the small ends tucked inside, leaving only an inconspicuous knot visible. Evidence also shows that the sunbonnet was almost as commonly worn as the turban by slaves, especially those who worked outdoors.

Bright red strap shoes were often worn, with bare legs, by black children in the South.

Figure 184 The bolero (sometimes called a Spanish jacket, corsage bodice, Zouave jacket, or Figaro jacket), remained in vogue throughout the decade for all ages of girls and women. Sometimes it was worn over a dress and at times was a different color from the skirt. Fashionable ensembles had a matching bolero and skirt, as shown here.

(184)

(185)

(186)

(187)

Similar to the suit in Figure 172, this bolero has three-quarter-length flared pagoda sleeves, with splits that reveal the full blouse sleeve beneath. Both bodice and sleeves are adorned with black braid and ball fringe. The dropped-shoulder seam is embellished with tassels inspired by military epaulettes. Some jackets had horizontal braid on the front, in imitation of those of state militia regiments.

Full skirts were pleated onto a pointed waistband decorated with black braid. Sometimes these pointed waistbands were separate belts that fastened in back. Black braid and ball fringe encircle the hemline to coordinate with the jacket.

Blouses of soft linen, muslin, or silk followed the fashion of the dropped-shoulder line and sleeves that flared out with extra fullness at the lower arm. The high collar, cuffs, and blouse front were always tucked or decorated with rows of lace.

The fad for plaid stockings, inspired by those of Scotland, continued. These have the plaid knitted straight rather than on the diagonal. In fact, the fascination with tartans produced plaid wool bolero suits for girls, much like that on the boy in Figure 218, page 142.

Figure 185 Young boys went to war too. A boy no more than twelve could serve as a powder monkey, to assist navy men in loading guns aboard fighting vessels. When the Civil War started, Congress appropriated funds to buy up any civilian ship that could be converted to a warship, from merchant steamers to tugs to riverboats. The Confederates used armored rams and gunboats early in the war, thereby revolutionizing naval warfare.

Powder monkeys were outfitted in middies and flared trousers patterned after sailor uniforms. Although photographs show variety in detail, the small uniforms were basically like this one. A yoke with a dropped-shoulder line goes across the chest, with an interesting small panel or yoke at the neck. This boy wears his black kerchief tied in back, but they were as often tied in front.

One boy's middy neck yoke had brightly colored crewel-embroidered designs of a heart and flowers. One can just imagine a mother's or grandmother's loving work on the small uniform, and the feelings she must have experienced at seeing one so young go off to war. His trousers, called slops, have a front fly and button-down pockets. They button onto the middy. His sailor tam is black, like his kerchief.

Very small boys were sometimes dressed in sailor suits like this, in imitation of adult sailors and powder monkeys.

Figure 186 Fabrics with printed borders were frequently employed in dressmaking, as in this arresting challis frock. The background is of polka dots, with dark bands of medallions of alternating size forming a border.

The liking for wide necks and drop shoulders persisted to the end of the decade. Here, a band from the border is darted to curve around the shoulders. Though short, the sleeves have the fashionable flare achieved by shoulder pleats. They are edged with the border. Another strip of the dark band forms a waistband.

Skirts were ordinarily pleated at the waist, rather than gathered. This one has small pleats. The older a girl became, the longer her skirts were, until, as an adult, they reached the floor.

Shawls and stoles were favored when wraps were needed. Wide-brimmed hats and sunbonnets were added for going to church or for an afternoon outing. In cold weather, a chemise blouse like that in Figure 184 might be worn underneath these low-necked, short-sleeved dresses, forming what we call a jumper today.

Toward the end of the decade, girls' hair was pulled back at the sides and front, but it fell long in back. Ribbon streamers hung down in back in imitation of hat ribbon streamers.

This girl's calf-length skirts reveal her horizontally striped stockings and lace-up black boots.

Figure 187 Young boys went to war as drummers for the infantry of both Union and Confederate forces. There are a number of paintings that show them to have been between ten to fifteen years old. Their uniforms were usually like those of the men in their regiment. During the early war years, they often wore state militia uniforms, like that in Figure 159, page 109. Toward the end of the conflict, they were depicted in regulation Union and Confederate uniforms and overcoats. Several period paintings show drummer boys wearing the same exotic Zouave uniforms worn by both northern and southern troops, as illustrated here.

Bright colored shirts with dropped shoulders and full gathered sleeves usually were either red, dark blue, or powder blue. Trousers were either red, dark blue, light blue, or blue and white striped. They were tucked inside tan canvas gaiters that buttoned up the sides. Black shoes were worn under the gaiters.

A white strap always held the brightly painted drum. This Zouave uniform cap is a kind of red stocking cap with a flat hard crown and a cord with a tassel hanging from its center.

One folk painting of Sherman's troops marching through Georgia shows two Union drummer boys in dark blue shirts, red trousers, tan gaiters, and red caps like this one. Their drums are tan with painted eagles, red metal strips, and black tension cords.

—6—

SAILOR SUITS &

BUSTLES

1870-1890

Train travel was considered so safe and efficient that children could travel without adults, as many did during the 1870s and 1880s. After the Civil War, travel increased dramatically, and the notion of taking one's ease in casual, sporty clothes brought in sports suits and shirtwaist blouses. When the fad for exercise and sports grew nationwide, many specialized forms were developed. As travel increased, so did the reasons for travel, fostering the idea of watering places or wintering places. Vacation resorts sprang up and the tourism industry was begun. Sailor suits, bathing attire, and the tennis shoe were seen at seaside and lakeside resorts before the end of the century. Railroad companies, steamboat and shipping companies, and sports vehicle manufacturers encouraged the resorts, while the vacation spots, in turn, encouraged travel.

The mushrooming interest in sports brought in many new ideas in sports shoes. The United States was already becoming a world leader in shoe manufacture. With the use of rubber and innovation of design, American shoes would soon outsell all others including French-made ones, in Europe.

Although it never became fashion, the baseball suit did become a classic sports symbol for little boys. In 1869, the first professional sports team, the Cincinnati Red Stockings, had been formed. During the early 1870s, their uniforms were designed in a style not too different from those of today. Immediately, boys of all ages were seen in baseball suits, particularly in magazine illustrations and advertisements. These would, in time, become identified with the American boy.

The mail-order business that began in 1872 would soon have an impact on children's clothing. By the 1890s, mail-order catalogs were offering the latest clothing fashions of the previous season. Descriptions of garments often stated,

"Made on the lines of the very latest fashion of last winter" or "was absolutely the newest thing last summer." Children in all parts of the nation could wear the same styles as those in any other region. No child in America lived in a place so remote that his parents couldn't order, and eventually receive, clothing made on the lines of the latest fashions of no more than a year or two ago.

There was a depression from 1873 to 1879, and violence during the railroad strikes of 1877. There was great suffering and hardship in the South during the reconstruction years by both whites and blacks. The flow of immigrants into America reached flood-tide proportions by the 1880s, with many staying in the East and others pouring into the West to homestead. By the end of the 1880s, there were hundreds of towns with European, including many Scandinavian, names, and at least a hundred newspapers in the United States were printed in languages other than English.

Even throughout all these hard times, writers and artists were presenting romanticized pictures of American children; young ones of all races and nationalities were depicted as innocent and delicate, in unreal settings. Toward the end of the century, the realists—"muckrakers," as many were called—began to depict mill children, slum children, and ethnic groups in terms showing the harsher childhoods of some children. Congress provided some funds to help start schools for black children, and reforms were begun in the slums, but they would be slow in improving the lot of many of America's young girls and boys.

It was still acceptable fashion, according to *Peterson's Magazine* for ladies in 1871, to use the good parts of old dresses to make a new basque bodice or jacket. The editors suggested that the bodice be worn over a dress or skirt and blouse.

The use of starch returned to children's fashion during the 1880s. Shirts, pinafores, aprons, sunbonnets, cotton dresses, and even coats were starched quite stiffly. When garments were folded and put away in a drawer, the resulting fold creases were like those seen in the seventeenth century, and were considered evidence of a clean, fresh garment. Starch was so cheap that all classes of children could have starched clothes. Even a poor child could look fashionably clean and crisp.

During the late nineeenth century, illustrations for children's clothing always stated the age for which the garments were intended. Dressing "according to one's age" was considered proper. A girl's skirt length was determined by her age, whereas a boy's trouser length and type told his. The older a boy became, the more closely his clothing followed adult male fashions.

The sudden and long-lasting fashion for sailor suits and their development parallels the history of U. S. Navy uniforms. Sailor suits had been seen occasionally at midcentury. But in the 1880s they became fashionable and swept the country. In 1881 the government began building a "new navy." Worn for many, many years by enlisted men, the pea coat finally became official regulation wear. Petty officers' double-breasted sack coats, or "reefers," were made regulation, too.

The development to have the most profound effect on fashion, however, was the publication of official uniform illustrations. Enlisted men's uniforms had not previously even been included in regulation illustrations. Now, enlisted men's uniforms were not only included but were illustrated in color, along with those of officers. People now knew just how the official uniforms were supposed to look, and fashion designers and clothing manufacturers seized upon the information with enthusiasm.

As if this excitement over uniforms wasn't enough inspiration, Congress commissioned four new ships of startling design, sailing ships with steam engines and smokestacks. The sails were maintained as auxiliary power in case the steam engines were to fail. Not only were boys' and girls' sailor suits directly influenced by navy regulations, but so were their toys. It became quite common for fashion illustrations to show little boys playing with boats, whether they were wearing sailor suits or not.

The bustle on girls' dresses began as merely large bows, then became more complex, with an overskirt pulled up into a swag and poufed out at the back. It started high, then gradually moved down during the 1870s. Between 1880 and 1882 it reached its lowest point, at the hips, and even at times was down on the thighs. After 1882 it began to move upward again, then grew to enormous proportions. Between 1885 and 1888, skirts extended so far out in back and bodies became so curved in front that girls looked like birds when viewed from the side. Their hats, with front brims and feather decorations, added to the effect. Bustles disappeared after this final extreme version, leaving by 1890 only pleated fullness in the skirt back.

Figure 188 Boys' and men's fashions were usually inspired by British fashion, especially in sporting clothes. This sports suit was the latest thing in the 1870s, with its four-button jacket and slender trousers. Only the top button was fastened by boys of fashion. Shawl collars were the most popular, but occasionally notched collars were seen also. Suits were checked, tweeds, or solid colors, stitched around the edges or bound with braid.

From 1870 to 1880

Canvas gaiters with metal clips often covered trousers at the lower leg for hiking or biking. Sometimes they fastened down the center front. The newly invented bicycles were huge and had no brake or chain, so only the tallest boys could ride them. The bicycle would continue to influence fashion design for both boys and girls until well into the twentieth century.

Vests were often of a different fabric than suits and might be plain or fancy. They always had a shawl collar and were straight across the bottom.

Boys' hats were inspired by the rolled brim panamas or the new derby with a rolled brim. Sometimes the crown was pushed in, forming a bowl-like depression on top, so the hat was referred to as a bowler.

(188)

(189)

(190)

(191)

(192)

128 /

Figure 189 Skirts were beginning to be drawn up into swags and poufs, as fashion designers experimented with their immense fullness. At first the fullness was merely drawn up, as demonstrated by this complicated outfit.

An overdress of taffeta has a wide low neck and brief flared sleeves curving up in a swag shape to repeat the skirt design. A dark binding edges the neckline, sleeves, and skirt hem. The flared skirt is drawn up at each side seam and twice in front and back, forming six shirred swags. The gathering lines are covered by heavy lace or braid continuing up at an angle over the bodice to the shoulders. An underskirt of coordinating darker fabric has a row of light-colored plain braid at the hem edge and another row of dark scalloped braid a little farther up.

Under the dress is a soft, lacy blouse with sleeves that flare out at the lower arm like that in Figure 184. In summer, or for formal appearances, the overdress was sometimes worn by itself.

Rust and blue were favorite colors for these frocks, with green, plum, and dusty rose also liked.

Lace-up boots with fancy tasseled ties were the vogue, often showing a red band around the pointed boot tops. It was stylish sometimes to wrap the long fancy strings several times around the boot before tying them.

Girls' hair was pulled up at the sides and front, then piled up in curls and braids decorated with ribbons or flowers. The back usually hung down in curls, as shown.

Figure 190 Exotic dress suits of wool or velvet followed lines similar to those of sports suits. This plum-colored jacket has a shawl collar like that in Figure 188. Fancy corded frog loop closures go across the double-breasted front to join the covered buttons. This one is belted, but jackets were worn straight as often as not.

Trousers of dress suits were held by canvas gaiters, as were those of sport suits. These are dark canvas with buttons at the sides. Scottish or Glengarry caps were very popular for boys and girls, too. This one is of the same fabric as the suit.

Wool with a quilted satin collar, cuffs, belt, and bindings, as shown here, was a favorite combination. Wool with velvet trim and velvet with satin trim were also favored. Wool suits with curly fur trim were considered quite handsome. White, flowered, or striped waists such as that in Figure 192 were worn underneath these jackets, as were collarless shirts like that shown in Figure 178.

Striped or plaid stockings were worn under short boots and knee breeches with these suits by younger boys, as illustrated in Figure 209.

A fashion print from *Harper's Bazaar* in 1874 pictures a boy in a similar suit, with epaulettes on the shoulders and wearing a plumed bicorne hat. Adding to his Napoleonic appearance, he wears a small sword and girdle attached to his belt!

Figure 191 Although tight bodices with corsets underneath and draped skirts were high fashion, girls still were seen in the full-bodied dresses of earlier decades. Necklines down off the shoulders and puff sleeves might be seen anywhere for casual attire. This dress was often pictured for play in the city at this time, as well as for wear in rural areas and for factory work. Such dresses appeared in southern areas, on the prairie, or along river fronts—in fact, just about anywhere in the nation, throughout the nineteenth century. Serviceable fabrics such as striped cotton, plain muslin, and printed calicos were used.

The sunbonnet of Figure 180 and the shawl from Figure 137 were seen with this dress, as were the wide-brimmed sailors in Figures 172 and 177. The dropped shoulder lines of the apron in Figure 183 make it particularly well suited to this frock.

Black children in the South were depicted in such dresses, with cloth sunbonnets or the apron and head scarf of Figure 183.

Figure 192 Boys' waists, also called blouse waists, were cotton or linen and made with a variety of collar styles. Their main characteristic was the fitted waistband worn on the outside of the trousers. They always had long, full sleeves gathered at both shoulder and cuff. Usually the cuff folded back. The new fly front was designed into tailored waists, whereas tucks and lace ruffles were a feature of dressy ones. Many had plain button fronts, as illustrated here.

One example (in the Brooklyn Museum) with a collar and fly front is made of a tiny red and white stripe, making it appear pink at a distance. The stand-up collar shown here was frequently seen, as was the lace neck ruffle on dressy waists. Sometimes a bow tie was added. Waists like this were worn for all occasions.

Trousers usually seen with waists were pleated at the waist, full at the hips, then tapered toward the ankles, where they ended in a cuff. They had the new fly front. Knee breeches and jackets, like those of Figures 216 and 217, were also suitable attire with blouse waists.

This young gentleman sports a broad-brimmed sailor hat of natural straw with a navy band and pointed streamers.

Figure 193 Two fresh ideas destined to influence girls' fashions during the coming years were the open collar and sports clothes. One can easily see an early development in the American shirtwaist blouse in this illustration. Exercise and sports dresses were already being seen in girls' schools in England and Germany at this time and were beginning to be accepted in America as physical education became integral to the educational process.

This skirt and blouse are worn over full bloomers. The blouse has radiating rows of tucks on the bodice and full sleeves gathered onto a drop shoulder line.

It is interesting to note that although the idea of special clothes for sports

(193)

(194)

(195)

(196)

(197)

131 /

had arrived, the idea of functional garments especially designed for freedom of movement had not. The drop shoulder line and fitted bodice did not permit ease of movement, especially with the arms raised, but this was a beginning. A fancy sash around the waist is embellished with the same fancy braid as that used on the cuffs, skirt, and bloomers.

This girl's shoes are noteworthy for their elastic insets at the sides. Her hair is contained in a decorative net and ribbon.

Figure 194 Walking suits or dresses for small boys were often Scottish-inspired, like this one of black and white plaid mohair, cut on the bias. The collar, pointed cuffs, and hemline are trimmed with black silk braid; jet buttons are used on the double-breasted front and sleeve cuffs. A sash tied around the waist widens at the ends, where it is ornamented with black and white silk fringe.

Knee breeches of matching fabric were generally worn under these dresses.

Curled-brim sailor hats of straw usually had bands and ribbon ties of navy blue or black. It was fashionable to cut the ribbon with points on the ends. Scottish caps like those in Figures 174 and 190 were often seen with these tartan dresses, as was the tam-o'-shanter of Figure 160.

A variety of little boots of wool, canvas, or leather might be selected to wear with either plain, striped, or plaid stockings.

Figure 195 Professional sports began in America in 1869, when the Cincinnati Red Stockings were formed. At first, the players wore smocks and loose pantaloons, but before long they were outfitted in baseball suits not too different from twentieth-century ones, and in no time after that young boys were outfitted in their own small-sized copies of them.

Striped shirts were the most commonly liked by early teams, but solid colors were worn too. Early shirts had small rounded collars.

Knee breeches or knickers for playing baseball were very important historically, because they were the first trousers to have loops for the belt. Sometimes they had only one loop in the center front and one in back but at other times had just one at each side. Belts were always black or brown. There was usually a stripe down the outseam to coordinate with the shirt colors.

Baseball shoes had elastic insets at each side of their canvas or buckskin tops. They were leather at the lower part. Spikes were not used on the soles until the end of the century. Early baseball players used neither mitts nor field gloves, but by the 1890s both were advertised in mail-order catalogs. The rather stiff caps were of the same fabric as the shirts.

Figure 196 By the late 1860s girls' bathing suits were pictured in ladies' fashion magazines. Articles about bathing (swimming) always cautioned parents to supervise their daughters properly and only to visit "respectable watering places."

Suits were always of wool flannel, which seems terribly hot to today's swimmers, but it should be remembered that early swimming places were natural springs, lakes, and oceans, which were quite cold. Full trousers were worn straight, as illustrated here, or gathered in like knickers. Swim dresses were either gray, navy blue, or red with braid trim.

Capes of flannel were wrapped around one's body, worn to the water's edge, then removed just before stepping into the water.

Gray or blue cotton duck slippers with cord soles were worn into the water, especially when the bottom was of pebbles. This little girl's low-cut slippers have two ties across the instep. Nets such as that in Figure 193, cloth hoods, or hair ribbons held the hair back during swimming.

Figure 197 Summer dresses were of poplin, winter ones of flannel. Here, a low-necked dress is worn over a guimpe or blouse of soft white muslin. Black velvet was commonly used as trim on children's clothes at this time, as demonstrated in this frock, gray with large magenta dots or "spots." Chevron-shaped bands of black velvet line the gray panels at each side of the bodice and skirt. The hemline and cuffs also are of black velvet, while the sash is magenta velvet to match the dots. A bustle bow at the back matches the black chevron panels. Skirt fullness has moved toward the back, leaving the front rather flat and fitted. It is easy to see the beginning of the bustle here.

The young lady models gray wool boots with black patent feet. Her hair ribbon is tied in back, after going across her head like a headband. Bunches of corkscrew curls are held close to her neck.

The jump rope is especially worth attention. Ladies' magazines at this time offered directions for crocheting or knotting fancy jump ropes with elaborate handles. They had tassels, pom-poms, and even little bells attached to the wool-covered handles. Bright colored woolen yarns were recommended.

Figure 198 After the mail-order business was founded in 1872, clothes could be mailed 🖋 people out west, on farms, and in remote mountain areas. Children everywhere could wear inexpensive factory-made garments and shoes. This was especially important for boys.

Young boys became heroes of popular novels and short stories by writers like Horatio Alger, Jr. and Mark Twain. Typical of those romanticized by such literature is this young boy. There is nothing extraordinary about his clothes, for he represents the average small town, big city, western, eastern, southern white, and southern black child. In other words, these clothes were seen in all parts of America on all classes of boys. Sometimes the jacket in Figure 188 was worn over this vest and scarf, and sometimes a red bandanna replaced the wool scarf. The hat might be a battered straw, or the billed cap described in Figure 135, or a baseball cap.

(198)

(199)

(200)

(201)

(202)

(203)

(204)

At this time, there was a small button attached to the scarf, to hold it wrapped around the neck. This meant that the scarf did not have to be tied and yet would still remain in place as a child ran and played.

Figure 199 Skirt fullness during the early 1870s was pulled around toward the back, where it was bunched up into a bustle. Guimpes or blouses of soft muslin were worn underneath dresses.

New dress styles always brought in new aprons to fit over them. This interesting style was worn over bustles by both adults and children. It has straps that loop around the neck, although apron bibs were still often pinned to the bodice front. The unique feature is the manner in which the apron widens at the hips, where long ties are fastened. They fasten around both the overskirt and bustle.

At first sight this garment might appear to be merely an adult-sized apron on a small child, but such large aprons appear both in engravings and fashion magazines. Sometimes there were two sets of ties, with one attached at the waistline as well as those at the hips. This practical covering gave protection to the sides of the dress during work or play, while being fitted in front.

Brown holland with scarlet binding, gray with blue trim, and white with red were the favorite color combinations.

Figure 200 "These aprons are in great favor with the little ones, as they will carry a lap-full, without using the dress, as children usually do." The ladies' fashion magazine that printed directions for making this apron went on to say, "It should be made of colored linen, and bound with colored braid around its scalloped edges."

The 1870s were years of creativity (and complexity) in apron design. This one seems very modern, with its toy pocket in the skirt. A buttoned tab in the center covers two small pleats that give fullness to the pocket and prevent its sagging when weighted with its contents. The back of the bib bodice is cut the same as the front and joins the waistband. It fastens in the center back with pearl buttons.

Sunbonnets were worn with the play apron out of doors, as were high-button shoes and dark dresses.

Figure 201 Little boys' aprons appeared in portraits during the 1870s, as well as in pattern sections of ladies' magazines. These aprons can probably best be described as smocks, because of their design. In fact, boys' aprons at this time were almost copies of girls' smocks of the 1840s, as shown in Figure 139, page 96. They had a high neck, sometimes with a standing collar or binding, and long or three-quarter-length sleeves. They fastened in back either with ties or buttons.

Intended to keep "good" clothes clean, these smocks (or aprons) were put on over plaid walking dresses like that in Figure 194, or dresses like that in Figure 206. Little bolero tartan suits like that of Figure 218 (worn with the jacket, or just the blouse and kilt) were protected under the smocks too.

Figure 202 Fine linen, cambric, or muslin was recommended as the appropriate fabric to make aprons for very little girls. This one, made from directions in a women's fashion magazine, has the front and back cut from the same pattern. The back opens to the waist. Ruffles are used for sleeves. Fancy triangular pockets are suggested. "Work tiny button-hole stitched scallops around the edges," advised the author, "or trim with worked edging." The apron is "plain enough for play," commented the magazine, adding, "but extra embroidery can be worked on the front for a dressy pinafore."

This little girl has a sunbonnet of the same fabric, trimmed with lace. The back is gathered in to form a ruffle at the neck to prevent sunburn. She wears the universally popular boots.

Aprons almost identical with this one sometimes had plain armholes, without ruffles. They were edged with the same trim as the neckline and hem.

The full drawstring apron of Figure 180 was still worn at this time, too, being much more everyday wear.

Figure 203 Although older girls, up to ten or eleven years of age, wore aprons too, theirs often were without bibs, and the apron skirts had no backs. Ladies' fashion publications referred to aprons as "being the fashion," meaning, of course, that they were considered more than just a protective garment for work or play. Of "Swiss muslin," this one has suspenders or braces instead of a bib. Ruffles of graduated width go over the shoulders and halfway down the braces. Gores are used for the skirt, fitted since it has no gathers, in keeping with the latest trend for narrow dress fronts. A ruffle surrounds the edges of the curved skirt, with cord covering the seam between it and the skirt.

Pastel satin ribbons and lace were applied to these aprons in a variety of ways, often extravagantly. Here the ribbons go over the braces and continue down to outline the ruffles. At the apron's lower hemline, five rows of inset ribbon and buttons decorate the skirt, and a bow is tied at the waist.

Braid, lace, or embroidery were sometimes combined with ruffles and ribbons. Ruchings, buckles, buttons, rosettes, tucks, bows, and scallops were employed in a variety of ways, making the apron as elaborate as the dress underneath. Some had only a waistband without straps or bib of any kind. For older girls, the waistband buttoned or was buckled in back or at one side, but was rarely tied.

Pockets might be heart shaped, round, square, or triangular, and set at any angle. Probably any design that one could create today would have a counterpart that was tried during the 1870s for these aprons. Under the apron, the young girl has on a print piqué dress.

Figure 204 Free government lands were available in quantity, and newspaper advertisements beckoned to thousands of immigrants. Advertisements appeared in the East and South and in foreign countries, such as Sweden, Norway, and Germany. America was made to seem like the Garden of Eden, and people came in droves.

On ships, riverboats, trains, and wagon trains were many children dressed in national costumes, such as those of Figures 140 and 135, page 96. This little girl also is typical of many who accompanied their immigrant parents on the long journey. Her dark dress is plain and worn with an old-fashioned kerchief tucked inside her apron. Some of the girls in old prints in the Library of Congress wear fringed shawls with embroidered designs in the same manner. Occasionally, a child pictured in the prints wears wooden shoes, while some are shown barefoot, apparently saving their shoes from wear. European peasant and regional clothes were a common sight in railroads, shipyards, and on river wharves, especially, but they might be seen anywhere in the United States, in cities or rural areas.

Figure 205 Capes and coats were as varied as aprons during the 1870s. It was not unusual for a garment to have three or even four different kinds of trimmings. Wraps were often combinations of capes, coats, stoles, or jackets of all shapes and lengths. This cape-coat of wool is edged with braid and white fur. The corners of both the cape and coat are rounded. Such coats were often of velvet or mohair.

This girl holds a matching fur muff and wears tall boots with fur around the tops. Her small hat sits forward on her head over a hair style similar to those of Figures 210 and 212. It has a curled narrow brim and ribbon streamers in back.

Although this wrap is thigh length, it was also worn in a longer length, like that in Figure 207, covering the dress underneath. Coats had to flare out in back out of necessity, in order to fit over the dress bustles. The jacket of Figure 210 illustrates the back construction. Bows or tassels were often added at the waistline, occasionally tassels were attached at the corners of the back flaps on short styles. One old fashion print shows a tassel attached at the back of each sleeve.

Figure 206 "A simple blouse-apron for either boy or girl of two to four years" was the way a fashion magazine in the late 1870s described this little frock (at the top of the stairs). Aprons for young children would remain the norm, with only a few changes throughout the nineteenth century and well into the next. Modish modifications would consist mainly of sleeve styles and skirt lengths.

Calico, madras gingham, white nainsook, muslin, and gray linen were recommended for these practical garments. The decoration applied to them was Hamburg insertion, hand-crocheted lace, or self-fabric bias bands. On plain ones, tucks might constitute the only decoration.

Belts were attached at the side seams, the center front, and back, because belt loops were not yet used.

(206)

(208)

(211)

(205)

(207)

(209)

(210)

(212)

High-button boots of black or bright colors were the fashion, as were striped, plaid, or dark stockings, either long or short.

Figure 207 This style of cloak was seen on children from early infancy to age twelve. It was cut into eight sections, with each one ending in a scallop. The hemline of the skirt sometimes repeated these scallops. There is a stand-up collar at the neck and buttons down the front of the coat, called a sack. Only a bow is used at the neck of the outer cape.

Braid outlines each cape section, the sleeve hems, and the skirt hemline. Fabrics were French merino or flannel. Favorite colors were blue, white, pearl (described in Figure 176), and the commonly seen black and white plaid. Narrow velvet ribbon was often used for trim, as well as braid. One fashion magazine recommended that these cloaks be made of "thinly crossed black and white plaid flannel with blue velvet ribbon trim."

One outstanding element of this little girl's costume is her crocheted gaiters, scalloped top and bottom, with a drawstring through the top and a strap under the foot. The crocheted drawstrings end in small tassels.

Her small, flat, curled-brim hat is worn forward like those of older girls. Her muff is fur. Muffs usually had a cord or ribbon at each side so they could be hung around the neck, or just one small loop for hanging from a wrist. She wears gloves in addition to the muff.

Figure 208 Princess dresses had returned to fashion at midcentury, reaching a peak by the early 1880s. The idea of a dress that followed the human form, without a waistline seam, and then flared out into full skirts had originated a long time before, in medieval Europe.

A kilted skirt, or pleated flounce, is added around the hem of this young girl's princess dress that closes down the center front with small buttons. Dresses now flared out, with extra fullness at the back forming a bustle, as in Figure 211.

Over the dress is added a cutaway coat or bodice, also without a waistline seam. It fastens in front with three buttons and has squared corners on the coattails. Velvet or wool was used for these tailcoats, with piqué for warm weather.

Boots are worn, as is the small forward-tilted hat that women liked. It is decorated with a bird made of feathers.

Figure 209 At the end of the 1870s and for a short time at the beginning of the 1880s, there was a fad for asymmetric designs. Braid usually pointed up the asymmetry, as illustrated here. This young boy models a double-breasted blouse-jacket, cut so that its front edge is on the diagonal from the left shoulder to the right hip. Braid not only accents the diagonal front but also the stand-up collar, cuffs, belt, and the outseam and hem of the trousers. Gray or navy blue flannel was recommended for these suits.

Lace-up boots often had decorative tassels hanging from their pointed tops. Horizontally striped stockings were often worn with these exotic suits, as were plaid ones. Although the wide-brimmed straw sailor hat is shown here, the caps of Figures 173 and 174 were often preferred.

Figure 210 The princess dress often had lace sewn over the seams down the side front. Yokes were often added at the shoulders of these dresses to break their long vertical lines, as were flounces and lace at their hemlines. Yokes were elaborately covered and edged with lace and ruffles, as were the sleeves and, in fact, the entire dresses. Most often single breasted, they were occasionally seen in double-breasted versions. Velvet and wool were favorite fabrics for winter, piqué and linen for summer.

In the back, the princess gores flared out, forming a bustle, which was usually decorated with a large ribbon bow. Here we see an interesting treatment, with the ribbon being sewn into the side-front seam and then pulled around to the back, where it is tied into the bustle bow. This back fullness would remain visible until about 1878, when dresses became quite fitted. They would remain fitted, almost tight, during the early 1880s.

The yoke and sleeves were sometimes omitted. The little shoulder ruffle or epaulette was sufficient sleeve for summer or party frocks. When a sleeveless, yokeless princess dress was put on over a blouse in cool weather, the effect was the same as this long-sleeved, high-necked dress.

Striped or solid color stockings were worn with black or pastel-colored boots in cool weather, or short socks when it was warm.

Figure 211 A basque bodice worn over a dress was the mode for girls from four to twelve years of age. It was essentially a suit jacket fastening in front with buttons, and a square yoke at the shoulders. It had a standing collar and flared sleeves.

In keeping with the trend for elaborate trim, it had a plain, wide black braid, a narrow curved braid, and a pleated ruffle. The ruffle is shown only at the yoke here, but it was often used on the sleeves and around the jacket hem. Fringe was also a stylish trim.

A simple one-skirt dress is worn underneath by this girl. A wide pleated flounce is topped with narrow braid in several rows. For cool weather, the dress underneath was much like that in Figure 210; in warm weather, it had small sleeves and a low neck for comfort. Dresses with draped overskirts, like that of Figure 212, were commonly worn under the basque bodice too.

The young lady's hair style is typical of the period: pulled up in front, high at the crown, and long and curly in back. Both boots and bright-colored slippers were proper accessories with these ensembles.

Figure 212 Formal or dressy frocks were of organdy, sheer muslin, linen, taffeta, or faille, often in pastel colors. Yellow, pale green, pink, or baby blue combined with white made "dainty" the best description for these frothy creations. This young lady's white bodice has rounded points both front and back, with a large pastel bow on the back one. A sheer lace neck ruffle frames her face, and several ruffles edge the very fitted three-quarter-length sleeves.

A sheer overskirt is drawn up at the side seams to form drapes and then poufed out into a bustle in back. The pastel taffeta or faille underskirt ends with a sheer flounce of several ruffles. Matching pastel flowers and ribbons decorate the bosom, sleeves, and skirt. These dresses were sometimes low necked and with briefer sleeves.

Black or pastel-colored slippers were worn by older girls, but boots were still preferred for the little ones. The latest hair styles with bangs on the forehead would remain popular until the end of the century.

Figure 213 Buttonhole stitching was painstakingly worked around the scallops of this skirt, overskirt, neckline, and sleeves. As if enough hours hadn't already been spent on this little dress, a braid was also applied in several rows of straight and looped designs. Both skirt and pointed overskirt are gored, so that they flare slightly in front but have extra fullness in back. Around the overskirt waist are tabs adorned with the same braid.

Both the low-necked bodice and small sleeves feature still more of the braid. A large ribbon bow forms a bustle at the back, and matching small bows are used on each shoulder.

White piqué was recommended for these elaborately worked dresses for summer use, with pearl-colored flannel preferred the rest of the year. Braid and embroidery were all-white for very young girls, with blue, red, and black for older girls. A white guimpe or blouse was sometimes worn underneath.

Little caps, often referred to as hoods, were as extravagantly embroidered as the dresses at this time. This one has a scalloped double ruffle around the face and a cape ruffle around the neck for protection from the sun. Embroidered "petals" are sewn on top and down the back of the head. These petals and all the ruffles are buttonhole stitched at the edges, like the dress.

In summer, black or colored slippers might be worn; in winter, the ever-popular boots were still favored.

Figure 214 Called a "hood and wrapper," very young children's cloaks were usually of white piqué or white or pearl flannel. This wrapper has buttonhole-stitched scalloped edges all the way around, with two rows of embroidery paralleling the scallops. Made in a half circle, capes were fitted at the shoulders and neck and full at the hem.

(215)

(216)

(214)

(218)

(213)

(217)

The attached hood was gathered onto the neckline, giving fullness to the back. It, too, is edged with buttonhole-stitched scallops and embroidery. Large satin ribbons at the neck are the cloak's only fasteners. A satin bow adorns the top of the hood, with streamers falling down in back. Dresses were like those in Figures 181 and 182.

Although commonly white or cream, these capes were occasionally tan or gray with scarlet or blue embroidery. The younger the child, the more likely the cape was to be white.

Baby carriages had become extremely popular by this time, when advertisements for English carriages were appearing in newspapers and magazines everywhere. The little girl of Figure 213 pushes a doll carriage patterned after the new full-sized baby carriages.

Figure 215 By the end of the 1870s, train travel was so safe and efficient that children could travel alone. Train travel helped to develop the idea of sports clothes. This nattily dressed young boy wears an overcoat with cape in a pale gray wool, top stitched around the edges. His gray suit with knee breeches is like that in Figure 217. Straight and slightly tapered in toward the knees, the breeches fasten with several buttons at the side.

High-button boots and dark stockings were proper attire with these stylish clothes. This cap is leather banded and visored, with a soft, gathered top. Little visored caps were also made of straw at this time. The derby was also proper dress wear for young boys, as shown in Figure 216, as was the wide-brimmed straw sailor.

When traveling, young boys of well-to-do parents carried binoculars for sightseeing from a train, stage coach, or riverboat. When not in use, the binoculars or field glasses were carried in a shoulder pouch, as in Figure 217.

Fashionable lads are known to have carried small walking canes, such as that leaning against the wall to the left of the infant. One railroad poster in the Library of Congress depicts a small traveler about six years of age, quite elegantly dressed, holding his ivory-headed cane. These sticks were not toys but actual child-sized canes. Other expensive ones had heads of silver, carved wood, and even gold. Boys carried black umbrellas, also.

Figure 216 Some boys' jackets were an interesting cross between the smock or blouse and the coat. This suit has a rather full jacket that blouses out when belted. Tabs are sewn down the front in an early form of the beloved Norfolk suit shown in Figure 242. The white collar belongs to the waist underneath. A large tie makes a soft bow at the neck. These ties or cravats were usually black but might also be red or even patterned silk.

Breeches were tapered ever so slightly toward the knees and cut straight. No bands or gathers were used, but buttons at the outseam fastened openings.

Tweeds, checks, plain flannel, and velvet were the favored fabrics, in gray, black, brown, or blue.

Striped stockings were very stylish, as were boots of various materials and heights. The new derby hat was the mode for gentlemen, so, naturally, young boys were seen sporting them too. Brown was a favorite color.

A small leather or canvas pouch was sometimes attached to the belt, instead of to a shoulder strap as in Figures 215 and 217. It was usually worn in the center front and held articles used during travel or hiking.

Figure 217 Ever since the Prince of Wales had visited the United States in 1860, interest in English sports clothes had grown. New jackets had four buttons and rounded coat corners. Although men's and older boys' jackets had shawl collars, those for younger boys had small round collars or none at all. The waist worn underneath had a large collar, always pulled out over the jacket, as illustrated here. Black cravats were tied into large bows under the collars.

While men and older boys fastened only the top button of their jackets, judging from paintings and photographs of the decade, little boys usually had all four buttons fastened. Tweeds, checks, plaids, and solids were the accepted fabrics, with velvet sometimes used for fancy interpretations.

Boots and dark stockings were commonly seen with these sports suits, as also were the canvas gaiters in Figures 188 and 190. Leather-billed caps were tremendously popular with boys of all ages all over the nation.

Of special interest is the binoculars shoulder pouch for sightseeing during travel. After the invention of the Pullman car, shoulder pouches were used for carrying toiletries and other overnight travel essentials, as well as the field glasses.

Little boys also traveled at home, on the new tricycle, just one of many novel wheeled toys now developed for children.

Figure 218 Kilt suits were one of the most important fashions for little boys from two to six years of age. Jackets varied in cut from the rounded bolero or Zouave style shown here to the tailcoat in Figure 176. The braid-trimmed blouse jacket of Figure 209, made in velvet, was seen with kilts also.

The kilt, pleated onto an underwaist with a vest and/or blouse over it, usually had a minature sporran in front. Trim was almost always of black velvet ribbon. Favorite fabrics were black and white plaids, brilliant combinations of lavender and green, or red and blue designs. Authentic tartans were seen too, with matching knee breeches or knickers worn underneath.

Of special interest are the accessories. An unusual tam-o'-shanter has ties under the chin and a tassel and cord attached to a button on top. The stockings are Scottish diagonal plaid or argyle, and the footwear consists of little dress slippers with ribbon rosettes.

Figure 219 Cloaks and mantles became quite complex in design in the 1880s, evolving into a combination of the coat, cape, and stole all rolled into one garment. Some looked like coats in front and capes in back, whereas others seemed to be capes that had been folded up under the arms. Many, such as this one, had sleeves forming a cape in back and were pulled up in pleats or poufs decorated with rosettes, bows, or tassels. They were made in short, medium, and long lengths, some having hoods in addition to the fancy sleeves. This one comes to below the knees.

Plaids and checks of various sizes, camel's hair, velvet, brocade, patterned velvet, silk, and piqué were the familiar fabrics. Quilted satin, fur, fringe, lace, and ribbons were the favorite trims.

This girl's hat is the rolled-brim sailor worn at the back of the head. Her striped stockings are noteworthy with their red, tan, and brown stripes. She wears the slippers that will be worn more and more toward the end of the century.

Figure 220 Starch, invented by the Dutch and immensely popular in the seventeenth century, returned to fashion in the 1880s. Blouses, aprons, sunbonnets, and petticoats were heavily starched and ironed, with creases visible. Linen, muslin, and piqué could be starched rigid, so as almost to stand alone.

The young girl here models an apron or pinafore that appeared in two different versions in paintings and fashion periodicals at this time. Here, the crisp muslin apron is shorter than the dress skirt, and its neckline and armholes are edged with small lace ruffles ironed flat. Another version, considered dressier, was as long as the dark dress worn underneath. Although this usually had no lace, it was made of fine linen or white piqué and was worn with a black contoured belt. Metal buckles or fancy clips might be used for fasteners, as well as ribbon bows.

Sunbonnets or plain straw hats were favored for play, while beribboned hats and rolled-brim sailors were preferred for dressy occasions.

Plaid and checked stockings were worn with boots; long or short stockings of black, white, or stripes were being paired with slippers.

Figure 221 Girls from three to twelve were dressed in dainty nainsook or fine muslin frocks with lots of lace and ribbon. In summer and for parties, weddings, and other special occasions these dresses had low necks and tiny or no sleeves. In cool weather, they usually had high necks and long or three-quarter-length sleeves. Waists were dropped quite low. This little girl's dress has several tiny ruffles around the neck and across the little sleeves. The long bodice is gathered at the neckline and hips in the center only, both back and front, so that the body looks slim from front or back but thick in a side view.

Skirts had from one to five ruffles, according to one's preference. This one has four of scalloped and embroidered sheer fabric. Imported lace could be pur-

(220)

(222)

(224)

(226)

(219)

(221)

(223)

(225)

(227)

chased, or one could buttonhole-stitch and work her own, as many American needle-women did. The wide sash is silk and tied in a very large bow in back, forming a bustle. These dresses had the very new belt loops that had recently come into use to keep the sashes in place.

Bonnet brims curved up quite high above the face, and the crowns were covered with ribbons and flowers. Brims were often covered and lined with shirred silk, like this one. The new short white socks and strapped white slippers were considered very elegant. Black slippers were popular too, as were colored ones to match the sash.

Figure 222 The newest thing in sports suit trousers was knickers. These first ones were not as full as they would later become. Sometimes they were worn with wool socks with fancy, knit fold-down tops. Either lace-up short boots were worn or the elastic inset shoe in Figure 173.

Although suit jackets always had four buttons, only the top one was fastened by older boys. Shawl collars like that in Figure 188 were still the vogue, but the notched collar illustrated here was in fashion too. Vests were not seen as much as in the past, and a boy could now be well dressed without one. Checks and tweeds were favorite fabrics in fall, with striped cottons for summer.

Small, narrow-brimmed straw hats with flat crowns had buckles on their ribbon hatbands. Field glasses or binoculars were carried in a leather shoulder pouch for sightseeing while traveling. Hiking was a popular sport, as was bird watching. These shoulder pouches were also used for other necessities of travel and sports.

Figure 223 Little coats with shoulder capes were used as long coats for infants and then became calf- or knee-length as the child grew. This was possible because toddlers usually grow only in height in the second year and even in the third year, without becoming much broader in the shoulders. Advertisements constantly reminded buyers of the practicality of these coats, which were handed down from child to child, because they were for both boys and girls.

Usually of flannel, coats might be tailored in thin stripes, small checks, plaids, or solid colors. Ribbon, lace, or braid always embellished the edges, with braid being the most practical and popular because it was more suited to older toddlers. This coat has three rows of narrow braid around the collar, cuffs, and front. It and the buttons are black.

Figure 224 Girls' clothes made practical use of the novel belt loop before boys' clothes did. (Early baseball uniforms utilized them, but they were not a regular aspect of boys' clothing until after the turn of the century.) The dropped waistlines needed loops to keep the belts from slipping down.

This tailored coat shows the liking for front pleats and tabs on both boys' and girls' clothes that would endure into the 1930s. It is of plaid, cut on the bias so that the threads run diagonally. This coat can be updated by raising or lowering the belt according to fashion's latest dictates. The cape, collar, cuffs, and hem are top stitched.

Hat brims now curved up in front and back till they resembled a small child's bonnet in front. Crowns were decorated with ribbons, plumes, or flowers. Although boots remained in fashion, slippers were gaining in popularity.

Figure 225 The princess dress changed little during the decade except in its skirt; that flared out at first, but at mid-decade grew slimmer. It usually fastened down the front, as does the dress in Figure 211. Flat little sleeves such as those illustrated here, puff sleeves, and long fitted ones, like those in Figure 227, were equally fashionable. One fashion print shows the Juliette sleeve, puffed at the top and fitted like a long glove from there down. An 1883 *Harper's Bazaar* offered one like this with tabs around the skirt, such as those in Figure 226. Several rows of lace ruffles formed the underskirt.

This sash is sewn into the side-front princess seam like that in Figure 211, but sometimes they reached all the way around. A great many color combinations were possible. Colors were usually combined with white or cream, and boots and shoes were sometimes dyed to coordinate with them. The girl's hair style is proper to the period.

Figure 226 Both boys and girls were outfitted in this ensemble, the main differences being in the belt and hat. This little boy wears a tailored belt and a wide-brimmed sailor hat. Girls' jackets had fancy ribbon belts with bows or rosettes front and back, and their hats were bonnets decorated with plumes or ribbons.

Girls' dresses usually had lacy collars pulled out to lie flat over the jacket collar. They were either round, square, or sailor style.

Black velvet was often picked for these jackets, but navy or gray wool was seen also. The skirt was often cut into squared tabs as shown here, though they might also be pointed or rounded. Boots and either patterned or plain stockings were proper attire with the ensemble.

Figure 227 This little garment, referred to as a coat in some fashion prints and a dress in others, is cut on the princess line and bedecked with lace, insertion, and ribbon. Collars might be round, square, pointed, or sailor style, as shown here. They fastened down the front with pearl buttons and could be single or double breasted. There was great variety in the manner of applying ornamentation at the neck, seams, hem, and cuffs.

Proper for girls and very little boys, these coat-dresses were usually of white piqué or pearl flannel, but blue, black, and maroon velvet were liked too. The lace was always white or cream, no matter what color garment was used.

This child sports white socks with little button boots, but white or dark stockings were preferred for cold days.

Boys' dresses had traditionally been referred to as coats during colonial days, and fashion prints still used the traditional term at times. Actually, during the 1880s, the difference was small between dresses and coats.

Figure 228 Coats and princess dresses for youngsters of both sexes were cut along basically the same lines as shown here. Although girls did wear tailored ones and boys often wore lacy, beribboned ones, older boys of four to six years were often dressed in plainer versions.

Pleats at the back seams flared out into three large box pleats or several smaller ones. The beginning of the fullness was accented by tabs of varying sizes and shapes, fastened with all kinds of buttons, buckles, snaps, and clips. Girls' coats often had gathered fullness and tabs with large bows. The center back or side seams might be top stitched for older boys or decorated with braid and lace for very little children.

This young boy wears the classic wide-brimmed sailor straw hat. His little boots are of canvas and leather.

Figure 229 Even pinafores were influenced by the appeal of the princess line. Flat kilted or pleated ruffles go over the shoulders and down the side-front seams before curving around toward the back at the hem of this princess pinafore. They face inward toward the neckline and center front gore. The same trim edges the neckline, back and front, circles the armholes, and completes the front hemline. Large sashes were sewn into the side-front seams a little below the waist at the beginning of the decade. (Just before mid-decade, sashes reached their lowest point and then rose again.) Extra fullness was added to the center back gore from the neck down and caught in by the sash, giving the apron a bloused look in back.

Pink and white striped cambric, pink-checked gingham, and white nainsook were favorites for these aprons. A high-necked style of apron was commonly seen, too, resembling a sleeveless version of the dress in Figure 234.

This girl's shoes, called Roman sandals, are particularly interesting. This boot-high shoe featured a series of straps across an open front, and buttonholes in the straps closed around small round buttons on the other side. The Roman sandal would grow in popularity until the 1930s.

The old-style apron of Figures 139 (page 96) and 201 (page 134) was still a common sight, but in a much more utilitarian model.

Figure 230 Although boys' coats might be single breasted, they were most often double breasted at this time. Coat bodies usually curved in at the sides and were cut on princess lines in the back, like the one in Figure 228. As did those for

(229)

(231)

(233)

(228)

(230)

(232)

(234)

(235)

girls, little boys' coats had fullness at the hips in back and even a suggestion of a bustle. They were either top stitched or trimmed with braid at the edges. Buttons were metal, bone, or pearl. Fabrics were solid flannels or cottons, with navy blue, brown, gray, and "coachman's drab" being the most liked. Here, two small capes, sewn together but separate from the coat, are fastened with a hook and eye on this coat. They are worn under the collar.

Striped stockings had been fashionable for many years and remained so at this time, appearing frequently on boys in ladies' fashion magazines. Checked and plaid ones were popular too. The straw sailor hat had become a classic for boys, as had button boots.

Figure 231 Suits were made of "striped summer cloth" for warm weather and navy blue or gray flannel for cold. Sometimes, instead of the corners being rounded, it appeared as though they had been cut off. The custom of putting pleats in the jacket front led to the development of the Norfolk suit, as shown in Figure 242. These pleats are stitched flat against the body, and pockets are set in right over them. There is a yoke across the shoulders. Although this jacket is plain in back, the Norfolk suit eventually had back pleats, too, and a belt.

This young boy's white shirtwaist collar is worn outside the jacket with a large scarf tie. His knee breeches button at the sides. With his button boots he wears textured stockings. His sailor hat has a rolled brim instead of the flat one in Figure 228, but the two styles were equally fashionable. Some new hats were fashioned of cloth, with curled brims stiffened by many rows of stitching. They were blue or a tan color that imitated straw.

Figure 232 After Congress commissioned four new sailing steamships and passed new uniform regulations, there was great interest in sailor middies, hats, coats, and anything nautical.

This dainty sailor dress is charmingly romantic, with its draped overskirt and full pleated skirt. Worn over a high-necked blouse, the middy bodice is slightly fitted. The dress is white with a blue swag overskirt and has a bustle that is not a bow. Rather it is a flat pleated length of cloth caught up in a large loop. The middy collar and cuffs are edged with navy braid; the kerchief and buttons are navy also.

The young lady's large curved-brim sailor hat is as romantic as her dress, with its navy bound edges and ribbon streamers. Her hair style, long in back with bangs at the forehead, is very fashionable, as are her canvas and patent leather boots.

Figure 233 Waistlines and bustles dropped all the way down to the thighs during the early 1880s. Dresses and coats were made on such interchangeable patterns that fashion magazines sometimes called them coat-dresses or dress and coat combinations. Straight rather than the curved princess style, this coat is double breasted, with a bias-cut flounce around the hem. The collar, cuffs, festoon, and pleated underflounce are velvet.

Small plaids and checks were the customary fabrics. Velvets or silks of co-ordinating solid colors were used for the trim. Piqué was worn in summer. A large flat bow serves as a bustle at the back of the festoon.

Tassels and coiled cords adorn the interesting little hat. The brim widens at the sides, where it dips in toward the ears. It curves back out again, staying wide around the back. This little girl's boots curve up into points at the tops.

Figure 234 Soft muslin and batiste were in large supply for children's dresses. Designs were usually dainty one-color prints of scattered miniature flowers or dots. This wispy little princess dress, sketched from the actual garment, has small blue flowers on a white background. Homemade, but machine sewn, it has plain white hemmed ruffles sewn into the front and back princess seams and another wider ruffle around the hemline. The ruffle around the neck is of lace.

Interestingly, it was cut with identical lines in front and back, but it fastens with nine pearl buttons down the center back. It could have been worn with the buttons either front or rear, if not for the two-seamed sleeves that curve toward the front, indicating that the buttons were to be worn in back.

Winter dresses were made on identical lines, in plaid woolens or flannel completely lined with calico to prevent them from being scratchy. The seams were finished with cording or braid instead of ruffles.

The apron-pinafore of Figure 229 was worn over these princess dresses, summer or winter.

Figure 235 New regulations for navy uniforms, as part of the "new navy" supported by Congress, were publicly announced at the beginning of the decade. For the first time in our history, the regulations included illustrations of the uniforms of enlisted men, sparking nationwide interest in sailor suits. While sailor suits were not new, official acknowledgment of them was.

This suit incorporates another new item of fashion along with the nautical look: knickers. Shown in a lady's fashion publication from 1881, they fasten up the side of the legs to the hip. They are quite full and gathered onto a kneeband hidden by their fullness. Knickers would remain a garment for boys with very high-fashion-conscious parents. They would not be commonly worn until 1900.

The middy is worn tucked inside the trousers in the "old-fashioned" way. It fastens to the waist in front with small black buttons such as those on the knickers. Dark blue braid edges the pocket and front opening, and white braid trims the blue collar and cuffs.

This boy's rolled-brim sailor hat has long ribbon streamers. It is made of canvas with the brim stiffened by many rows of stitching, like the new regulation navy hats. His boots dip down in a point at the center and he sports short socks of white cotton.

For a short time, boys' shoes had an interesting metal tap for protection and longer shoe wear. It came up over the edge of the sole and onto the tip of the upper toe. Called blakeys, they were probably inspired by the dancers' taps from the popular minstrel shows. The fad was short-lived, apparently, because they proved to be damaging to floors and rugs, not to mention the ears.

Figure 236 Dark colors were commonly used for children's clothes during this decade. This dress, of black, red, and green striped taffeta, has a dropped waist-line and three-quarter-length sleeves. A wide pleated black sash is arranged in a large flat bow in back. Narrow white lace edges the neckband and sleeves. Over the dress is added a separate lace collar, with points in back and front. It fastens with hooks and eyes down the front.

Without the lace collar, the dress has a decided home-sewn look about it that gives it a certain small-town, rural, or western quality. Similar dresses appear in pictures made in New England and Nebraska. It could have been made anywhere by a loving mother.

The young girl wears black stockings inside plain boots. Her long hair is cut in bangs at the forehead and pushed behind her ears.

Figure 237 Reefer suits had the popular nautical lines but were made in bright colors as well as navy blue. They might be red, black, or green and were usually of velvet. They were seen on boys up to about age nine.

Jackets were double breasted, though always worn open, as shown here. This velvet jacket has a very large sailor collar with a smaller silk one of another shade of the same color. Fold-back cuffs and covered buttons are of the same silk.

The knee breeches have silk bands but no gathers and the same silk-covered buttons as the jacket. A short overblouse worn underneath was of white or horizontally striped fabric. Very small boys wore pleated skirts with these jackets.

Hats made of cloth were popular during this decade. This one is of the suit fabric, with a silk rosette on the up-turned brim. Sometimes striped stockings matched a striped blouse. Either long stockings or short socks were seen with these new oxford shoes with elastic insets at the sides, though boots were still fashionable, too.

Figure 238 The long full waists of these little dresses are revealed, upon close examination, to be slightly flared at the bottom where they were gathered onto the skirts. The side seam angled outward a bit and the front and back center curved down slightly. The gathers were only front and back, not at the sides.

Made of a creamy batiste or fine muslin, this frock is trimmed with hand-made eyelet or cut-work embroidery. A square yoke at the chest is outlined with

(238)

(241)

(236)

(237)

(239)

(240)

(242)

(243)

154 /

flat eyelet, whereas the neckline is edged with a gathered ruffle bound at the edge, so it lies down. Double-scalloped eyelet is stitched flat down the center front bodice, and the sleeves are also edged with eyelet and have both front and back seams.

Two skirts are stitched to the waist. The top skirt has a wide eyelet band sewn at the edge of a one and one-half-inch-deep hem, while the underskirt has a self-ruffle extending below. A pastel silk sash ties into a large bustle bow in back.

This little girl wears short silk socks and the new white slippers that tie across the instep with satin ribbons. Sometimes expensive socks were embroidered at the sides or around the tops.

Figure 239 Infants' dresses were elaborate and long, and christening dresses were often extreme in length.

This dress or "robe" has the enormously wide sash seen at the time on girls' dresses. A baby's physical build made the long-waisted look a bit whimsical, because the wide sash ended up going around the entire torso. This neckline is wide and low, and the sleeves are long and slightly gathered. Made along popular princess lines, the dress has lace insertion and sheer pleated ruffles down the side-front seams. An apron was simulated by joining the two lines of ruffles by a ruffle across the bottom, then running bands of insertion across the center all the way up to the neckline. Sashes were a component of infant dresses throughout the 1880s and into the early 1890s, when dresses were left full and flowing from the chest or shoulders.

One fashion magazine at this time showed a pair of interesting baby boots of Roman sandal style, as those in Figure 229. They had an open center front fastened with three satin ribbon bow ties. There was also a small ribbon bow at the toe of these soft white high-top shoes. Another periodical showed a quilted flannel lace-up pair, with white fur around the tops.

Figure 240 The practice of folding down the tops of short white socks was begun at this time, when one-strap slippers were being seen more and more.

This little boy is dressed in a tailored white piqué dress eventually referred to as an apron. It has starched pleats running from the shoulders to the hem, held in place with a self-belt at a lowered waistline. Its wide, capelike collar is edged with white eyelet embroidery, its only embellishment. This self-belt fastens with two little buttons, but white or black patent leather belts were also seen. The apron fastens in front with small pearl buttons.

This hat is a large rolled-brim sailor straw. Little boys' hats sometimes had plume or ribbon decorations, making them look like those worn by young girls. Occasionally the underside of the brim was covered with shirred silk.

Noteworthy are the bangs of this child's hair style. Bangs were commonly seen on both girls and little boys, sometimes cut clear around to the ears, where they abruptly ended. The back hair hung long from the ears back. This style was not common but can be seen in some old photographs.

Figure 241 Pearl flannel, an exquisite, lustrous cream-gray color, was still a favorite for toddlers' and infants' clothing. This little sacque, sketched from the actual garment, is of a flared design resembling the coats of the 1860s. All the edges have perfectly measured little scallops, each about the size of a dime. They are buttonhole stitched with a shiny white silk thread that matches the embroidered flowers and leaves down the front and around the corners. The back of the sacque, which is quite flared, comes down to a point at the center, where it displays a large spray of dainty white embroidered flowers such as those at the front.

A little white cap of the same fabric has a matching scalloped edge and silk ribbon ties.

The dress under the sacque has the popular center front panel edged with lace insertion. Several rows of tucks and lace encircle the hem.

Shoes for infants were cloth versions of the boots and shoes worn by older children. They might be of quilted satin, cashmere, or flannel, in high-button styles, or slippers. Pearl buttons were always used for baby shoes.

Figure 242 The trend toward pleated or tucked fronts on boys' jackets had by this time developed into the classic Norfolk suit still worn in the twentieth century.

Shown here is a Norfolk with three small pleats at each side running from shoulder to jacket hemline. Aside from the characteristic pleats, the top stitching on the belt, collar, cuffs, and breeches hem is the only trim. It is charming in its simplicity, which may explain its long popularity.

Another characteristic of the Norfolk is its lowered waistline. Although that has moved up or down according to fashion, it has always lodged at least slightly below the natural waist.

Made of flannel for winter and linen for warm weather, the Norfok generally came in light colors like tan, cream, gray, and white. Dark blue was used occasionally, but light colors were preferred, probably because tucks are best displayed when they cast a shadow.

Now, knee breeches were up to or above the knee. These have a top-stitched hem and three pearl buttons at the side. Wide-brimmed straw sailors, as shown here, or billed caps such as those in Figures 215 and 217, or the narrow-brimmed straw of Figure 222 were appropriate accessories. These high-button shoes have the metal taps called blakeys described under Figure 235.

Figure 243 Brocade, satin, faille, soft batiste, and muslin were sewn into confectionlike creations for summer and special occasions.

This young lady shows a frock of batiste with much lace, shirring, and ribbon. The waist is quite long and cut with a center front panel with shirred fullness. A lace sewn-in ruffle defines the seams down each side of the panel. Dainty sleeves are made of rows of gathered narrow lace across the shoulders. The back is cut to duplicate the front, but it has several rows of shirring just below the natural waistline, so that the fullness blouses out at the waist in back rather than at the hips, as it does in front. This was the main difference between dresses for girls over age eight and those for very little girls (as shown in Figure 221), which were identical in back and front. Their style gave older girls a swayback silhouette from the side. To visualize the difference, imagine the front panel, shown here, turned upside down so that the band of shirring comes at the lower back rather than at the neckline.

A ribbon bow is attached below the front panel, and a wide silk sash is tied in back, forming a bustle. The skirt illustrated here is formed of two flounces of eyelet embroidery, but any number from six small ones to just one might be used. Sometimes the top flounce was flared and cut into flaps or points like the skirt of Figure 226, with full ruffled skirts showing underneath.

White slippers with tongue flaps and little ties were fashionable, which resembled those of the eighteenth century. This girl has the becoming hair style of the period, with its bangs and pulled-back sides.

Figure 244 Children's coats and dresses of the mid to late 1880s had the incredibly large bustles of adult clothes. The bustle, which had reached its lowest point at mid-decade, quickly went back up and out again into what was described as a horse's tail shape. It lasted only two or three years, then became smaller in 1889 and, by 1891 was nothing more than just back pleats.

Cape-coats were still the vogue, some with the sling sleeves in Figure 219. In fact, when the extreme bustle is added to the earlier cloak to give it the new silhouette, it becomes representative of the late 1880s styles.

Of pinstriped or checked tweeds, these coats have the back bustle of Figure 248. Braid or velvet bands adorn the cape, skirt, and front, as well as the shoulders and standing collar. The shoulder braid has the look of military epaulettes. A large velvet bow is tied at the neck here, but one fashion print of 1888 shows a second bow at the waistline of a similar coat, with its streamers falling to about three inches above the hem. The description with the above-mentioned fashion print suggests that the coat be made of "camel's-hair cloth in a myrtle-green tint, striped with brown, ivory, and gold." It added, "Any pretty cloth or flannel may be used with dark velvet trim."

Hats at this time were high-crowned affairs with tall decorations at the front or sides. This one has a shirred-velvet-covered brim that widens at the front. Feathers or "quills" stand up in front. The young lady carries a fancy parasol and wears dark stockings with boots.

(244)

(245)

(246)

(247)

(248)

These coats were made of waterproof fabrics also, when a rain umbrella was carried instead of a parsasol.

Figure 245 Young boys up to five or even six years wore coats much like their sisters'. Usually double breasted and fastened with very large metal buttons, like this one, they sometimes even followed the extreme bustle style illustrated in Figure 248.

The coat shown in a rear view in Figure 228 illustrates the low bustles of the early part of the decade. When the bustle moved up at mid-decade, the skirt fullness was released just below the natural waistline rather than down over the derrière.

Several capes of varying sizes, often added, were detachable so that the coats could be changed in appearance. Sometimes only one large cape, like the girl's coat in Figure 244, was seen on little boys' coats and, of course, some coats had no capes at all.

Braid was rarely used on boys' coats, top stitching being more common. One, two, or even three rows of stitching ordinarily embellished the edges of collar, capes, cuffs, front, and skirts, as illustrated here.

Waterproof fabrics were employed for all-weather coats or mackintoshes. One of the characteristics of the mackintosh coat was its plaid lining, a tradition continued today. Plaid woolens were used for winter coats, as were tweeds and checks. Navy blue or gray were favorite solid colors.

The game of "Pin the tail on the donkey" was copyrighted in 1888, another tradition continued today.

Figure 246 Kilt suits for little boys remained the mode for many years, but constantly changed in detail, as did coats, to conform to current silhouettes. Here we see the kilt skirt with the extreme bustle of women's and girls' clothes from the last half of the 1880s.

A vest of matching tartan laps over diagonally in front, copying the traditional shoulder plaid worn by Scots soldiers. The jacket is fitted to the waist in back, then flared out with pleats to accommodate the large bustle. It is like the coat in Figure 248 in back. The high-necked white blouse worn underneath has the full shirred front of girl's dresses and blouses, barely visible here.

Worn with the kilt suit is a "highland bonnet" or tam, with the checkered rim or band and a pom-pom on top. There was a fashion being worn by elegant gentlemen at this time called a collar, which was just a short white spat over the shoe.

Scottish Highlander troops wore gaiters over their plaid stockings. This little boy wears white gaiters over his black shoes and dark stockings; they were probably inspired by one or both of these styles of adult footwear. Plain black button-boots were also appropriate accessories for these suits.

Figure 247 Girls' dress bodices curved out in front while they curved in at the back. The huge bustles added to the curves, giving young girls the look of a bird when seen from the side. As if the clothing silhouette weren't already sufficiently exaggerated, the current posture dictated at the time (and the corsets) required that a girl's chest be pushed out and the back curved in in swayback fashion.

Feathers on the hats added to the look, as did the hats themselves, with their brims sometimes wider in front than in back, as shown here.

This young girl's dress has a pointed yoke and stand-up collar of the same fabric as the cuffs and belt. The waist is below the natural waistline but not as low as during the first half of the decade. The belt is lower in front than in back, because of her curved posture. Two box-pleated skirts balloon out over a large bustle.

Stripes and checks were favorite fabrics in both wool and cotton. Colors were often dark and dull. Sometimes the yoke, belt, and cuffs were in a solid color to contrast with a striped dress. Checked or striped yokes were coordinated with solid-color dresses too.

Roman sandals occasionally had ribbon ties instead of button straps, as in Figure 229. Some dressy shoes had short ribbons tied in a series of bows down the front of the shoe rather than laced up as shown here.

Figure 248 Coats always had to conform to dress shapes, so this one has the same curves and large high bustle as dresses of the last half of the 1880s. It has a high standing collar, with another large collar that forms a hood in back. Made double breasted, it has covered buttons down the front and on the buttoned-tab belt. The bustle has a series of large box pleats. (When such a bustle is constructed, the extra length it requires must be added to the skirt at the top, not at the hem.)

These coats were either top stitched or edged with braid. Checked wool was commonly used, as was striped, while waterproof fabrics were popular for all-weather coats. Capes of all sizes were used on coats, often in twos or threes, or more. They were usually detachable, for convenience and variety.

Hats were seen with hooded coats and plain ones. Mannish styles with high crowns were decorated with feathers and ribbons usually pointing toward the back, for back-view appeal. Those with straight broad brims in front presented a billed appearance, as seen in Figure 247. They were worn at the back of the head or squarely on the top. Brims sometimes widened in front while flaring at the same time, creating a bonnet effect, as illustrated here. Some even tied under the chin, like a young child's bonnet.

Hair styles grew quite long and wavy in back, with some fashion prints showing the hair coming down to the waist. The side hair was always pulled up and the front cut into curly bangs.

Figure 249 As industrialization increased during the first decades after the Civil War, conflicts between capital and labor grew. Sudden slums festered in the cities as immigrants poured into America. Four million ex-slaves were still having difficulty finding employment. It was a time of great growth, but of equally great hardships and unrest as well.

The similarity in the clothing of a laborer's daughter in Robert Koehler's 1886 painting *The Strike* and the young black girl in Edward L. Henry's *Kept In* of 1888 reveal that children of the cities and of the rural South were both still wearing dresses with the natural waistline and full skirt of the 1860s and 1870s.

Sleeveless and low necked, the dress of the Southern black child is worn over a guimpe or blouse. It is bright red with a tab across the low neck and rows of braid trim around the skirt. The white child in a city's industrial section wore a plain gray dress, without trim of any kind.

Another interesting similarity between the clothing of these two children hit by hard times can be seen in their shoes. The black girl's are too large, with the laces wrapped around the outside and tied in front, as illustrated here in Figure 249. Her stockings are black with the knees worn through; her shoes are brown. The Koehler painting's white child's low-cut shoes are also too large and without sufficient laces. Her stockings are brown, the shoes are very scuffed and grayed black.

The old-fashioned smock in Figure 139 was still a familiar sight over plain dresses like this one. They might be blue, brown, or gray and had a binding at the neck rather than the drawstring.

Figure 250 Princess dresses of plaid wool, lined with tiny print calicos to prevent their being scratchy, were worn under pinafores of muslin, linen, and novelty weave cottons. Both dress and pinafore here are constructed in front like the dress in Figure 234. Woolen dresses often had a low waistline seam across the back, as illustrated on the pinafore. It occasionally extended to the side-front seams, although at times it appeared only at the side-back and side-front gores, leaving the center front and back gores unbroken.

This pinafore, sketched from the actual garment, is made of a cotton cloth woven in a thick–thin checked pattern. A variety of these novelty weaves could be achieved by alternating stripes of loosely woven and closely woven bands. Some weaves were striped, whereas others were checked, as a result of using both woof and warp threads in thick and thin patterns. Various twill and herringbone patterns were woven into these unbleached and white cottons, too, as well as waffle patterns.

The back of this pinafore or apron fastens with small pearl buttons and hand-worked buttonholes. The flared skirt's corners are rounded and come together at

(249)

(250)

(251)

(252)

(253)

(254)

the center back without overlapping. Dressy aprons had sashes sewn into the side or side-front seams.

This child wears the short striped socks, sometimes pictured in fashion plates at this time, with button shoes. Her hat, on the chair, has the popular brim that widens in front. It was sometimes worn straight on the head, like the one in Figure 247, but usually it perched at the back of the head, like a bonnet for little girls.

Old-fashioned aprons such as those in Figures 139 (page 96) and 201 (page 134) were still commonly seen at this time, especially in winter.

Figure 251 Dresses of coarse-weave cottons in stripes, checks, and flowered designs might be seen in any part of the country. They were usually plain versions of the long-waisted styles, with little or no ornamentation. Dark and subdued colors were more likely to be used for work clothes than pastels, although light blues and grays were also seen.

This girl's dress is casually open at the neck. Its sleeves have the slight fullness at the shoulder that appeared near the end of the decade.

Simple work aprons usually had ties around the neck as shown. (The pinned apron bib was now worn only by personal maids and household servants.) This simple garment might be seen in the garden, kitchen, in the country, or at home for doing any of numerous chores. Gray, tan, blue, or unbleached muslin were preferred, with white also seen.

Country straw hats in a kind of flower-pot shape, such as this one, were made to fit the head with a "bonnet string," or tie threaded through the straw that could be drawn up to fit any size head. The cloth sunbonnet was commonly seen with such outfits too. The straw hat resting on the chair has a brim that widens in front. In the country, it was sometimes decorated with flowers or a bandanna.

Romantic "old-fashioned" hats such as those of Figures 25 (page 28) and 100 (page 73) might have been worn for a picnic in the country or for working in a patch of flower garden.

Figure 252 When long it was an apron, when short, a bib. This apron has a one-piece long front with a wide neck and little cap sleeves. The back comes down to just below the armholes and fastens with three pearl buttons. For a bib, the neck was made higher and the front smaller. Gray, red, blue, and brown cotton were used for everyday, while fine white linen was lace trimmed and embroidered for dressy versions. Sometimes play aprons were trimmed with braid or scalloped at the edges. Pockets were often added.

When intended for a bib, this garment was made of quilted linen, cotton, or even satin.

Play dresses were often of dark cottons, plaids, checks or calicos. Woolen winter dresses were always lined with printed calicos to forestall chafing and scratching. Sometimes museum examples show two or even three different prints inside, indicating that scraps and remnants were saved for linings. These exhibited dresses invariably have holes at the front hem, especially in the linings, where the baby's knees and toes wore away the fabric while the child was crawling or trying to stand up.

Dark button shoes and either short socks or long stockings were appropriate for play. Short socks were seen in gray as well as white at this time, and striped stockings were now available in short and long lengths.

Figure 253 Seen on boys on Nebraska homesteads, along the rivers, on farms in the South or New England, and in large cities, this simple outfit was universal. It cannot be tied to any one age, ethnic group, or class of youngsters, because it was as likely to be worn by a newsboy in New York as by a black farm worker in Georgia or a prairie farm boy.

Plain shirts made in a variety of fabrics and colors were often worn without the detachable collar. Vests of all kinds of material from leather to silk were worn over them. Trousers, too, might be homespun, hand-me-downs, new, or even of fine quality, depending on whose child was wearing them and where he happened to be.

Immigrant children from Scandinavia and other parts of Europe dressed in much the same manner, and usually wore the cap in Figures 215 and 217. But rural straws, well-worn derbies, and cowboy hats were also seen with these clothes, as were stocking caps. Shoes of the heavy oxford type, high-top lace-ups, riding boots, cowboy boots, or bare feet might accompany them.

By the 1890s, there were over four hundred towns in Minnesota alone that had Swedish names. Norwegian was often the common language in the Dakotas. The 1890 census revealed that there was virtually no more frontier left, since any area with two or more people per square mile was considered settled.

Figure 254 During the 1880s, immigrants from western Europe and Scandinavia were joined by those from central and eastern Europe, as millions poured into Ellis Island.

This girl wears the clothes seen in Charles Ulrich's *The Land of Promise— Castle Garden* painted in 1884. Her dress is made like the ones seen on the small-town or rural girl of Figure 236, but without the sash. It has no ornamentation of any kind and the fabric is a dull, solid brown. She wears a dark, fringed shawl wrapped around her shoulders, crossed in front, and tied in back. Like girls in many other areas, she favors high-top shoes with laces, and dark stockings. Her hair is pulled back and held with a plain ribbon band. (In the above-mentioned painting, the girl's mother is dressed in a traditional European folk costume.)

This outfit is surprisingly like those homemade ones seen on the western prairies as well as in almost any city or rural area in the nation. Its simplicity has a certain no-nonsense appeal. The cloth sunbonnet was commonly worn with it, as were wide-brimmed sailors and country straws.

Figure 255 When fashionable hat brims widened in front and flared, cloth sunbonnet brims followed suit. The old sunbonnets (Figures 97 and 180) had cylindrical or straight brims.

This flared bonnet brim is stiffened with numerous rows of top stitching. The crown is full, as is the protective neck ruffle. Although this one is plain, brims often had ruffles around the edges at this time.

New bathing dresses followed the same princess lines as many dresses of the 1880s. Seams were usually covered with cording or braid, and nautical motifs such as stars and anchors were popular. Navy, white, and red were so consistently employed in swimming attire that they became traditional swimwear colors for several decades. The open collar on this swim dress gives it a very modern look, as do the little sleeves. Bloomers were worn underneath.

Long flannel capes, often hooded, served as bathing robes. They were a necessity in days when vitually all swimming was done in natural lakes, streams, rivers, and oceans where the water was quite cool or even cold.

Figure 256 Pullover middies soon evolved to join the popular front-buttoned ones. These newest ones were more authentically replicas of U. S. Navy uniforms of enlisted men, as discussed in Figure 235. New regulations in 1886 required that the white middy be worn outside the trousers, so it followed that young boys' middies were worn outside, too, in no time. When five-year-old Franklin D. Roosevelt visited Grover Cleveland in 1887, he was dressed in a white sailor middy worn outside his white knee breeches.

Middies were rather short and straight at first but would later take on the full-bloused look of feminine fashions, as little boys' clothes had done for so long. This middy has a low shoulder line and cuffs but no braid trim. A black kerchief is tied under the collar. Since the whistle was regulation for United States sailors, it was also a part of boys' nautical outfits. The whistle, one of the oldest children's toys, seems to have naturally great appeal for little boys.

Knee breeches were straight and loose, without a kneeband. They came down to the middle of the knee or just above. Dark stockings were preferred with them, with black high-top shoes that laced up the front. Short socks were worn in summer.

Hats worn with these sailor suits were navy tams or the visored yacht cap, as illustrated. The latter were made of navy blue flannel, broadcloth, or white duck.

(256)

(258)

(260)

(255)

(257)

(259)

Figure 257 Tourism blossomed into an industry in the 1880s, as seaside and lakeside resorts proliferated. "Watering holes" were the fashionable places at which to be seen.

Boys' bathing suits were styled like those of their fathers. Knit of wool, they were usually two-piece. Necklines might be high or low and suits might be sleeveless or with short sleeves, as shown. Most suits were navy blue, some black. Bands of either red or white went around the neck, sleeves, or armholes, shirt hem, and the hem of the trunks. Suits could now be ordered from the new mail-order houses, so the same styles might be seen at any seacoast or resort in any part of the nation.

Wool was considered the only healthy fiber for swimsuits, advertisements always claiming that wool would "prevent chills." Cotton knits were available and at a cheaper price, but they had a slight tendency to stretch.

This boy has the new side-part hair style seen on fashionable young men and boys at this time but not yet commonly worn.

Boys older than this one were seen in identical swimsuits, as were young men. They were also worn for other sports like boxing, track events, and gymnastics.

Figure 258 Tucks and pleats were prominent on boys' waists of all styles. This young boy has on a suit that is similar to the Norfolk suit jacket, with its pleats on each side of the blouse front. Its wide collar almost touches the armhole seam. Either a waistband or a drawstring holds the fullness in at the waistline, where extra length allows the waist to fall down, curve, and then continue up to the shoulders. A soft waist-blouse was sometimes worn underneath these tailored suits, with lace or self-ruffles showing at the neck and sleeves.

Loose knee-length trousers have pockets set into the sides and openings at the knees where they fasten with four buttons. Boys under four years of age usually wore pleated kilt skirts.

Boots and high-top shoes of various lengths were proper footwear for these suits. These boots are rather high and have an interesting curve forming a dip where the overlap for the buttons begins. Stockings are dark, but short or long ones in a variety of patterns and colors were liked.

Bangs became a favorite hair style for little boys, with curls of various lengths worn at the sides and back. The long page-boy cut of Figure 259 was familiarly seen with this suit, also.

The visored or yacht cap frequently topped off this suit, as did rolled-brim and flat sailor straw hats.

Figure 259 Sailor middies eventually were accepted by every member of the family before the decade came to a close. Even very little boys and girls had fashions inspired by the "new navy" middy, which was required to be worn outside the trousers.

This very small boy is decked out in a middy with an extremely low neck opening. The sailor collar comes down almost to the hem. A striped blouse or vest is worn underneath, and the horizontal stripes add to the nautical feeling. Braid adorns the collar and cuffs.

A pleated skirt, always referred to as a kilt or kilted skirt, was generally preferred for boys four and under, as illustrated. Older boys were attired in identical middies, with the knee-length trousers shown in Figure 258. The hem of this kilt is trimmed with braid.

Large rolled-brim sailor straws were suitable accessories, as were flat brimmed ones. A visored cap known as a yacht cap at this time was worn with sailor suits.

Button boots, still the favorite footwear for little boys, were worn with long stockings or short socks. Striped stockings or socks sometimes matched the striped vest or blouse.

Figure 260 Fashion articles advising on popular "watering holes" and swimwear always reminded parents about properly supervising their daughters while at the beach. Bathing suits were still considered shocking by some people.

Girls' bathing suits were like those of adults, with their bloomers and overdresses. The tunic or overdress was full-bodied and belted at the natural waist. Necks might be square, V-shaped, or round, as is this one. Sleeves were quite small, even just a binding or ruffle. Trim was often of braid for a tailored or nautical look and of ruffles and lace for the more frivolous styles.

This young lady wears a dress edged at the neck and armholes with self-ruffles having shirred headings. Various braid and tab designs (similar to that used on the little swim dress in Figure 255) were sometimes applied to the hem and neckline. Red and navy blue were popular colors for swim dresses. The full trousers of Figure 196 were still in fashion, as well as the bloomers.

This cap is especially interesting. It is the full mob cap style made from a gathered circle of cloth, with a cloth visor added at the front and a small bow decoration. One fashion print showed a similar cap with a ruffle across the back of the neck as well as the visor, making it look like a helmet from the side.

The slippers, too, are interesting. Made of canvas, they are the Roman sandal style, with straps and bows across an open front.

Beach robes were long flannel capes, sometimes with hoods and large tassel and rope ties. They too were trimmed with ruffles and braid. In natural waters of low temperatures, they were a necessary afterswim garment.

— 7 —

"TURKISH TROUSERS" &

TURTLENECKS

1890-1900

Several new ideas in clothing were introduced during the 1890s. A unique form of trousers called jodhpurs was a combination of knickers with gaiters or leggings. Their name came from a state in Northwest India, where they were worn by British troops, as later in Australia.

Originally relegated in America to bike riding, they served well as a solution to the problem of trousers getting caught in bicycle chains. At first, jodhpurs fastened all the way to the ankle but were later shortened to calf length. In a short time, their practical design was realized to be suitable for other sports as well, like hiking and horseback riding. Young Franklin Roosevelt was photographed wearing this very new fashion, with gaiters and high lace-up shoes, around 1896.

Girls had their own new (and to some, shocking) form of costume at the end of the century. Cycling had been increasing in popularity since the 1860s. The new safety bike, with its chain and brake, made biking a national pastime, because it enabled girls and even young children to ride, too. It was bicycling, in fact, that eventually made pants or trousers respectable garb for girls. They were called "Turkish trousers" and were always worn with gaiters. Resembling what we refer to today as culottes, they were enormously full and, in the beginning, were usually gathered at the knee.

In the previous decade, high-waisted pantaloons with straps had been put on over other clothing for protection during work. The idea for the overall soon evolved. Since denim trousers were called overalls, the new overalls were named apron-overalls. Although they soon were considered merely work clothing, during the 1890s they were advertised as bike-riding attire. They were usually of black twill, since denim was reserved for horseback riding. The overall would eventually become known the world over as an American folk garment and even find its way into fashion one day.

Little children began wearing the Brownie suit (overalls), ushering in a new concept in children's clothing. Specially designed, action free, comfortable garments grew into the modern industry of children's playwear.

Still another new item of fashion was to sweep the country and the Western world: the sweater. Its earliest form, the pullover, had a fold-down (turtle) neck and was of a heavy knit. Almost immediately, its potential began to be realized, and a variety of open-necked and collarless pullovers were designed. By the turn of the century, the coat sweater or cardigan would be seen.

Already a national craze, nautical fashions for children continued their popularity. During the Spanish–American War in 1898, new regulation tropical white uniforms were issued to United States Navy personnel. Officers' white coats and enlisted men's white middies were both inspirations for children's fashions. It was the first war in which American sailors had officially worn the middy on the outside of the trousers. The whistle on a rope around the neck was one regulation that had immediately appealed to children. Virtually every description of sailor suits in advertisements and fashion pictures pointed out that "a whistle comes with the suit." As in the real uniforms, children's middies had a pocket especially for the whistle.

Canvas hats with stitched brims were regulation naval attire also and influenced youngsters' hats. Stitched-brim rollers were sold in white, navy blue, or tan, to be worn with sailor or regular suits. Officers' caps with patent leather visors were imitated in both boys' and girls' fashions, usually being recommended for biking, yachting, or tennis.

All ages of children, both boys and girls, were seen in "reefer coats." They became so common that eventually any coat with nautical braid or a wide collar was labeled a reefer. Originally, though, the reefer was a short box or sack coat with a double-breasted front closing and a large squared collar. They always had lots of pockets, as did the reefer coat of naval petty officers.

Girls' dresses and coats had a nautical flavor even when not actually sailor dresses or coats. Boys' clothes also had a nautical flavor, either by use of a large collar, the addition of braid, or by the straight shape of the jacket or blouse. The navy theme amounted almost to a national uniform or costume during the 1890s.

Girls' sleeves of the 1890s had as startling a growth in size and then as swift a decline as the bustle had during the 1880s. There were a number of distinguishing characteristics in clothes of this decade, such as the flared skirts with back fullness and the rounded bosom, but the huge sleeves are what first come to mind.

About 1889, sleeves began to take on a little fullness at the shoulder. They grew gradually from 1890 through 1892 until, by 1893, they were quite large. Although large during the early 1890s, they sloped downward from the shoulder, with the main fullness on the arm. They then began to take on a stiffness, at first expanding horizontally, then actually growing upward from the armhole and rounding over by 1896.

By 1897, the fullness began to recede. It should be noted that, even though *Harper's Bazaar* was showing new, smaller sleeves in 1896, the Sears Roebuck catalog still offered the enormous sleeves in 1897.

At the end of the nineteenth century and into the twentieth, millions of beautiful birds were killed for their feathers to decorate ladies' and girls' hats. President Roosevelt became interested in conservation and began a program that eventually led to establishing national parks and wildlife refuges in the United States. Natural furs would, however, continue to be used as trim on children's coats and hats.

The practice of designating certain styles, lengths, or waistlines for specific age groups was continued. Every garment was carefully described as being proper for one group or another.

Girls from four to fourteen were to be attired in dresses with waistlines at the natural waist or only slightly below. Girls from three to five were dressed in Empire-waisted dresses, and toddlers up to three or four wore the full-flowing frocks of infants.

Baby carriages were so much in demand that even mail-order houses published special baby carriage catalogs. Made of reed, they had bentwood handles and steel axles. Upholstery was imported brocatelle or silk plush. Fancy cushions and rolls were decorated with tassels, and both they and the upholstery were quilted in elaborate patterns matching the reed designs of the carriage. Brussels carpet covered the floor and all this could be custom-made in any color requested.

Carriage parasols were silk satin, lined with satin, and adorned with silk fringe or valenciennes edging. They could be closed or moved to various angles as needed. Advertisements always stressed, "our own patented self-locking automatic brake." There was no doubt about it: American tots rode in carriages fit for royalty.

Figure 261 By 1890, British troops in India and Australia were wearing jodhpurs. The U.S. Cavalry would adopt them before World War I and call them simply riding breeches. (It was during a cavalry mission into Mexico in 1916 that the U.S. Army used airplanes for the first time, so that our first aviators wore cavalry uniforms. Airmen continued to wear jodhpurs during the war in all branches of the service and made them famous.)

This young gentleman is nattily dressed in a tweed sports jacket, checked vest, and shirt with tie. Over his high-top shoes and jodhpurs, he has leather gai-

(261)

(262)

(263)

(264)

ters that fasten with snaps up the side, ending with a small strap and buckle at the top. His jodhpurs fasten with buttons, but laces were used by 1910. His shirt collar is soft and pulled out over his vest.

The hat considered proper for this outfit was the touring cap shown on the boy in Figure 264. Turtleneck sweaters, also a novelty at this time, were proper attire with jodhpurs, with or without the jacket. Leather gloves were usually worn.

The Norfolk jacket in Figure 231 was worn with jodhpurs for hiking or bicycle riding.

Figure 262 It was bicycling that made divided skirts or full bloomer-trousers acceptable for girls. They were now considered respectable for physical education and other sports. But, though they had become fashion, many adults of both sexes still considered them in coarse taste and antifeminine. For this reason advertisers repeatedly assured prospective buyers that they were "so full that the division is not noticed."

There were two styles available: the flared skirt style with box pleat in front and back, known today as culottes, and the other, the enormously full bloomers called Turkish trousers. Even the *Ladies Home Journal* accepted advertisements for them. Both styles were so voluminous that, as the ads promised, they looked more like skirts than trousers. The bloomer style was gathered or pleated all around the waist, then gathered onto a leg band just below the knee. The fullness dropped down below the band before curving back up toward the knee, which explains why they were called Turkish trousers.

This young cyclist wears a fashionable pointed belt and suspenders with her Turkish trousers. Her blouse is the new shirtwaist style eventually known the world over as an American creation. It has a tucked front and the new gathered sleeves that, starting in 1889, gradually grew in size from 1890 to 1892.

Her cap is the old shako worn by boys for so long in America. It came to be called a yacht cap at this time and was worn by girls for most sports activities. It differs from the boys' new touring cap in Figure 264 in that it has a stiff band all the way around the head and a patent leather visor. An "engineer's cap" (like a baseball cap) was pictured in fashion prints with divided skirts, as was the tam-o-shanter and the sailor hat.

Canvas or jersey gaiters, referred to in girls' clothing as leggings, were almost always worn. Like the gaiters in Figures 188 and 190 (page 128), they came in gray, tan, blue, or black and were advertised as glove fitting. Leggings were calf high, knee high, or even well up on the thigh for wintertime.

Bicycle suit advertisements often showed the reefer jacket in Figure 271 with divided skirts, blouses, and hats like these. Velveteen was often used for such suits.

Figure 263 Another new concept in garments first manufactured during the 1890s was "bib trousers" and "apron overalls." So far an overall had simply been work or military trousers without bibs and was worn over the regular trousers to protect them. Apron overalls would eventually become our modern overalls, and the overalls (denim trousers) of the nineteenth century would become our blue jeans.

Overalls as we know them were sold in mercantile stores and through the popular mail-order catalogs. Blue denim was recommended for horseback riding, black duck for bike riding. Blue and white stripes, gray and white stripes, and white duck would eventually become associated with certain trades such as railroading, carpentry, mining, and other "blue-collar" work.

For kids in rural areas all over America, these clothes would be primarily for chores and play. In many small-town and rural areas, especially in the west and south, they were worn as school clothing, too, by both black and white boys. It began life as just a rugged garment intended to save one's "good" clothes, but the overall was destined to become one of America's best-known folk symbols.

This young boy is dressed in the plain overall originally known as the "Brownie suit," for boys from four to fourteen. Sometimes there was a pleat or a special facing at the side of the bib, as shown. At first, the straps were riveted to the bib and had to be dropped down to remove the overalls. By 1900, elastic would be added for comfort.

This shirt has the same soft collar as the dress shirt on the boy at the left. It is buttoned, but no tie is worn. Red bandannas were sometimes tied either under or on top of the collar. The hat is an "old-fashioned" straw. The cap of Figure 262 was commonly seen with overalls, and the cowboy hat was seen occasionally, too.

Boys' shoes were lace-up high-tops designed for rugged wear, sometimes advertised as hard-knock shoes.

Figure 264 At the beginning of the 1890s, there were already 10 million people in America riding the new safety bikes with balloon tires, brakes, flat pedals, and two wheels of the same size.

The turtleneck, or roll-neck, sweater was designed for bicycle riding, and American mail-order catalogs were soon selling them. In the catalogs, they were called bike sweaters, but they were soon taken up by golfers, newsboys, hikers, football players, and schoolboys of all ages. Catalogs, however, continued to label them bike sweaters, and offer them in wine, black, navy blue, and tan.

The sweater proved to be such a popular item of apparel that eventually open collars were designed, and decorative white stripes ran around the hips or across the chest. By the beginning of the twentieth century turtlenecks were sometimes horizontally striped all over.

Knickers or jodhpurs were sometimes worn with roll-neck sweaters for sports.

The jacket of Figure 261 was often put on over the sweater. High-top shoes and thick stockings were worn, and occasionally canvas or leather gaiters.

The new touring cap was constructed of pie-shaped gores or sections sewn onto a narrow cloth band. There was a cloth visor in front, and the crown fell out over the band onto the visor, giving the cap a forward tilt. There was always a button on top. The cap of Figure 262 was seen on boys too.

Many cities and towns had street lights by the end of the 1890s, and boys and girls could bike even at night. They could bike in rain, too, as soon as some stores began to stock a bicycle slicker or "cyclists' cape." A kind of poncho of oilcloth, it came in a leather case that could be fastened to the bike.

Figure 265 During the first two years of the decade, sleeves gradually grew larger, as illustrated here. There was a preoccupation with collars, necklines, and sleeves, and everything seemed to add width at the shoulders. Waistlines were pulled in tight, as young girls continued to wear corsets. The bodice was full and rounded, with fullness always added at the center front waist.

Skirts were flared, with pleats at the sides and back. Although the bustle was gone, there was still much fullness pleated into the back, causing the skirt to appear to be moving even when the wearer was standing still.

The nautical theme was still common, as shown here. A young lady wears a white dress trimmed with red braid, over a red and white striped blouse or vest-ee. The collar extends out over the armhole seam at the shoulder, as did most collars of the day.

Hats were placed straight on top of the head, squared sailor shapes being the most popular. Without the ribbon decorations, this girl's hat is duplicated on the young boy in Figure 268. Narrow-brimmed sailors were popular, too. Buttoned boots remained the most commonly seen footwear for children, although slippers might be substituted for special occasions.

Girls' suits with jackets like that worn by the young boy of Figure 266 were popular. They appeared with tailored blouses, either plain or striped, and frilly white ones with tucks and lace.

Figure 266 By the mid-decade, boys' sailor suits had become quite varied in design and sometimes quite elegant, as illustrated here. This three-piece suit is of wool broadcloth in a medium blue, with black braid trim. The pea jacket is double breasted; its shiny brass buttons have eagles embossed on them. It obviously was not intended to be worn fastened, since it has only two small buttonholes at the chest. Through these would pass a cufflinklike fastener made from two buttons. The collar is quite large, extending out beyond the armhole seam at the shoulder. Several rows of black braid edge the collar and cuffs. Stars embellish the sleeves and an eagle, star, and wreath are further nautical motifs on the matching blouse.

(265)

(266)

(267)

(268)

(269)

These blouses were often just dickies or vestees sewn into the jacket. Sometimes they were striped, like that in Figure 237.

Black neckerchieves were sometimes tied under the collar, but during the early 1890s they might fashionably be omitted. Advertisements usually suggested this suit for boys from three to eight, but mail-order catalogs and some stores recommended it for boys up to ten.

Trousers were knee length with a slight taper, and buttons were often used purely as decoration instead of being functional.

Wide-brimmed sailor straws remained the favorite hat for young boys, as did boots and dark stockings. This boy sports the fashionable side-part hair style.

The jacket of this suit, worn over a pleated skirt or kilt, was advocated for little boys of two to five years. "Fancy" suits of almost identical design were also advertised, the only difference being in the length of the jacket, the fancy ones being shorter. These suits were worn over feminine, even frilly, white blouses that fell down below the jacket.

Figure 267 Boys' sailor suits eventually became more authentic in design, based on the famous navy regulations of 1886. This young boy's middy has the blue collar and cuffs with braid trim and sleeve insignia of regulation uniforms. It also has the official whistle on a cord, knotted in the navy manner, and kept in a special pocket. The seam down the center front is further copying of navy middies, but the fullness in the body and gathers at the sleeve tops are the result of feminine fashion influence, an element always present in small boys' clothes. It is interesting that virtually all sailor suits for boys during this decade are pictured without the neckerchief.

Trousers were short and tapered toward the knee. Buttons were sewn at the sides, sometimes merely as decoration and sometimes for genuine use. Some suits at this time came with an extra pair of trousers.

Fabrics used in summer were blue and white striped piqué with light blue collar and cuffs, striped white or twilled duck, navy blue and white "pencil striped wash goods," twilled tan nankeen with red trim, navy blue duck with white trim, and heavy cream sateen with a blue duck collar and cuffs. Winter advertisements offered flannel, "wool tricot flannel," heavy navy blue duck, broadcloth (wool), and wool cheviot. Colors offered were navy blue, light blue, white, slate, tan, brown, and "drab."

Hats, too, were often counterparts of the rolled-brim cloth hat of navy regulation, as shown here. Wide-brimmed sailor straws were also in general use, as was the yacht cap.

One 1897 advertisement showed an interesting sailor suit made of red and blue striped duck. The collar, cuffs, and pocket cuff of solid blue were scalloped at the edges and bound with white cord. Mail-order catalogs occasionally offered long trousers in sailor suits.

Figure 268 Made of piqué or duck for summer and flannel for cold weather, these blouse suits were recommended for boys from three to eight. The blouse fastened down the front on a top-stitched or braid-edged panel. Elastic in the hem caused it to fall out over the trousers. Collars were squared, though short in back, and trimmed with two or three rows of braid. Breast pockets were always provided on these blouses, and young gentlemen were encouraged to carry handkerchieves in them. Small silk ribbons were tied into bow ties at the neck.

Trousers tapered to the knees, where they fastened with three buttons, though often the buttons were merely decorative. Some trousers had braid down the outseam, but most did not.

Either wide-brimmed or rolled-brim sailor hats were appropriate accessories, as was the yacht cap. For Sunday or dressy occasions, boys often were dressed in oxford-type shoes fastening with large tailored bows over the instep. Horizontally striped stockings were occasionally seen, but dark, solid colors were most often preferred.

The Norfolk jacket with pleats was still popular and sometimes worn over these blouse suits, and the coat from Figure 270 was added over them in cold weather. Mail-order catalogs occasionally showed the bolero-type Zouave jackets of the 1860s (shown in figure 174, page 115) over these suits, too.

Figure 269 Coats, like dresses, had wide collars and huge sleeves by 1893. The princess style of Figure 245, worn both by girls and boys in the previous decade, was reserved for girls during the 1890s. It had changed little except for the new balloon sleeves. Capes and princess coats with full capes were popular too.

Full styles with yokes or large squared collars, such as this one, were shown in style periodicals. Expensive ones had brocade velvet collars either with fur trim, fur collars, or embroidered yokes and collars. Velvet was a favorite fabric, along with plush and velour. They usually fastened only at the neck or yoke and hung free from there to the hem. Muffs were often carried in winter, expensive ones matching the fur trim on the coat. In the spring, white piqué or light-weight flannel were the preferred coat fabrics, with lace ruffles around the yoke or collar.

Less dressy coats for spring or fall often came in plaids or checks. Coordinating solid colors might be used for trim. Advertisements show these flared coats in several lengths, falling either to the knees, finger tips, or even only to the hips.

Hats were wide-brimmed sailors as in Figure 265, with ribbons, plumes or flowers, or the curved-brim style illustrated here. This brim dips down on each side and then turns up in back, giving the hat a forward tilt.

Strap sandals with large bows were worn in warm weather and for dressy occasions. They had very pointed toes called needle toes and could be bought in black or white kid. Stockings sometimes had dots or flowers embroidered in all-over designs, or just on each side, or up the front.

Figure 270 Reefer suits and coats became immensely popular for all youngsters during the 1890s as a result of the navy regulations that had also made sailor suits so popular. The regulations permitted petty officers to wear double-breasted sack coats. The old pea jacket, worn since the eighteenth century by merchant seamen and sailors, had now become official attire for enlisted men.

This little boy is dressed in a reefer with a large nautical collar broken by the lapel of the double-breasted front. The collar is edged with several rows of braid, a characteristic of reefer coats. Plenty of pockets were always put into these coats, including a watch pocket like those on petty officers' coats. They were usually advertised as being made of "all wool cassimere or cheviot." Favorite colors were navy blue, gray, brown, and a dark gray-brown tweed.

Reefer suits always had knee-length trousers for boys from three to eight years, and pleated skirts for boys under three.

Wide-brimmed sailor hats were accounted proper coordinates, as were the rolled-brim sailors. High-button shoes and dark stockings were always worn with reefer suits.

Little boys' summer suits were made of white piqué, their collars and cuffs edged with large eyelet ruffles.

Figure 271 Girls wore reefer coats fashioned after navy coats, too, but theirs were not as authentically styled as those of the boys. They were double breasted and had sailor collars, but the sleeves followed their mothers' sleeve changes. These represent the huge sleeves of 1896, but reefer coats can be made with any of the sleeves of the 1890s.

Collars were always edged with several rows of braid, as were cuffs and pocket flaps. Six buttons of pearl, horn, or brass were usual, although a few reefers had only four. Metal buttons with embossed eagles were favored.

Skirts were always flat in front, but large pleats at the sides and back flared out over full petticoats. Popular colors for reefer coats were navy, dark red, tan, and green. Small plaids and checks in dark colors were popular also.

Tams were wool, hand-knit, or straw in rather stiff interpretations of the soft ones. Tams would remain in favor into the 1900s, growing larger and floppier during the decade. This one has a pom-pom on top. Dark stockings and high-button shoes of leather, cloth, or combinations of the two materials continued to be the most familiar footwear.

Figure 272 Young girls from the toddler stage up to age five or six continued to wear frilly white clothing, much like that of infants. As a rule, little boys remained in baby clothes only through age two or sometimes three. Most advertisements for infants' clothing reminded parents how the long cloaks and coats would "grow" with the child, so the younger the child, the longer the cloak. Since chil-

(272)

(273)

(271)

(275)

(270)

(274)

dren grow primarily in height during the first few years, a coat might be worn two or even three seasons in some instances, growing shorter each year.

White piqué was a favorite for spring, and white or pearl cashmere in the fall. Lace and eyelet embroidery, often hand worked, were applied in abundance to dresses, coats, and capes. This little girl models an ensemble of dress, coat, and bonnet. The dress is constructed like that in Figure 278, with eyelet embroidery around the hem. A shorter coat, also bordered with tucks and eyelet, was added over the dress. It also has a round yoke, with shoulders edged in embroidered eyelet. The full sleeves have eyelet cuffs. Two buttons fasten the coat only at the yoke.

Bonnets at this time had ruffled brims that became wider at the center front, making them appear quite tall. Adding still more height were the silk ribbon bows at the bonnet top. Some bonnets were as tall again as the child's face length. They had round crowns at the back with shirred sides and top, and then gathered brims. (A side view can be seen in Figure 279.) Bows were added at the back or sides, as well as on top. Sometimes the ribbon ties hung to the waist even after being tied, as shown here. In addition to all this, there was often a neck ruffle at the back.

Either white or black button shoes were customary footgear, as were bow-tied slippers and strap shoes. Either long stockings or short socks were worn.

Figure 273 Infants' cloaks or wrappers were quite long during the 1890s and almost always had large cape collars. These capes usually hung to just above the wrist, but occasionally a fashion print shows one longer. One characteristic of 1890s capes is the shirring or smocking around the neck. They were made from a straight piece of fabric drawn up to fit.

The coat had a yoke at the chest, with two or three buttons, then fell open to the hem. They were usually about a yard long, but very expensive ones might be longer. Both the coat and its cape were beautifully embroidered, even on inexpensive mail-order cloaks. They were made of piqué for summer and cashmere for winter, and were always white. Embroidery was silk, and much white satin ribbon was used for bands around the skirt and cape. Sometimes the ribbon was run through eyelet embroidery.

One advertisement offered a cloak with five rows of ribbon around its cape collar. Wool flannel embroidered with silk could be purchased by the yard and sewn around the hems, if one had no time or perhaps lacked the skill to do the embroidery. The lining was always of sateen.

Baby bonnets were similar to those of little girls, being sewn onto a small circle at the crown like the one in Figure 279. The brim ruffle on an infant's cap was smaller, and there was rarely a neck ruffle, but the tall ribbon adornment on top was often used, as shown here.

Dresses usually had a round yoke with a ruffle and long sleeves. Sometimes the dress was sleeveless and low necked, worn over a guimpe giving much the same appearance. Baby boots were fashioned of quilted satin or soft kid, made on the same lines as the high-topped shoes worn by most children.

Figure 274 Collars, yokes, capes, epaulettes, and various other design elements focused attention on the neck and shoulders during the 1890s, growing more squared during the last half of the decade.

This tiny girl has on a white coat of a somewhat tailored design with squared epaulettes at the shoulders, over the sleeves. It has no yoke but flares from the shoulder seams. A small round collar edged with an eyelet ruffle is its only frill. A hook fastener holds the coat together at the neck, while the sides barely meet over a center panel held by two huge buttons on each side. The coat comes to just above her ankles; it might have reached the floor a season ago, when the little miss was even smaller.

White piqué and duck were the preferred spring fabrics, white and pearl flannel or cashmere wool being favorites for fall. Pearl buttons were prominent as decorations as well as fasteners.

With only minor changes, this coat could be made to conform to the latest style trend. At the beginning of the decade, the little capes of Figure 245 (page 158) might be used. At mid-decade, round yokes like that in Figure 272 or the large collar of Figure 280 would be more likely choices. The squared epaulettes were the mode during the last three years of the 1890s. During the entire decade, a ruffle might replace the epaulettes, or the cape of Figure 273 might be worn. This, of course, is not an absolute rule, since there was such variety and overlapping of modes, but it is a general rule based on trends shown in expensive fashion magazines and advertisements of the time.

The dress under the coat is like the infant's of Figure 278 with its ruffle-edged shoulder yoke. The large floppy hat is typical of those of older girls. Brims would continue to droop until 1910. Plumes, ribbons, and flowers were used extravagantly around the crown. High-button shoes in either white or black were customary accessories.

Figure 275 For boys from four to fifteen, suits of the 1890s were characterized by knee-length trousers. Instead of braces or suspenders, buttons on the shirtwaist were used to hold the trousers up, though advertisements at this time offered a "patent waistband with buttonholes and extra elastic loops." Advertisers always mentioned the three buttons at the knee, too, despite the fact that sometimes they actually fastened nothing.

Another important characteristic of new trousers was the crease. The custom began in the 1880s but was seen only on very fashion-conscious gentlemen. By the 1890s, no fashion print would show boys' trousers without sharp creases.

Jackets were always double breasted and straight, with several pockets, including a watch pocket like those on men's coats. They usually had six buttons showing, with two more under the collar that were rarely fastened. Younger boys' shirts had soft collars, while older boys wore stiff collars with only the points turned down.

Ties were sold already knotted and on an elastic band, with a metal clip in back. For spring, fabrics were "satinette" and striped cotton. But "Michigan hard twist cassimere," cheviot, corduroy, mixed cassimere, and all-wool serge were brought out for fall. Brown, navy, and gray were the favorite colors. Gray and brown tweeds or brown and white checks were common, too.

The most fashionable hat was the derby, illustrated here, but various styles of caps and hats were seen, especially the yacht cap, the touring cap, baseball caps, and western cowboy hats. High-topped shoes were still the mode, with older boys having laces instead of buttons, and pull tapes at the back.

The turtleneck sweater often replaced the shirt on cold days or for sports wear. The overcoat with shoulder cape and plaid lining, like that in Figure 215 (page 142), was still a favorite, as was the Norfolk jacket.

Figure 276 Frilly blouse waists were advertised as being appropriate for boys from four to twelve when made of sateen, percale, calico, or "chelsea cloth." When fine white lawn and sheer eyelet embroidery were used, they were suggested for boys three to eight years old. Although of different fabrics, they were all of the same cut.

Sometimes these white waists were advertised as "little prince" blouses, apparently to identify them with the popular Little Lord Fauntleroy book of 1886. Velvet suits were black, blue, dark green, or burgundy.

Blouse collars were large and made even larger by the addition of wide self- or lace ruffles. A double ruffle covered the front opening, curving at the bottom. It was constructed so that it went down one side, turned, and made its way back up the other side. Large ruffles edged the cuffs, too. Blouse bodies were always extremely full and gathered in by a drawstring or elastic through the hem. Large bows were often worn at the neck, as shown.

Percale blouse waists were available in "French indigo, garnet, pink, blue, tan, and assorted colors and patterns." Black sateen waists were routinely pictured in mail-order catalogs. Other fabrics advertised were dark blue with random white stripes, cadet blue with white and black figures, and "light and dark colors in stripes and fancy patterns." Only boys under eight wore lace edging; older boys' waists had self-ruffles.

Blouse waists were always paired with knee-length trousers tapered to the knee and creased in front. Young boys were outfitted in high-button shoes or bow-

(278)

(276)

(277)

(279)

(280)

tied oxfords, as illustrated, with dark stockings. Long page-boy hair styles with middle parts or bangs were the mode for little boys; older boys preferred the short side-part style.

Boys of two or three were dressed in pleated skirts.

Figure 277 Most families "allowed their sons to declare their sex by age two or three," according to ladies' fashion publications. Up until the age of three, it was difficult for the outsider to tell boys from girls, because their clothing was virtually the same. This very young boy is outfitted in a box-pleated kilt with a very deep hem falling to his shoe tops. The skirt was always attached to a body of sateen or muslin to hold it up.

These frilly little jackets were called reefers, although there was very little about them that was nautical. Their double-breasted style and large collars gave them their name.

This boy's reefer is white like his skirt and trimmed with white eyelet embroidered ruffles. It is double breasted and fastens with pearl buttons. The cuffs, hem, and jacket front are topstitched, giving the suit a tailored look in spite of its frills. In summer, white piqué or duck was favored; in fall, they were stitched from white cashmere or pearl flannel.

Girls' suits were made on the same lines, but with more eyelet or lace. Their skirts usually had lace or tucks around the hem, and the jacket was often scalloped down the front and around the hem. Their collars were a bit smaller, too, as a rule. The blouse-waist of Figure 276 was worn with pleated kilts like this by boys from eighteen months to three years.

White or black high-button shoes were natty accessories, as were sailor hats.

Nursing bottles advertised in this period still had the nipple on a long tube of rubber. Glass bottles were flask-shaped.

Figure 278 Infant dresses, also called slips or robes, were either one piece with a yoke or low-necked frocks worn over a guimpe (blouse). They looked much the same, except that the jumper type of dress ordinarily had a ruffle around the arm-hole, or small puffed sleeves. This one has the armhole ruffle, indicating that it is worn over a guimpe. One advantage of the two-piece set was that, in summer, it could be worn without the blouse. The bodice of the guimpe is made up of rows of lace stitched together, while a strip of lace forms the neckband. The sleeves are full and gathered in at the lace-edged wrists. Sheer embroidered eyelet forms the full neck and armhole ruffles of the dress.

General agreement on infants' dress lengths was that the younger the baby, the longer the dress must necessarily be, to allow for growth. During the first few months, dresses might be as much as three or four feet long. Toddler frocks reached to the ankles, sometimes to the floor, and by the time the child was two years old, frocks had risen to the boot tops.

Made of fine cambric or lawn, these dresses were always white, with white trim and satin ribbons. The white cloak and bonnet of Figure 273 were put on over the dress when needed. Crocheted sacque sweaters were commonly worn, too. Advertisements and catalogs offered these in pink, blue, or white. Crocheted booties and caps were made to match. Baby shoes were made on the same lines as older children's high-button shoes but were fashioned of soft kid and quilted satin or wool.

In his hand the infant holds a toy made to look like a miniature maypole, with tiny bells attached to the end of each ribbon. The stick is candy striped, with a ribbon rosette at the end.

Baby carriages, as elegant and plush as the finest horse-drawn carriage, were in such demand that stores and mail-order houses published special catalogs showing them.

Figure 279 Coats or cloaks were sometimes quite elaborate, as were bonnets. Made of piqué or cashmere, they were almost always white, with those of older girls occasionally being peach, pale blue, or cream. This little girl's cloak has a large cape collar constructed by gathering a straight piece of lace-edged fabric onto a curved, fitted yoke around the neck. Some cloaks had small collars, some had none. The coat body was usually made with a yoke at the chest like the infant's coat of Figure 273, especially during the mid and late nineties. At the beginning of the decade, the coat sometimes consisted of a full skirt sewn onto a slightly dropped waistline.

Imported lace and embroidered piqué, flannel, or sheer eyelet were available from most stores and mail-order houses. Or mother sometimes did her own cut-work embroidery with silk thread. Cream lace was usually applied to pastel cloaks. Cording was stitched into the seam between the lace and flannel or piqué, around the yoke, and at the collar edge. Pearl buttons were standard, and the lining was always sateen.

Bonnets had a circular crown with a shirred band across the head. Brims were created from ruffles that grew wider at the center front, so that the bonnet appeared quite tall. Ribbons, looped on top of the head, gave it still more height, while ribbon bands went over the head and around the back with a bow in center back. Many bonnets had ruffles at the neck, too, and they, as well as the brim, were edged with lace.

Figure 280 Up until the age of six, in this era, a girl was usually dressed in high-waisted dresses and coats. Dressy versions were white, frilly, and beribboned, as in Figure 272. For more casual wear, both coats and dresses had large sailor collars and tailored pleats as shown. U.S. Navy uniforms had had a dramatic impact on children's clothing in America during the 1880s and 1890s. Now entered one more maritime influence, in a fad for gold braid on little girls' coats. But gold soutache was rarely used alone; it was always paired with several rows of bright red, green, or navy braid.

Everyday coats were red, navy, brown, or tan wool solids. Checks were very popular, too, with green, black, navy, bright blue, and brown the favorites. Combination plaids in several shades of the same colors were advertised with collar and cuffs of a coordinating solid tone. Ads usually pointed out that a coat "has three rows of braid" or that it "is trimmed with gold and colored soutache."

Tams were still advertised, with the latest ones turned up in front and adorned with a ribbon rosette and a "quill" standing up at a very steep angle, as shown. The hat of Figure 265 also was often pictured in ads with these full coats. Shoes were high-button styles or bow-tied slippers worn with dark cotton stockings for warm weather, and wool in winter.

Everyday dresses for girls between three and five were almost identical with coats, featuring Empire waists, large collars, and full sleeves. They were often plaids or checks in cotton or wool, depending upon the season.

Figure 281 Rubber diaper covers, at the turn of the century, would have a profound and lasting influence over the design of children's clothes. At first, Brownie suits were advertised in mail-order catalogs and newspapers as suited to boys from four to fourteen years. But, within a few years, the new rubber pants would enable toddler boys to wear trousers before they were toilet trained. Denim was the fabric used for the practical and tough little Brownie suits, advertised as "a boy's everyday go-as-you-please suit." Stores proclaimed, "They are worn everywhere this season," and "Let your boy play in the healthy outdoor air this summer in a Brownie suit!" Colors were blue or gray solids, or gray and white striped (heavy duty).

These first overalls had a cuff at each side of the bib to make it fit around the curve of the torso. A metal clip fastened each strap. Two pockets were attached at the front hips, and the trouser legs always folded up into a cuff. At first, they were thought of as summer attire, but eventually the idea of putting them on over shirts or sweaters showed they would be practical all year round. During this decade, the coverall with collar and sleeves, made of gray and white denim, was manufactured in Wisconsin.

It would be only a few years before little girls would also be allowed to play in this form of trousers.

One of the most outstanding contributions to child development resulting from rubber diaper covers and young children's overalls was in the area of crawling and walking. Children had previously learned to walk while in skirts; old dresses in museums showing worn out front hems tell the story of how difficult it had been. By comparison, how easy and comfortable it has been for twentieth-century children to learn to crawl and walk in overalls.

(281)

(282)

(283)

(284)

(285)

Figure 282 Tremendous emphasis was placed on shoulder decoration during the last years of the century. Ruffles of various sizes were scalloped, braid trimmed, and embroidered. Occasionally, they were long and capelike, as in Figure 314, and often they were squared, like those of Figure 274. Whatever their shape, they are characteristic of feminine clothing during the last decade of the nineteenth century.

At this time, sleeves began to decrease in size, after reaching their peak during 1896 and 1897. The waist was changing, too, having moved up to the natural waistline or slightly below it early in the decade and then dropping down again. Long waists would return to fashion after the turn of the century.

This dress and apron demonstrate not only the new sleeves, but the descending waistline, also. The bib is full in center front, like dresses of the 1900s. These aprons were almost always made of white lawn in this period. They might be tucked or lace-trimmed when worn by little girls. At times, the popular shoulder ruffle or squared epaulette was on the apron as well as on the dress.

High-button shoes and black cotton or woolen stockings were commonly seen with these clothes. Straw sailors, cloth sunbonnets, and rural straw hats were seen with them too, in all parts of the nation. Hair was arranged with upswept sides, front bangs, and very, very long back hair.

Figure 283 Tailored frocks or smocks were favorites for two- and three-year-old boys because, even though they were skirts, these had a certain masculine simplicity about them. Pleats started at the shoulder line or yoke, extending all the way to the hem. They usually were sewn in place down to the hips, where they were released to form box pleats in a full skirt. At times they were released from a yoke and caught only briefly at the hips, before their ultimate release.

A tailored belt was always worn, either of the frock fabric or of dark leather. During the 1890s, large maritime collars such as this were favored. During the early 1900s, a standing collar without a yoke would be preferred. (The girl's dress in Figure 313 is what little boys' smocks would look like during the coming decade—they would grow shorter too.)

Fine smocks were made of white piqué and trimmed with embroidered eyelet ruffles. Often they were made from figured percales or piqué, in patterns with white backgrounds, like those used for men's shirts. Braid was often used around the collar, cuffs, and belt, but sometimes top stitching was the only trim. Belts usually had buttoned fastenings rather than buckles, and belts were now contoured to curve around the body and ride on the hips. They were usually anchored by stitching at the center back; belt loops were still rarely, if ever, used on boys' clothing.

Little button shoes were always worn in either black or tan. Dark stockings of cotton or wool were standard accessories. High-button shoes were sometimes of patent leather or kid, with patent toes and heels. Little boys wore lace-up shoes, too.

Flask-shaped nursing bottles with rubber nipples fitting directly onto the mouth could be purchased now. The new design had ribbed and valved interiors to prevent suction from collapsing them. When the little one released the nipple, air could return to the bottle. Before the end of the decade, some new bottles were produced with measurements indicated on their sides.

Figure 284 Although rarely shown in fashion magazines, there were simple little frocks and aprons seen on beaches, in one's own yard, or at vacation spots and family gatherings. They appear in paintings of this decade, as well as in advertisements. They were so simple and informal that they were taken for granted and certainly not considered fashion.

Basically, they were hardly more than a straight piece of fabric, with vertical slits or horizontal crescent cuts forming little cap sleeves. Either a drawstring was used or a binding was sewn on at the neck to make it fit. They either tied at the back of the neck and fell freely from there to the hem or were caught one or two times down the back with other ties. One little frock appearing in the *Ladies Home Journal* in 1895 had eyelet insertion through it. Fabrics were muslin and piqué in white, or miniature patterns printed on a white background.

The only other necessities were the diaper and sometimes cloth or knit diaper covers. Most paintings show little bare feet, but when shoes were shown, they were worn with short white socks.

This toddler holds an ivory teething ring with a nipple attached, an early pacifier, although it was not yet called that in advertisements or catalogs. Other teething rings had beautiful silver ornaments attached, in the shapes of animals, bells, or shells. These lovely old teething rings preserved in collections today usually show dents in the silver ornaments, either from being bitten or banged against something.

Frocks were also seen in the new "play yard," advertised for sale at this time. We know it today as the play pen. The wooden ones of recent years are virtually unchanged from those of 1890.

Figure 285 Dresses with waistlines at the natural waist, or just slightly below, were reserved for girls from four to fourteen years of age. Some were fitted in the bodice, but most had full-bloused bodices, as illustrated here. They varied in the degree of fullness, from those bloused only slightly to bodices that fell so far out over the waistband that they touched the skirt before moving back up to the shoulders.

The extra length of fabric in the bodice allowed the dress to "grow" with the child, increasing the amount of wear one could get from it. Interest was, in general, centered on the chest, shoulders, and neck through the use of yokes, collars, epaulettes, and ruffles. This dress has a huge sailor collar that is set into the center front button panel. It has a high neck along with the collar. The bodice blouses out a bit onto the waistband, and the full skirt is pleated.

Sleeves varied from large to enormous. The point at which the fullness was released also varied. Some were full only to the elbow, some gradually decreased in size toward the wrist, and others, like these, were full to the middle of the lower arm, where they fell out over a deep cuff. Another sleeve, not shown, was full like this one all the way to the wrist, where it was gathered onto a small cuff. Any of these sleeves might also have a ruffle at the wrist from a dainty almost-nothing-width to down-over-the-hand, supplying still more variations. Sleeves reached their peak in size in 1896 and 1897, then began to grow smaller.

Fabrics were French percales in pastel colors, imported madras plaids, "zephyr" cloth (lightweight, plain-weave wool), printed chelsea cloth, calico, and gingham. Solid and plaid flannel were saved for winter.

— 8 —

KNIT CLOTHES &

NIGHT SUITS

1900-1910

Three hundred bicycle factories in America were turning out a million bikes a year, and sweaters were still called "bike sweaters" in advertisements and catalogs during the early 1900s. The immediate acceptance of the sweater as fashion during the 1890s had ushered in the modern age of knit clothing. Coat sweaters for all ages of boys and (a little later) for young girls were seen everywhere. Baby clothes of all kinds were knitted or crocheted, as were petticoats and slips for little girls. By the end of the first decade, girls would even be wearing hand-knit or crocheted dresses and knit "drawer-leggings."

In 1907, President Teddy Roosevelt dispatched sixteen American battleships on a world cruise lasting fourteen months. It had been planned to show potential enemies our Great White Fleet, but it naturally stimulated still further the already tremendous interest in nautical clothing. Girls continued wearing the middy to the point of making it almost an American schoolgirl uniform. Little boys' sailor suits became quite authentic in design, in some cases even to the long flared trousers.

Knickers, though not new, came into fashion, too, at this time. At first they were quite full and ended above the knee, but soon they moved lower on older boys. Belt loops, soon to be standard on nearly all trousers for men, were being added to the new knickers at the beginning of the new century.

Button shoes were no longer seen on boys, as lace-ups in both high-top and oxford styles became commonplace. Button styles came to be associated with girls and babies of both sexes. New rubber-soled tennis shoes with canvas or suede tops were here to stay. (Could anyone have imagined at the time how important the tennis or sports shoe was destined to become during the 1980s?) High-topped tennis shoes were seen at the end of the decade and in a few more years would be classic sportswear for American boys everywhere.

The concept of specialized sports shoes and equipment inevitably led to the evolution of specialized protective clothes for sports. For many years, unfortunately, most protective equipment had been designed for adult sportsmen, before it was realized that growing young bodies needed protection from injury, also. Girls were wearing bloomer gym suits with tennis shoes for school sports, with knickers under their skirts for hiking.

In a short time overalls had become standard play wear for young children. On older boys, they began to be associated with the west and south for play and work clothing, and as rural and work garments in most areas of the country. Still another new form of play clothes branched off from the overall. Coveralls, called romper suits, had been meant primarily for very young boys and girls. As a modern concept, they were designed for comfort and freedom of action for a child's growing body. Still enjoyed today, they are now known as jump suits and coveralls.

Rubber diaper covers had not only influenced the design of infants' and children's fashions but were, in a sense, responsible for adults' changing attitudes as well. For the first time in Western culture, very small boys could wear trousers before being toilet-trained. No longer would a young male child have to wait till the age of two and a half to five years to "declare his sex," as in the past. And with his skirts went most of his frills, as little boys' clothing became more masculine.

Boy and girl infants would continue to dress alike during their first few months of life, but the age at which a boy's clothing asserted his maleness was growing younger and younger. By 1910, a baby boy might be put into rompers, boys' tailored aprons, sunsuits, or overalls, before he could walk.

Rubber and rubber-lined silk diaper covers continued to have an impact on the fashioning of children's clothing, with the introduction of pajamas or children's sleepers. Staying warm and dry at night had always been a problem for babies and toddlers. Now it was easy. The new sleepers called "night suits" were of Canton flannel, constructed with drop seats and "moccasin feet." Advertisements also offered them with fold-down cuffs to cover the hands on cold nights. Remarkably like modern sleepers in appearance, this very early twentieth-century garment would eventually be made of cotton knit and change little during the coming decades.

Complementing the pajama or sleeper of the early twentieth century was the teddy bear. For decades, popular illustrations have depicted a sleepy child clad in sleepers usually holding, hugging, or dragging his bear. The craze for the soft toy began in 1905 and peaked in 1908, with millions being sold. The teddy bear was important evidence of the still-changing attitudes toward children. In earlier times, a boy playing with a doll was subject to ridicule and his bewildered parents reacted with shock or concern. Teddy was to change that, for as many bears were sold for boys as for girls. There was much debate and concern, but educators and toy manufacturers asked, "What can be sissy about a bear?" There was also concern that Teddy might "destroy the maternal instinct" in little girls, but soft bears and other stuffed animals soon proved to be so lovable that everyone had to admit they might actually even encourage parental instincts. At any rate, the teddy bear was part of the changing attitude toward toys.

It was at this time that the educational possibilities of toys began to be recognized by both parents and educators. At last, learning could be fun. Not only were novel toys designed with learning in mind, but so was reading matter. The new children's magazines were extremely popular, being hailed as "fun and entertaining pastimes for rainy or winter days." Older boys and girls read the exciting dime novels that sold in the millions. The funny papers, or comics, were introduced into newspapers at this time, also for children's amusement.

The changed attitudes toward children were apparent in photographs showing families sharing their fun during vacation, on outings, or crowded into the new family automobile. Celebrations, band concerts, parades, and picnics were favorite times for taking snapshots, and the pictures usually reveal happy faces, laughter, and pranks. The newly invented box camera made picture taking easy enough for the average person just to snap a picture and record the children for posterity.

Public schools afforded at least some education for all children, though punishments were still harsh by our standards. Whispering, or daring to chew the newly marketed chewing gum, could merit a "whipping." Amid all the new material comfort and fun was a darker side for some American childhoods. At least 1,700,000 children under sixteen employed in factories and fields often worked nights and weekends. Laws were passed in 1907 prohibiting young children's being made to work more than sixty-six hours a week and from working nights! Immigrant families were still pouring into the nation in huge numbers, usually into crowded city slums that offered little to children except hard work, discouragement, and prejudice.

Whatever our faults and virtues at the beginning of the twentieth century, we thrust our children almost immediately into a world of stylish, machine-made, varied, comfortable clothing. There have been few new concepts in children's clothing design since then, only variations on and improvements in those already conceived.

From 1900
to 1910

Figure 286 Labeled variously as military blouses, Buster Brown suits, and Russian suits, these high-necked overblouse and knicker suits were worn by boys of two and a half to six years, as the new century dawned. They opened either down the front, at the side front under one of the pleats, or at the back. Sometimes they had sailor collars along with high-standing collars (like the blouse to the right

194 /

(287)

(290)

(291)

(286)

(288)

(289)

(292)

of this little boy). Embellishments at the side front might be braid, tucks, self-tabs, or pleats, and either restricted to one side or on both.

A novel knitted version of this popular overblouse was called the Buster Brown sweater, available in red or blue with a white knit stripe down each side instead of the tab or pleat. Sometimes the belt ran across the tabs, and then went through loops at the back and side seams rather than the front pleats. In Russian peasant styles, the blouse was a bright blue, red, or white, with colorful embroidered braid sewn down one or both sides of the front. The belt was usually covered with the same braid.

Striped fabrics were very prominent, as were solid white, navy, or red. Occasionally a printed cotton calico suit in this style appears in a photograph. Wool flannel in navy, gray, brown, or red was a favorite in winter, together with checked wool.

This little boy is wearing long leggings over his black shoes. Although some were dark, most were cream, gray, or tan, made of jersey or wool. Leggings came in a variety of lengths, from ankle spats, to calf length, just under the knee, just over the knee, as shown here, and to well up onto the thighs. Two or three little straps with buckles at the top adjusted the fit. Long white or black stockings were often worn with high-topped shoes, as were short socks of stripes or solid colors. Big, floppy tam-o'-shanters and sailor straws were preferred headwear along with the billed cap. The little coat and hat of Figure 294 were proper for these suits.

Girls' dresses were just longer versions of this blouse.

Figure 287 Girls' "allover aprons" were advertised as being "excellent protection for children's dresses." For children aged two to six years, they were usually of blue, brown, or red checked gingham. They were full and flared, with long sleeves and a medium- to large-sized collar. A back belt, sewn into the side seams, fastened in back with a pearl button; these were also used for fastening the apron down the back. There was always a handkerchief pocket, or even two, in front, on aprons that might be edged with braid or left completely plain. Some of these garments had a yoke at the chest, but, generally, they were flared from the shoulder, as shown.

Black cotton or wool stockings were customary, but short gray socks were seen also. This little girl's high-button shoes are white kid with black patent toes and heels. These shoes could also be purchased with pink or blue tops. However, bright red shoes were advertised as the latest style. Girls were sporting lace-up shoes as well as button styles, and the new red shoes usually had laces.

The hair ribbons are noteworthy, being of striped silk ribbon. Plaid, checked, dotted, and floral ribbons were liked, too. Wide- or rolled-brim sailor hats, mob caps, cloth sunbonnets, and rural straw hats were all proper accessories for these practical aprons. In cold weather, little girls were pictured as snug in the high jersey leggings of Figure 286. Their dresses were often just longer versions of the little boys' overblouses.

Figure 288 Sailor suits were modified through the years to suit current taste, just as they still are today. Although all the sailor suits of the 1880s and 1890s were still being worn during this first decade, middies took on several new forms, too. Double-breasted blouses became as popular as pullover middies. Many were made without braid, the only trim on most double-breasted blouse-waists being placed on the shield or dickey that filled in the neck. Necks on both single- and double-breasted styles were sometimes extremely low. Sailor suits were recommended for boys of three to six years. Pearl buttons were the usual fasteners, and sailor-style whistles often came with the suits.

Trousers for young boys were full knickerbockers; they ended just above the knee, with some fullness falling down over the knee. Advertisements always stressed the modern elastic at the knees and side pockets. A novel item for sale in stores and from mail-order catalogs was stocking knee protectors, "for boys and girls who wear their stockings out quickly." Of padded jersey cloth, they looked much like those used for skateboarding and basketball today, with their straps buckled around the leg. President Teddy Roosevelt reported that his son Archie used to wear out his stockings by crawling around on his knees. There is a famous photograph in the Roosevelt archives of Archie with large holes in both knees of his black stockings. Stores also offered heel protectors. Black or brown lace-up shoes were the usual accessories.

White linen was a favorite summer fabric for these suits. Duck was also common. Chambray suits were advertised in blues and grays for warm weather. Black and white stripes were available in both summer and winter fabrics, as were black and white and tan and white checks. Gray, navy, and brown solid color woolens were also recommended for cold weather.

Tam-o'-shanters, billed caps, rural straw hats, and, as illustrated here, the rolled-brim sailor straw were all appropriate headwear with these most charming little suits.

Figure 289 Fullness fell either from the shoulder seam or from a yoke across the chest on young girls' dresses. Although this pattern was usually recommended for ages one to six, the dresses were seen on older girls, too, in expensive interpretations. After they were no longer offered in catalogs or stores except for little children, they continued to be offered in exclusive shops and as beautiful handmade creations for those who could afford them for dressy occasions.

Made of lawn, silk mull, embroidered net, and fine handkerchief linen, they were edged with imported or handmade lace and eyelet. This frock has the fashionable standing collar and elbow-length sleeves of adult gowns. In place of a yoke, it has many tiny tucks that release their fullness at the chest. Several rows of tucks and wide lace encircle the hem, while narrow lace edges the collar and sleeve ruffles.

These dresses ranged from simple to elaborate in their amount of lace and handwork. Although usually white, they were occasionally pink, yellow, or blue. Taffeta was the favorite lining, and sometimes it was pink or blue under a white dress.

The full mob cap of colonial days returned to fashion and was worn squarely on top of the head, in keeping with current fashion. It was always edged with lace like the dresses, and often had pink or blue ribbons around it. Parasols could be covered to match dresses, for a complete ensemble. Either one-strap slippers or white canvas or leather oxfords with ribbon ties further enhanced an already becoming fashion.

Photographs as well as fashion prints show black stockings with these delicate outfits as often as they show tan ones and short socks.

Figure 290 The invention of night drawers or night suits with sewn-in moccasin feet and drop seats afforded toddlers sanitary and protective warmth they had not previously had at night. In 1900, these new sleepers were recommended for children from two to ten. By 1902, they were advertised for one year olds and younger, because of another new concept called diaper drawers that were waterproof rubber or rubber-coated silk diaper covers. Advertisements now read, "It makes no difference whether the children kick out of the bed-clothing or not." Made of either gray knit merino or unbleached Canton flannel, they fastened in back with pearl buttons. They had cuffs that could be folded down over the hands for extra protection in cold rooms.

Long nightgowns of flannelette in solid white or pastel stripes were still common and would remain so. They had shoulder yokes in front and back, either a lace ruffle or a small collar at the neck, and long full sleeves like old-fashioned gowns of today.

The advantages of the new sleeper, quickly recognized, sold the country on the idea of healthful and comfortable nighttime apparel for children, and the idea was here to stay. In addition, new diapers were now available in quilted bird's-eye *contoured* shapes, though still with only three corners.

Originated around 1905 and already a national craze by 1908, the teddy bear, named for President Teddy Roosevelt, became almost an accessory to children's bedtime clothing of the twentieth century.

Figure 291 Pinafores, along with nautical middies, were virtually a schoolgirl uniform during the first decade of the twentieth century. Most had a wide neck like this one, with a curved bertha around the shoulders, though less often they had gathered ruffles. Cut with a flared shape, these pinafores flowed out over the full-skirted dresses in a graceful line.

They fastened in back, sometimes only at the top, or halfway down with buttons or ties. Back views show that in some patterns they slipped on over the head, with no fasteners of any kind. They were as likely to have sleeves as not, and the sleeves might be long or short. Photographs show pinafores with short puffed sleeves worn over long-sleeved dresses or guimpes, producing a Juliette sleeve effect. The body might be pleated or gathered, as shown here. Sometimes a dress shows at the hemline in photographs, but most often does not. This full-style apron could easily "grow" with a child, revealing more of the dress skirt during successive seasons.

White cotton was the favorite, with gray material being used for work aprons at times. Lace or braid occasionally edged the bertha.

Plaid, check, and calico dresses were favorites for school wear, sharing popularity with solid navy and brown. Large straw sailor hats were the most popular accessory for school, church, or for nearly any outing or occasion. Sunbonnets were seen, too.

High-button shoes were the most widely accepted footwear in all parts of the nation well into the twentieth century. Most were leather with black patent toes and heels, or just patent toes. Bright red lace-ups were the latest style. Black cotton stockings were worn in summer and black wool ones in winter. Also worn in winter were the wool jersey gaiters shown in Figure 286.

Figure 292 Long-waisted frocks, referred to as "princess dresses" at this time, were quite similar to those worn during the 1880s. Wide collars or ruffle-edged yokes gave them their up-to-date appearance. Worn by girls of one to six years of age, they were constructed of white lawn or nainsook. Advertisements and catalog descriptions always stressed as a selling point the number of tucks at the front or yoke, stating, "twelve tucks on each side of front insertion extending from neck to flounce," or "four rows of tucks on each side of open work embroidered front panel."

Princess dress skirts were referred to as flounces at this time. Pastel ribbon sashes were added for special occasions, but many of these dresses had no sash or belt of any kind. A narrow row of insertion or cording was sometimes sewn into the waistline seam. Beautiful scalloped eyelet was added to the large collars, cuffs, and hemlines. Sometimes a ruffle like that in Figure 289, rather than a cuff, edged the sleeve.

Black patent leather slippers had eyelets in the strap, in place of buttons or buckles, so that satin or grosgrain ribbons could be tied through them, as shown, for a very dressy effect. The white canvas or kid oxfords of Figure 289 were also the mode, as well as high-button shoes. This young girl wears short blue socks to match her sash and hair ribbon. The socks could also be purchased in pink, red, and black.

Figure 293 Knitted jackets, known today as cardigans or coat sweaters, soon joined the bike sweaters of the 1890s as comfortable, sensible apparel for children. It is interesting that the coat sweater was at first reserved exclusively for men and boys; then, a few years later, it was sold for infants.

The notion of sweaters for little girls took almost a decade in coming. Early photographs of girls wearing sweaters indicate that the idea may have resulted from their inheriting their big brothers' hand-me-downs. At first, sweaters were not considered fashion but fell more into the category of everyday play and work clothes. Early ones were ribbed around all the edges, as illustrated. In 1908, one could buy the new button sweaters for toddlers in blue or pink, with white ribbing. Those for older children were usually in navy, scarlet, royal blue, and white.

Knit clothing for children would be seen more and more in the twentieth century as its advantages were realized. Another novel idea developed in the first decade was the knitted "legging drawers" or "combination leggings." A drawstring with tasseled ends was threaded around the waist, and knit or elastic straps went under the shoe. They were worn under the skirts of girls and young boys.

Knitted toques or stocking caps had tassels on the ends that flopped over. They were available in pink, blue, navy, or red combined with white stripes, either all over or just on the cuffs.

Young children also wore the pullover sweater with a turtleneck or mock turtleneck like that seen on the boy of Figure 264. The colors were the same as those of this knitted jacket.

Figure 294 Little boys' coats, worn over the full short knickers and overblouses in Figure 286, were only slightly longer than the blouses. They allowed the knickers to show just a bit, as illustrated. Usually double breasted, they might have either shawl collars or the popular large sailor collars. One of the principal characteristics of little boys' coats of this time was the wide belt, always lower in front than in back. It was just slightly below the waist in back, but curved down under the tummy in front.

Belt loops were employed on children's clothing before their fathers realized their potential. They were a necessity on the lowered waistlines of small girls' dresses during the 1880s, but, for the most, were forgotten during the 1890s when waistlines moved up. With the new lowered waists and fashionable belts of the early twentieth century, the belt loop's uses were again examined, although they were still primarily decorative.

Navy blue, brown, tan, and sometimes red were the approved colors for these coats.

This small boy's coat has loops at the sides and side-fronts to accommodate

(294)

(296)

(298)

(293)

(295)

(297)

(299)

his large leather belt. The belt, large pearl buttons, and sailor collar give it its simple and pleasing lines without further ornamentation. Fur collars and cuffs were sometimes added in winter, and brass buttons with an anchor or eagle on them were popular, too.

Accessories are black stockings, high lace-up shoes of black, red, or brown, and woolen mittens. His hat is the familiar rolled-brim sailor with the brim standing up in front. These sailors were navy blue straw in spring and fur felt in fall. His hair style is the classic pageboy.

The reefer coat in Figure 270 was still commonly liked. New fabrics were corduroy, plush, or duck, in black, brown, gray, "drab," and black and white stripes. Braid trim was seldom employed anymore, but fur or plush collars were stylish. Reefers were usually advertised at this time as being "blanket lined" and sometimes as waterproof. Although braid was not used as much as in the previous decade, emblems on the left sleeve were. They might be eagles, anchors, stars, or teddy bears.

Figure 295 Embroidered emblems on the sleeves of small children's coats became prominent at the turn of the century and continued so for several decades. Although eagles and anchors were the most common, it should be noted that there was also a teddy bear emblem set available at notions counters. The set consisted of two stars and a two and one-eighth-inch teddy holding an American flag. It was offered in navy, light blue, red, or white, and was a part of the craze for the new toys that continued to sweep the nation.

Little girls' coats still had the large sleeves of 1890s styles. They were full in the body and could be purchased in dress length or in the shorter style of Figure 280. In fact, coats in the 1900s had changed little from the previous decade, except that the yoke was rarely seen anymore. Large collars were still in favor, along with smaller notched and shawl styles. In summer, light corded cottons were common, along with whites in piqué, poplin, and butcher linen. In winter, woolens in navy, royal blue, or red solids and black and white checks were preferred.

This coat has a shawl collar and cuffs edged with soutache braid. Double breasted, it has large buttons and a popular emblem on the left sleeve. Brass buttons with anchors or eagles were commonly used on these little coats, as were white pearl ones.

This little girl models a large floppy hat similar to a mob cap. These hats were sometimes made of cloth, or a combination of straw brim with a cloth crown, of linen, eyelet sheers, silk mull, poplin, or valenciennes lace. Trim usually consisted of ribbon bows or lace edging. She also models three-strap Roman sandals of black patent, and short socks, which were available in black, blue, white, pink, and red.

Figure 296 Mackintoshes of various waterproofed fabrics made practical raincoats for boys and girls. Wool serge coats in navy blue, black, or red were lined with plaid in line with the tradition for the mackintosh. Black oilcloth and rubber in black or red were made into children's coats, too. Although cowboys wore yellow oilcloth slickers, the thought of making children's raincoats in yellow had apparently not yet occurred to manufacturers. It would be some time—after the automobile became a common danger—before the safety value of the yellow slicker would be perceived.

One to three detachable capes were often a feature of these coats, but plain ones without capes were pictured too. Buttons were still used, although men's coats were already using various "patented" clips. These would eventually also appear on children's raincoats.

As a rule, black rubber boots had shiny insteps with dull "pebble finish" uppers. Sometimes the name of the rubber company was molded or printed on the sides. They always had pull tapes on each side, at the top, to assist the child in pulling them on. One boot advertised as snag-proof was made of tough rubber-coated duck, but all boots were lined with jersey, wool flannel, or fleece. Floppy tams like that shown in Figure 299 and stocking caps as illustrated here were the most popular accessories for raincoats.

At this time, illustrations in magazines and books often showed one or more young children under huge black umbrellas apparently belonging to their fathers, sometimes with the umbrella turned inside-out by the wind. All had a timeless charm about them.

Dressier mackintoshes were made of waterproofed fine woolens in checks or solids. They were tailored, top stitched with fold-down velvet collars and pockets with flaps, in both double- and single-breasted styles.

Figure 297 Infant cloaks now had a yoke sewn at the cape shoulders with a gathered flounce added to it, bunching less bulk at the neck than previous cloaks. (The cloak of Figure 273 shows the former method of gathering in or shirring all the cape's fullness at the neck.) Sometimes small round collars were added. The coat under the cape has a yoke, as in the past. Made of cashmere, silk, corded cotton, or eiderdown, they were always offered in either cream or white. Linings were silk, cotton twill, sateen, or "shaker flannel."

Open-work embroidery done with silk floss was used extravagantly, as was satin ribbon and lace insertion. Advertisements often stated, "They are made full length, but when changing Baby's clothes from long to short these cloaks can easily be altered to the desired length, either at the yoke seam or skirt hem." The skirt embellishments were often set several inches above the hem, to facilitate one or more alterations.

Baby bonnets had become snug and quite simple, in contrast to the conspicuous ones of the 1890s.

Although the old flask nursing bottles with their long tube nipples were still in use, a good deal of experimentation was being done in impoved nipple and bottle designs. To the infant's left can be seen the new wide-mouthed nursing bottle with its marked measurements and large rubber nipple. This would eventually make earlier ones obsolete.

Figure 298 Belted Norfolk suits were worn by boys from four to sixteen while they were in short trousers, and then all through their adult years with long trousers or knickers. Two chief characteristics identify the Norfolk jacket: the belt, and the vertical pleats or tabs on the front and back body. Some Norfolks had a yoke at the chest, though others did not. Tweeds, checks, small plaids, thin stripes, and solids, in blues, grays, and browns, were the fabrics of these suits. The jacket had no set number of pleats front or back. Sometimes the body was pleated all the way across. Back pleats were either restricted to center back or appeared at each side, like the front.

Buttons varied from four to six, and the top one might either be fastened or worn open, as shown. Young boys were often pictured wearing the jacket open, with the ends of the belt swinging down in front. Occasionally, the jacket was unbuttoned but the belt fastened. Although it was a suit with a great deal of elegance appeal, it was, nonetheless, a sports suit, so casual was the word.

Trousers had risen to above the knee for boys up to age sixteen. They were tapered in shape toward their hems, where three buttons were always sewn, whether they fastened or not. The fly front was standard now, as were side pockets and pressed creases.

The dress suit in Figure 275 was still in fashion, and so were the sports suit of Figure 261 and the sweater of Figure 264.

Touring or golf caps, yacht caps, derbies, fedoras, and jockey caps were appropriate for young boys.

This young fellow carries his schoolbooks with the leather bookstraps and handle preferred by boys over the bookbag carried by girls in Figure 299. Drawstring bookbags like those of early colonial days (Figure 24, page 28) were still available in most stores, made of multicolored striped fabrics.

Figure 299 Dress skirts showing below coat hems were a part of the fashion look in this period. Even so-called full-length styles were only as long as illustrated by this girl's coat. Short coats were sleeve length, or a little longer, reaching as low as the knuckles of the hand. Virtually all coats and jackets for girls were double breasted during this decade. Collars were notched like Figure 270, or wide seafaring styles, or shawl collars like that of Figure 295.

This girl's collar is held up around the neck by her wool scarf. Older girls' coats and jackets sometimes had embroidered emblems of anchors or eagles on the left sleeve, like younger children's. Patch pockets were applied with fancy cuffs, or, alternatively, the newer slash pockets, set in at an angle, were incorporated.

This young lady shows the tam-o'-shanter, grown to such huge proportions now that it flopped down at the sides. Yarn or fur pom-poms adorned the crown. Her hair is teased so that it is bouffant on top and sides, then caught with ribbons at each side in a fashionable schoolgirl style.

Her over-the-knee leggings are strapped under the instep to hold them in place. Of pale gray wool jersey, they fasten down the sides with small buttons. Some leggings opened only at the ankle and were slipped on over the foot.

She carries a metal lunchbox in her right hand and a brown canvas schoolbag with leather bindings in her left. These bookbags were available with leather shoulder straps, too. The old drawstring schoolbag of colonial days was still sold in mercantile stores and through mail-order catalogs, as were slates.

Figure 300 Specialized clothing for sports by now was becoming big business. The concept of protective clothing was being explored, to cut down on injuries. Baseball uniforms for adults and professional players set the styles, of course, for those of young boys. It is interesting to remember that baseball, a form of the English game cricket, had originally been considered a children's game. During the last half of the nineteenth century, it had become not only a favorite of adults, but had pioneered the notion that professional sports could attract paying fans.

By the beginning of the twentieth century, sports equipment and uniforms of all kinds, such as quilted knickers and all manner of gloves, mitts, catcher's masks, and cleated shoes, could be purchased. Although the old squared cap of Figure 195 was still worn by some teams, there was a new gored, fitted one called the college cap that was especially liked by young boys. They wore it even with their regular clothes. New shirts had names of favored teams or schools printed across the chest. Extra baseball socks without toes or heels were put on over the regular socks; they had striped or patterned fold-down tops.

Baseball trousers had originated the belt loop during the 1870s. But it was not until the twentieth century that belt loops became a standard fixture on men's and boys' trousers. This boy has a webbed belt laced through the loops. Besides the new-style cap, with its ventilation holes in each gore, he wears the new rub-ber-soled sports shoes. They had cloth tops trimmed with leather and would, by 1910, evolve into the high-top tennis shoe so closely identified with American boys during the twentieth century. Even though adults had professionalized the game, baseball would always remain primarily "young boys' country."

For football, boys dressed in turtleneck sweaters, knickers, black stockings, and high-top lace-up shoes. The protective leather helmet was just beginning to be promoted.

Figure 301 Naval action in the Caribbean required white summer uniforms, be-cause of the heat. New uniform regulations at the turn of the century allowed more flare in the trousers of enlisted men, so it was no time at all before boys were

(302)

(304)

(300)

(301)

(303)

(305)

dressed in white sailor suits with bell-bottom trousers. (They didn't abandon the short knickers, however, which remained in favor, too.)

Anchor motifs and metal military buttons are still used on children's clothing, up to the present. The new middies were not too changed from the styles of the 1890s, as seen in Figure 267, except that they had grown longer. They still often came complete with a whistle. Necklines dipped quite low and middies again utilized the navy tie, which had been omitted for several years.

Canvas tennis shoes with rubber soles were available by mid-decade. The first ones were black, but they were soon available in white also. Sailor tams had U.S. NAVY printed on the band. For a short time a most interesting hat in fashion was a square tam. Worn with corners to the front and back, it looked much like a mortarboard. The rounded tam shown here was regulation navy headgear for many years.

Figure 302 Bathing suits for boys were now offered in more different styles than in previous decades, sleeveless or with "quarter sleeves" as choices. They could also be found in either one- or two-piece styles. The one-piece suits fastened at the shoulder with buttons. Lengths varied in both shirt and trunks, with the newer trunks being generally above the knee. Colors were either black or navy, and trim either white or red. Expensive suits were worsted wool. The cheaper ones were of cotton. Advertisements often promised, "If you wear our worsted suit, you will not experience that chill so disagreeable to bathers."

This young boy wears a navy two-piece suit with a sailor collar and sleeves. The collar, sleeves, and hemline are trimmed with bands of white. But plain, round, or V-necks were seen too.

By now, boys were allowed to wear just the trunks during very hot weather. Trunks, either alone or with a shirt, were made to fit by use of a drawstring at the waist.

Figure 303 Very little boys bathed (swam) either in plain wool trunks or bathing suits with little overall bibs. They were usually navy blue but now and then came in red. Plain knee-length trunks were available in assorted designs and stripes through mail-order houses. They were wool with a drawstring at the waist.

Advertised water wings, "to hold the child at the proper level," were described as "of the greatest assistance to beginning bathers." There were also kapok "swim jackets" for keeping a child safe while swimming. It should be remembered that many more dangers existed in natural "watering places" such as beaches, lakes, rivers, and swimming holes than at modern-day supervised pools. Also, these natural waters were much colder than modern man-made pools that can be heated, so illness starting with chills was a real possibility. Woolen suits were always advertised as insurance against "shivering and chills," and promoted as being healthier than cotton.

Figure 304 Although most girls' bathing outfits still had skirts at this time, very fashion-conscious mothers were dressing their daughters in new bloomer suits, without a skirt of any kind. The newest style was the one-piece step-in suit that opened down the front. It had to be pulled up over the feet. Navy blue, white, and black were the favorite colors, but printed fabrics in dots or stripes were being seen at fashionable beaches and spas.

This young girl's bathing suit is of a dotted fabric, with a yoke and sewn-in waistband onto which the waist and bloomers are gathered. Navy braid trims the navy and white suit. She holds the fashionable drawstring beach bag made of rubber-coated fabric in either blue or black.

Wool and duck were the standby fabrics, advertised for their ability to shed water and with the assurance that they would not cling revealingly to the female figure.

Conservative mothers dressed their daughters in almost identical suits, but with full skirts over their bloomers.

Figure 305 Sailor dresses were so popular as school attire that they amounted almost to a national educational uniform along with the full pinafore in Figure 291. Nearly any school group photograph of this decade will show the majority of young girls wearing one fashion or the other. Waists were full and waistbands curved down in front, helping to promote the popular swayback posture of the time. Always either navy or dark red, these maritime-type dresses were sometimes trimmed with as many as four to six rows of soutache braid. A fad for "Scotch plaid bands," similar to plaid bias tape, followed production of plaid ties matching the braid trim: White ties were paired with white braid trim. Ties were always advertised as being four-in-hand style. Either an anchor or eagle adorned the dickey at the neck.

Skirts were always pleated quite full, and store ads called attention to the "deep hems" that would "grow" with the girl. Fabrics were linen, chambray, or wool flannel.

Noteworthy are this young girl's white canvas tennis shoes with rubber soles. In this period, they were strictly for sports or picnics and would not have been worn to school, as tennis shoes are today. They were intended for tennis, boating, and other sports, and worn primarily by men and boys. But fashionable girls and women were wearing them, and would be seen in them more and more in coming years.

The young girl holds an ice cream cone, newly invented, enabling one to eat ice cream outside or almost anywhere. Chewing gum was another new fad sweeping the nation.

Figure 306 Overalls were denim trousers usually worn over other clothing as a protective garment. Apron overalls were those with an apron bib and suspenders, as shown, forming the garment referred to today as overalls. When made for boys from four to sixteen, they were constructed identically with adult apron overalls.

This young man is clothed in a Brownie suit, the name given to the first children's overalls introduced in the 1890s. By 1900, they had double stitching and sometimes metal rivets at stress points. Two pockets in back and front provided places to carry items of importance to young boys. Suspenders were detachable at both ends and could be removed when the overalls were laundered, in order to protect the four-inch elastic ends. This was an important factor because clothes were usually boiled during laundering.

Although apron overalls were still often put on over other clothing, the idea of wearing them in place of other trousers was taking hold. This practical garment was coming into its own as an accepted item of American costume. Blue, black, and red-blue denim were the fabrics of overalls in the beginning, along with gray and white striped duck. Advertisements of Brownie overalls urged parents, "Let the boy romp about and play without being afraid of spoiling his best clothes." They also led the way by pointing out, "They require no other trousers."

Under his overalls, the boy has on a striped collarless shirt over his red union suit. All manner of shirts and sweaters would be paired with overalls, according to the activity and the weather. For shirt styles and fabrics, see description of Figure 311.

Figure 307 Aprons for girls aged two to twelve covered the entire dress in order to "form excellent protection to the dress," as manufacturers proclaimed. In fact, aprons were actually dresses worn over other dresses.

This little girl shows the standard everyday wear that, today, we would refer to as a smock. Checks were always used for these cover-up aprons at this time, with blue, red, or brown ginghams being the most commonly seen. Even though meant for everyday use, they were bound or corded at the edges of the collar, cuffs, pocket, and belt. They buttoned down the back, with the belt fastening both back and front and secured even at the apron's sides, to hold it in place. Some aprons had belts across the back only, that either buttoned or tied like a sash.

Straw sailor hats, rural straws, or cloth sunbonnets were generally seen with these little aprons. Black or red high-button shoes were worn with black stockings in winter and short socks in summer.

Over a million children in the nation were employed in factories and fields doing hard labor for long hours and even at night. In 1907, laws were passed to control, at least, the number of hours a child could be made to work. Some photographs of these children show girls working in aprons of gray or brown made on lines similar to this one, without trim of any kind. These little working girls always wore black stockings and well-worn lace-up shoes, rather than the buttoned shoes of more fortunate girls.

(307)

(309)

(306)

(308)

(310)

(311)

Figure 308 "For little brother or sister to play in and save their good clothes," read one 1900s mail-order catalog displaying children's overalls. The Brownie suit of the 1890s was now being sold for girls to wear, too. Descriptions usually mentioned that overalls "allow children lots of freedom for action."

The first Brownie suit of the previous decade was recommended for boys from four to fourteen; now the new overalls were suggested for both sexes, aged one to eight. Toddlers could now wear trousers because they were equipped underneath with rubber-coated silk diaper covers. Before this time, little boys had always had to wear skirts until they were trained.

Smaller sizes came in blue chambray or denim, and the customer could have either red or blue trim on the bib, pockets, and cuffs. Suspenders, separate from the overalls, had elastic at the ends and also came in either red or blue. The overalls that clothe small children today are not too different from those of 1905.

Either plain or frilly blouses were worn under overalls. The new roll-neck sweaters and cardigans were natural accessories for them, too, offering the same comfort and freedom. This little garment and the waterproof diaper cover had, in one decade, revolutionized adult views on children's clothing needs.

Figure 309 Neck and shoulder interest remained in fashion throughout most of the decade. Shoulder flounces and berthas were sometimes so large that they were labeled shoulder "capes," and often a small ruffle sat on a larger one. Ruffles were edged with lace, braid, rickrack, or embroidery. The yoke was always embellished with rows of insertion, tucks, and braid, as was the waistband.

The waistline still curved down in front because of the swayback posture and fullness of the bodice front. Skirts were full and flared, with only a few gathers, and were worn over full petticoats. Dresses might be one-piece, or what we refer to today as a jumper dress, worn over a guimpe blouse.

In summer, madras plaids, checks, stripes, polka dots, and prints were favored in percale, duck, gingham, or lawn fabrics. Blouses were lawn or piqué. In winter, the same designs were made up in cashmere, wool flannel, and velvet; navy, red, or brown led as the favorite colors. Wool plaids served for trim on plain dresses as well as being used for entire dresses. Velvet trimmed many flannel dresses. The trim and fabric determined where these frocks were to be worn, with the dressier ones being reserved for Sunday and special occasions.

This young girl's side-part hair style and large ribbon bow are new. But middle parts and bangs were still in fashion, too. Her shoes are patent leather slippers with tailored bows. Oxfords and high-button shoes were preferred for school and everyday wear.

Figure 310 Both boys and girls from one to six years old enjoyed the very new romper suit. It seems that children's clothing had arrived in the twentieth century before adult clothes. Advertisers consistently pointed out how "serviceable and practical," they were. They never failed to mention, either, the freedom of movement these rompers afforded the child.

For winter, rompers were constructed of gray and white striped duck; in summer, they were cut of gingham, in either pink, blue, or red checks. They could be purchased with a collar or a plain neck, and white binding usually edged the collar, cuffs, yoke, pocket, and belt. The rompers fastened in back with pearl buttons; the belt fastened both in front and back. There were sometimes belt loops (at the side seam only), but usually the belts were secured by stitching at the sides. Trousers were gathered at the ankles with elastic. A pocket was very important for carrying the handkerchief.

All the hats and shoes of this decade are proper accessories for this garment, depending upon the occasion, of course, but straw sailors and cloth sunbonnets are particularly charming. Strap slippers or high-button shoes in red or black were the usual footwear.

Figure 311 Boys' shirts came in a wide assortment of styles and fabrics during the first decade of the present century. By this time, they had developed a yoke at the shoulders both front and back, but still only opened to the chest rather than all the way down in front. With this exception, there was, in fact, little difference between them and today's shirt. One style, the negligee shirt, had a white neckband but no collar (see Figure 306). Sometimes two detachable stiff collars were included with the purchase. Boys' shirts also came with attached soft collars, in both dress and sports styles (the latter shown here). Both soft collar and collarless styles could be purchased with tucked or plain fronts.

Negligee shirts came in "finest percales with handsome black, blue, or pink checks, stripes, and figures on white backgrounds." Dressy negligee shirts were solid white corded cottons and novelty weaves.

Soft-collared dress shirts were of cream-white or tan pongee. They also were available in "fancy stripes, checks and patterns," as worn by this boy. He also sports the soft bow tie.

Soft-collar styles came in blue, brown, gray, or tan flannel for winter. There were also work garments of black and white drill, blue or patterned chambray, and black sateen. Flannel and work shirts could be bought with "double or military yokes" that were the fancy-shaped ones referred to today as the western style.

Belt loops, not yet standard on trousers, were nevertheless in use on some fashionable sporting clothes. Advertisements still listed suspender buttons among the features of men's trousers, and only occasionally listed loops for belts. At the end of the decade, mail-order catalogs and department store ads were still mentioning buttonholes for shirts or buttons for suspenders for boys' trousers, with no mention of belt loops. It is interesting that little boys' clothing utilized the belt loop first, but on blouses and jackets rather than on trousers. This boy has suspender buttons as did older boys. But little boys' trousers still buttoned onto the shirt or underwaist.

The hat worn by this boy is the plain high-crowned straw or black felt commonly encountered in all parts of America since the early nineteenth century. Usually it was creased or peaked in western regions, but left rounded in the north and east.

Figure 312 Knickers had been around for fashionable "sporting" suits since the 1880s, but during the early twentieth century they were accepted by more and more boys for ordinary wear. Little boys were still dressed in either the very full short knickers, above-the-knee knickers, or short tapered trousers. Schoolage boys in the preteen years took up the sporty knickers their fathers had been reserving for biking, golfing, hunting, and automobile driving, and made them their own.

Trousers (knickers) for sportswear now had belt loops, side pockets, back pockets, and button-fly fronts. They came to below the knee, where they were gathered onto a knee band. However, they were tapered like the knee pants that had been so popular, so that they somewhat resembled jodhpurs. They were yet to evolve into the extremely full knickers of the 1920s. Plaids, tweeds, and checked fabrics were favorites. Knickers were always lined to prevent them from scratching.

Sports jackets had not changed much during the previous decade, nor had double-breasted dress-suit jackets. Both styles would now serve as coordinates for the fashionable new knickers.

Knit socks and oxfords replaced the black stockings and high-top shoes and gave older boys a more grown-up look. Socks had fold-down tops of novelty knit patterns, or stripes and checks in color. A few socks styles were patterned all over, but most had designs only on the tops. They were usually of neutral or dark colors, with white and bright accents. This fellow sports the touring or golf cap that would increase in popularity along with the knickers. V-neck sweaters were often worn like vests under the jacket on brisk days. When riding in the new automobile, he would wear a close-fitting cap and goggles.

Figure 313 One of the most characteristic sights of the first ten years of the twentieth century, along with "the nautical look," was the simple tucked frock with lowered belt and high neck. Many variations of this pleated dress were produced for all ages of girls. Sometimes there was a yoke at the chest and at times the neck was low, as in Figure 314, with a high-necked guimpe underneath.

All the sleeves shown during this decade appeared on the pleated dress, too, as well as all the necklines. This basic form of the popular frock was often white in summer, with a dark or self-belt. Pink, blue, and yellow were also seen. One charming variation was a deep cream dress with pale blue neckband, cuffs, and belt. Belt loops were employed as decoration either at the side seams or at each

(312)   (313)   (314)   (315)   (316)

side in front. In winter, solid flannels, plaid or checked woolens, and velvet were made into cold-weather variations.

Wide-brimmed sailor hats were still commonly seen, but often now with a flower or two added in front or back. They were worn a little to the back of the head.

Oxfords and slippers, as seen in Figures 314 and 316, were shown in most fashion prints and catalogs as the latest styles. Just the same, high-top shoes in both lace-up and button styles continued to be the most commonly worn shoe, according to contemporaneous photographs.

Figure 314 The name jumper suit was now used for dresses worn over guimpes (blouses). Jumpers had round, square, V-shaped, heart shaped, and even high necks. "Circular" sleeves, as illustrated here, were the most popular, but puffed or long sleeves were seen too. Sometimes a kind of cap sleeve, or just a ruffle around the armhole, might be preferred in summer.

The bodice was always full and long, so that it bloused out in front; the effect was achieved by curving the bottom of the waist. Pleats, rows of lace or insertion, braid, and tucks enhanced the bodice. This girl's jumper has several tucks at each shoulder. Either the fashionable patent leather or a self-belt was preferred, with self-belts often trimmed with the same braid or lace as the dresses. Skirts were pleated or gathered, but always cut with a wide flare that fanned out over ruffled petticoats.

Guimpes usually had full three-quarter-length sleeves with either cuffs or flounces at the elbow, like this one. Of white or cream lawn, they were tucked and embellished with rows of lace and insertion. Elastic or drawstrings at the waist created a peplum underneath the dress and petticoat.

Oxford shoes of leather or cloth usually had patent leather toes and wide laces forming bows, as shown. White, pink, black, or red stockings might have embroidered dots, flowers, or other designs. Or patterns of mesh, lace, or stripes might be woven into them.

Leghorn straw hats with floppy brims were heavily adorned with flowers and ribbons. They were worn on top of the head, but canted just slightly toward the back.

A full-pleated skirt with wide suspenders, called the suspender dress, was sometimes worn over the guimpe. The waistband and suspenders were embroidered or adorned with braid and grew wider at the shoulders, in keeping with the shoulder interest of this time.

Figure 315 Once the idea for knit sweaters was hit upon, variations soon followed. It was not long before the coat sweater or knit jacket (the cardigan) came on the scene.

Cardigans had ribbing knit around the neck, front opening, cuffs, pockets, and hemline. Colors were navy, wine, gray and brown. Some coat sweaters had collars; others were double breasted. There were sweaters knit in a Norfolk style, like Figure 298, with a belt. Worn over a shirt and tie, the cardigan took the place of the sports jacket but was rarely, if ever, worn with an open collar. Even when the tie was omitted, the collar was buttoned.

Pullover sweaters with turtlenecks were even more popular during this decade than they had been in the 1890s. They had developed stripes, either all over or just on the neck, cuffs, and across the chest. Sometimes white bands set off the hips, too. Necklines were opened into collars, and both pullovers and cardigans literally swept the country.

Little boys still preferred short tapered trousers or full bloomer-style knickers, but older boys were being seen in the new knickers described in Figure 312. Fold-down socks and oxford shoes gave knickers a modern look, and the touring or golf cap was being adopted by boys in all parts of the country. Boys' and men's clothing had arrived at a twentieth-century style that was to change little for decades.

For a drive in the country in the new family automobile, this young man would don a close-fitting car cap and goggles not too different in shape and style from those to be worn by World War I aviators during the following decade.

Figure 316 Soft frocks were the mode for spring, summer, and special occasions. Most of the time they had a yoke at the chest and a high neckband. Sometimes lace and insertion went the full vertical length of the waist. Round, square, or pointed yokes were employed in variety. Sleeves might be three-quarter-length, long, short and puffed, or circular, as those in Figure 314.

Skirts, full and flared, were shaped with a few gathers at the waist. Flounces around the skirt, about halfway up, were always added to dressier frocks. These flounces were applied with a ruffle heading standing up. Either lace or self-ruffles were applied to sleeves, yoke, skirt, and neck, while silk or taffeta sashes added color to the dresses.

Lawn, batiste, silk mull, or embroidered net were used for these soft, delicate dresses. Lawn was available in sheer plaids or checks, as well as dainty figured patterns, on white, cream, or pastel backgrounds. Many designs featured pink roses with green leaves or tiny scattered polka dots. Sometimes the patterns were so tiny they could be discerned only from close range.

Black patent leather shoes had one strap across the instep, decorated with a bow. Some bows had tiny rhinestone buckles at their center, lending them a bit of sparkle. Pastel or white stockings were coordinated with the dress and sash.

This young girl's hat is a large floppy leghorn straw with the crown surrounded by silk flowers and ribbons. Hair styles were often as long as to the waist. Ribbon streamers on the hats hung down to the waist at times, too. This hat, like that in Figure 314, was sometimes placed squarely on top of the head, but young girls often tilted it to the back in a charmingly romantic gesture.